STANLEY COMPLETE
PAINTING

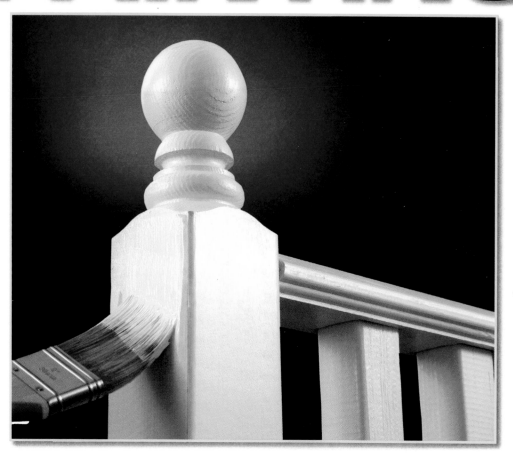

Meredith® Books
Des Moines, Iowa

W9-ANI-299

Stanley Complete Painting
Editor: Larry Johnston
Copy Chief: Terri Fredrickson
Publishing Operations Manager: Karen Schirm
Senior Editor, Asset and Information Manager: Phillip Morgan
Edit and Design Production Coordinator: Mary Lee Gavin
Editorial and Design Assistant: Renee E. McAtee
Book Production Managers: Pam Kvitne,
    Marjorie J. Schenkelberg, Rick von Holdt, Mark Weaver
Contributing Copy Editor: Don Gulbrandsen
Contributing Proofreaders: Ellen Bingham, Becky Danley,
    Paula Reece
Indexer: Donald Glassman

Additional Editoral Contributions from
    Art Rep Services
Director: Chip Nadeau
Designer/Technical Direction: LK Design
Writer: Martin Miller
Photographer: Mike Dvorak
Illustrator: Rick Hanson Illustration

Meredith® Books
Executive Director, Editorial: Gregory H. Kayko
Executive Director, Design: Matt Strelecki
Managing Editor: Amy Tincher-Durik
Executive Editor/Group Manager: Benjamin Allen
Senior Associate Design Director: Tom Wegner
Marketing Product Manager: Brent Wiersma

Publisher and Editor in Chief: James D. Blume
Editorial Director: Linda Raglan Cunningham
Executive Director, New Business Development: Todd M. Davis
Executive Director, Sales: Ken Zagor
Director, Operations: George A. Susral
Director, Production: Douglas M. Johnston
Director, Marketing: Amy Nichols
Business Director: Jim Leonard

Vice President and General Manager: Douglas J. Guendel

Meredith Publishing Group
President: Jack Griffin
Executive Vice President: Karla Jeffries

Meredith Corporation
Chairman of the Board: William T. Kerr
President and Chief Executive Officer: Stephen M. Lacy

In Memoriam: E. T. Meredith III (1933–2003)

Special thanks to:
American Sandblasting; Bennett Lumber; Bill Voss Construction;
Carpet Mill Connection; Dave's Floor Sanding; Eco-System
Painting, Tim Shaw; Eric and Aaron Sechler; Hirschfield's; Jaide
Salon; Jeff and Lynette Podergois; M&W Painting; Michael
Hayes Co.; Mozet's Concrete and Masonry; Re-use Center;
Richtone Painters, Tim Shaw, Greg Allen; Rust-oleum; Tom
Madsen Painting; Wagner Spray Tech; Werner Ladders

All of us at Meredith® Books are dedicated to providing you
with the information and ideas you need to enhance your home
and garden. We welcome your comments and suggestions
about this book. Write to us at:
    Meredith Corporation
    Meredith Books
    1716 Locust St.
    Des Moines, IA 50309-3203

If you would like more information on other Stanley products,
call 1-800-STANLEY or visit us at: www.stanleyworks.com
Stanley® and the notched rectangle around the Stanley
name are registered trademarks of The Stanley Works and
subsidiaries.

Note to the Readers: Due to differing conditions, tools, and
individual skills, Meredith Corporation assumes no responsibility
for any damages, injuries suffered, or losses incurred as a
result of following the information published in this book.
Before beginning any project, review the instructions carefully,
and if any doubts or questions remain, consult local experts
or authorities. Because codes and regulations vary greatly,
you always should check with authorities to ensure that your
project complies with all applicable local codes and regulations.
Always read and observe all of the safety precautions provided
by manufacturers of any tools, equipment, or supplies, and
follow all accepted safety procedures.

CONTENTS

COLOR & DESIGN 4

Understanding color 6
Establishing a color scheme 8
Style and color 12
A gallery of interior design 14
A gallery of exterior design 20
Furniture, trim, and accessories 24
Hiring a pro 26

ABOUT PAINT & PAINTING 28

The chemistry of paint 30
The case for quality 32
Picking the perfect paint 34
Primers and sealers 36
Texture and speciality paints 38
Problems and cures—interior 40
Problems and cures—exterior 42
Painting preparation at a glance 44
Brushes and paint pads 46
Rollers 48
Sprayers and other tools 50
Good painting practices 52
Cleaning up 58
Maintaining painted surfaces 60

PAINTING EXTERIORS 62

Planning and estimating 64
Getting the site ready 66
Preparing siding 68
Preparing masonry surfaces 72
Ladders and scaffolding 74
Ladder jacks and accessories 78
Setting up scaffolding 79
Painting soffits and siding 82
Painting windows and doors 86
Painting masonry and
    other surfaces 90
Finishing cedar shingles and siding 92
Finishing fences and gates 94
Selecting finishes for
    a deck or porch 96
Preparing and painting
    decks and porches 98
Applying a clear deck finsh 100

INTERIOR PAINTING 102

Planning and estimating 104
Getting the room ready 106
Removing wallpaper 108
Cleaning and sanding 110
Smoothing textured surfaces 111
Preparing and repairing walls 112
Preparing trim 116
Protecting surfaces 120
Ladders and work platforms 122
Priming tips 124
Painting ceilings 126
Painting walls 128
Painting interior windows 130
Staining and varnishing trim 136
Painting interior doors 138
Painting a basement wall 142
Painting a basement or
    garage floor 144
Painting a wood floor 146
Staining or varnishing
    a wood floor 148
Painting vinyl flooring
    and ceramic tile 150
Painting steps 152
Painting cabinetry 154

HOW TO PAINT JUST ABOUT ANYTHING 158

Painting iron and steel furniture
    and ornaments 160
Painting plastics 166
Painting wood furniture 168
Special applications 170
Whitewash, distemper,
    and milk paints 172
Painting a swimming pool 174

APPLYING STAIN & VARNISH 176

Preparing wood 178
Stain, dye, and varnish 180
Stripping paint and varnish 184
Applying stain, dye,
    and clear finish 186

Glossary 188
Index 189

COLOR & DESIGN

Of all the tools you can employ to redecorate a room, paint is the least expensive, most versatile, easiest to apply, and most expressive. With careful planning—particularly in your color choices and sheens—a new coat of paint can produce dramatic results, transforming a dull room into an exciting space that draws you in and makes you want to use it.

Paint can make a small room look larger. It can brighten a dark room or set the perfect tone for showing off design features. Paint can even create its own items for display, making accents of elements that otherwise would remain unnoticed. That you can find all this potential in a container no bigger than a milk jug makes a simple can of paint something of a small wonder.

Of course, it's not just the paint that brings about this transformation; you play a big role too, and for many people, that's where things can seem complicated. After all, most homeowners are not trained as interior designers. So how are you going to know that the colors you choose are the right ones? And how are you going to get the paint on the wall and not on everything else? Wouldn't it just be better to let a professional make your color choices and apply the paint too? This book will help you make the right choices when you answer those questions.

Any room you design yourself more truly reflects your personality, and that brings a certain—even if intangible—enjoyment the moment you walk into it. You feel at home surrounded by your colors, patterns, and textures. That's not to say you shouldn't seek professional advice if you need it. But good interior designers know that their job is not to impose their personalities on your space. Their job is to help you discover what you want. So if you turn the entire decorating challenge over to someone else, you will probably end up with a result you like, but you might feel something is missing—your personal touch.

The same goes for applying the paint. Once you've chosen your color scheme and prepared the room for painting, you've arrived at the easiest part of the job. Painting skills are relatively easy to master. And when the job is done, nothing beats the reward of standing back and looking at a beautiful room, knowing that what you're admiring is the quality of your own workmanship.

A room you design yourself makes you feel at home in your own colors, textures, and patterns.

CHAPTER PREVIEW

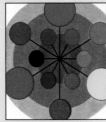

Understanding color
page 6

Establishing a color scheme
page 8

Style and color
page 12

A gallery of interior design
page 14

Paint colors are key elements in setting a room's mood and style. Together with the furnishings, paint can create a calm and serene setting like this; a bold, brash room; or anything in between.

A gallery of exterior design
page 20

Furniture, trim, and accessories
page 24

Hiring a pro
page 26

UNDERSTANDING COLOR

Technically, color is light. Because the white light spectrum contains all colors, the color you see for any object is the portion of the spectrum that is reflected back to your eyes.

But beyond that technicality, what's more important when choosing paint for a room is how various colors (sometimes called hues) are created, how they relate to each other, and what effect they have on other colors and the overall mood of the room.

The color wheel

Understanding the color wheel is a key to understanding color. When you first look at a color wheel, it might seem confusing. But viewed one part at a time, it becomes clear.

First look for the **primary colors—red, blue, and yellow.** These are the basic colors that cannot be made from or broken down into any other color. They are pure hues. All other colors are created by mixing primary colors with each other in various combinations. They are spaced equidistant from each other on a color wheel, making the points of an imaginary triangle. They are the largest circles on the wheel at right.

The next series is the three **secondary colors—orange, violet, and green.** These are created by mixing equal amounts of two primary colors. To get orange, you mix red and yellow; for violet, mix red and blue; and for green, mix blue and yellow. On the color wheel, the secondary colors are midway between the primary colors from which they're made (the medium-size circles on the wheel shown).

The **tertiary colors** are mixtures of a secondary color with one of its primary colors: red and orange make red-orange, yellow and orange make yellow-orange. These are the smallest circles on the wheel above right.

Warm and cool colors

Colors also have a perceived temperature value. Reds, yellows, and oranges are considered warm colors; blues, greens, and violets are usually cool colors.

Using the color wheel

The color wheel helps you see what colors work well with each other. You may already know that there aren't any rigid rules you

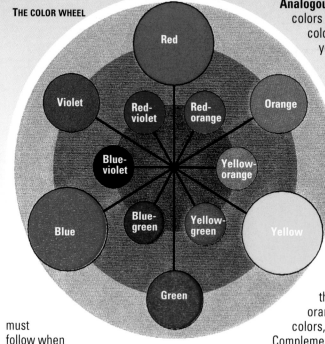

THE COLOR WHEEL

must follow when choosing a color scheme. You can, however, rely on combinations based on the color wheel to develop appealing color schemes.

Analogous colors are any three colors next to each other on the color wheel. For example, yellow-orange, orange, and red-orange make an analogous arrangement. So do blue-green, blue, and blue-violet. Analogous colors work well because they are closely related to each other, each containing some of the other color. This makes a harmonious color scheme.

Complementary colors lie directly opposite each other on the color wheel. Blue and orange are complementary colors, as are red and green. Complementary combinations are opposite in tone and work well because they balance a warm color with a cool one. They can produce dramatic effects but can overpower a design if you use intense hues.

Shades, tints, and tones

If your color choices were limited only to the major classifications, designing a room would be a pretty dull business. Luckily, the range of colors at your disposal is practically endless, thanks to the possibilities created by adding just small amounts of colors to each other. You can also add white, black, and gray to any color to produce further variations called **values.**

Adding white to a color creates a **tint** of the color. The more white you add, the lighter the tint. Pink, for example, is a tint of primary red. On the color wheel at right, you'll see tints inside the hue, growing lighter toward the center with the addition of more white.

Adding black to a color creates a **shade** of the color. Shades are darker versions of any color, and on the color wheel you'll find them on the outer rings, becoming darker as they move away from their color of origin. Forest green, for example, is a shade of primary green produced by adding a small amount of black.

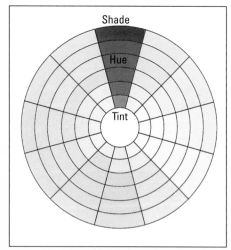

Another way to alter a color is to add gray. This makes a **tone** of the color—a subtle variation of it. Yellow with some gray added produces a mustard color. Using a slightly different value of gray can make an almost imperceptible change in tone.

Triadic colors lie at equidistant points on the color wheel. Greens, oranges, and violets make a triadic combination. So do the primary colors, red, blue, and yellow. Use care with any triadic combination. It's a high-energy scheme but can be dizzying with colors of high intensity.

Monochromatic combinations employ one color in various intensities and values to keep the mixture from looking dull. Adding different textures to the mix also makes the combination interesting and can create a very sophisticated design.

Neutrals

White, black, and gray (a mixture of white and black), though often referred to as neutral colors, are not true colors. That's because white reflects all the colors in the visible spectrum, and black absorbs them all.

It's all in a name

The names of colors on the color wheel are technically descriptive, but you'll get a puzzled look from the paint-store staff if you ask for gallon of blue-violet. You'll have to look at the color chips for that brand of paint and ask for the name or number of the color that's closest to blue-violet. Manufacturers develop thousands of names each year for their paint colors as part of their marketing strategy, an indication of the extraordinary variety of colors available.

When you start developing a color scheme for your room, start with the basic combinations shown here. Choose base colors that go together well, then you can branch out with other choices for accents, adding a little at a time.

ANALOGOUS COLORS

ANALOGOUS COLORS

Red and red-oranges are the main colors in this scheme. Red is the dominant color in the arrangement.

MONOCHROMATIC COLORS

Shades and tints of a single color create a calm, serene scene, but you need some accents for interest.

TRIADIC COLORS

Tints of three primary colors make a lively color scheme. Here the colors are used about equally.

COMPLEMENTARY COLORS

Purple and yellow, opposite each other on the color wheel, create a strong, balanced scheme.

ESTABLISHING A COLOR SCHEME

Picking new colors for a room can be difficult because it's hard to know where to start. You can begin color selection by taking two steps: Determine the mood of the room, then decide whether you want the walls to grab attention or just serve as a backdrop for the rest of the room.

Choose a mood

Colors generate emotions; language is full of pertinent examples. People are said to be green with envy or they feel blue after suffering a disappointment. Colors have a psychological impact, so one of your first choices should be to choose colors that will help establish the mood you want for a room.

Red is bold and energetic—perfect for a room designated for activity, such as a family room or recreation space. It draws the eye toward it and makes an excellent accent.

Blue and green are passive and restful, quiet and receding, formal and fresh. Above all, they're easy on the eyes, especially in lighter tints. That makes them a good choice for rooms, like bedrooms, designed for relaxation and sleep.

Yellow and orange are warm and cheerful. They can bring the feeling of sunshine to a space, especially a room that is shaded or has small window areas.

Remember that these descriptions are general and your choices will seldom be limited to the pure hues of any color. You will more likely think about ranges of colors that could establish the kind of atmosphere you want for the room.

Yellow gets your attention and keeps it. The color is associated with sunlight, so it helps lift moods and brightens dimly lit rooms and hallways. Be careful of intense yellows, which can cause anxiety. Pure yellow suggests hospitality and brings a sense of well being. Muted hues suggest a soft, glowing light and are less noticeable.

Red walls make this room warm and inviting. Red can actually increase blood pressure and heart rate. It often produces feelings of intimacy, energy, and passion. Orange, a secondary color of red, is more friendly and less passionate. Pure orange is bright and bold, while tints and shades generate a more subtle glow.

Blue and its secondary cousin green are cool colors, peaceful and relaxing. They also recede, making rooms look larger. Muted blues, as in this room, mimic sunlit skies, and shaded blues generate a sense of comfort and ease. Pure green is reminiscent of colors in nature. Muted variants encourage contemplation and relaxation.

Focal points or backdrops?

Walls are a good place to start color selection because they are the largest area in a room. They can be the dominant design element or serve as a backdrop for the rest of the room. The choice will affect other decorating decisions.

If you want focal-point walls, pick their color first, then design the room around it. The "emotions" of a color are important, but also consider the size of the room and how much light it receives. Light colors are generally best in a dimly lit room, and dark tones work well in a well-lighted room. To make it easy, choose your favorite color and build a theme around it with contrasts, complements, and variations of intensity.

For backdrop walls, select the other major decorative elements first, including rugs and furniture. Then select a wall color that balances and complements these colors and lets them take center stage. It's a lot easier to match a paint color to a rug or carpet than to find a carpet that matches a particular paint color. A good place to start is with a tint or shade of another color in the room or a complement of the dominant color.

Red and orange two-tone paint makes this wall the focal point of the dining room. Outlining the false window with paint is an informal touch.

Neutral walls serve well by providing a simple background when the room furnishings are colorful or ornate.

Living with colors you love

If you have trouble deciding where to start when selecting colors, there's a simple solution—pick a color you love as a starting point.

Selecting a favorite color is the least complicated method for choosing colors for a decorating project. You can pick almost anything—a pillow, a painting,

a comfortable chair, a piece of clothing—with colors that are attractive to you.

You don't need to give it a lot of thought: Why the object appeals to you really doesn't matter. What matters is that there's something about its color that you like or that makes you feel good.

Finding this favorite color makes the rest of your color selection easier because it gives you a reference point on the color wheel. From there you can consider the combinations on pages 6–7. The color scheme you create this way will truly reflect your taste and not someone else's.

Select color chips that fit into the scheme at your home center. Or use any of the paint manufacturers' websites that feature digital color selection aids.

You can then use the colors in your palette throughout the house as you select paint colors, furnishings, and accessories.

ESTABLISHING A COLOR SCHEME *continued*

Making connections

While it's important to create unities of style within each room, each room should feel like it's part of a consistent design throughout the house. Color is an effective tool for connecting rooms, especially in open-space floor plans.

For example, painting the molding throughout an open-space home the same color ties adjacent spaces together, while their different floor and wall coverings maintain the individuality of each room. Employing the same technique with built-in bookcases and cabinets in different rooms integrates the rooms, even though they are used for entirely different functions. Another way to achieve a cohesive design is to use different amounts of the same tone in different rooms or vary the tones of one color. Even though each tone is different, the fact that they originate from the same base will create a subtle unity—a definite, even if unconscious, effect.

Quick solutions with color

If you get stuck on the road to developing your color scheme, some simple steps may help get you going again.

Consider active colors such as yellow, orange, and red for rooms designated for social or entertainment activities. Yellows can jump-start your creativity, which is good for home offices and kitchens. Passive colors, members of the cool collection—blue, green, and purple—go where rest and rejuvenation are important, in bathrooms and bedrooms. Neutral colors bridge other colors. Dark neutrals tone them down, while whites make them stronger.

Monochromatic color schemes create a calm, unruffled appearance. And they're easy to create; all you have to do is to come up with variants of the same color that mix pleasingly with one another. You'll need some contrast, but use it carefully. Different textures and fabric patterns can work as accents too.

Although the range of colors is endless, you need only two or three, with one of those an accent color that is used sparingly. If you're working with a monochromatic arrangement with three tones, try a really dark variation for the accent. For a complementary scheme, pick an accent

Light, neutral walls, a white ceiling, and white woodwork make this room seem bright and airy, though the windows are relatively small. The large mirror adds to the sense of brightness. Black accents in the window muntins and wall shelves add contrast and keep the room from being bland.

from the opposite side of the color wheel. And if you've decided to paint the walls as a backdrop, select an accent color that goes with the furnishings.

On the other hand, if you're painting with completely different colors, you risk the possibility of jarring contrasts. To protect yourself from this color shock, use colors of the same intensity. Most colors will work well together when they have the same or similar values.

What about white?

This all-time favorite has some drawbacks. First, manufacturers make an astounding array of whites, all different from one another. Some have noticeable color casts; make sure the one you've chosen goes with the other colors in the room.

Second, almost any white can dramatically alter the way other nearby colors look, a consequence you may not discover until after the paint has dried. Avoid this pitfall by using test boards for all your colors. (See "Make a test board," right.)

STANLEY PRO TIP

Make a test board

Paint is a chameleon. It changes color under three conditions—on large expanses of wall, when it dries, and when lighting conditions change. This idiosyncrasy can affect your color selection.

To make sure you're seeing the color correctly, get several sheets of 24×30-inch foam core from a picture-framing shop and paint them with the colors you're considering. Let the paint dry thoroughly, then set the boards against the surfaces where you would use them. Look at them at various times of the day and night. Sunlight will render the truest color. Most fluorescents will tinge the color with a slight blue (although you can get fluorescents that more closely resemble sunlight). When you're sure, cut pieces from the boards and take them with you when you buy the paint.

Light from a pair of sconces washes the striking purple walls in this room. The complementary orange trim and dark furnishings add warmth to balance the cool wall color.

Bright primary red and blue enliven this child's room. White trim and wainscoting give a fresh look, and painted stripes above the wainscoting introduce more colors for interest.

Analogous colors on the walls and trim lend a sense of calm to this room. The choice of furnishings can make the room serene or active. A white ceiling helps brighten the room.

Color tips

■ Add color variety to your room by installing a chair rail and painting the lower section of the wall a different color than the upper area. Or install picture-frame moldings and use a slightly different shade inside them.

■ Stick to one style— modern, traditional, or whatever matches the overall style of your house. Research colors for periods such as Victorian, Colonial, or Arts and Crafts and use them to unify the style of your home.

■ If you're painting different hues on the walls of different rooms, use neutral colors in the hallways as transitions.

■ Consider the sun. A large expanse of south-facing windows may beg for cool color tones. A shaded or north-facing room might warm up with reds, yellows, or oranges.

■ Alter the perceived size of a room with color; light walls and a white ceiling make a room seem larger and the ceiling higher. So do stripes (good for kids' rooms), cool colors, and semigloss paints. Dark walls and ceiling make the room seem smaller and the ceiling lower. So will satin or eggshell paints and warm colors. Dark tones also feel more intimate—perfect for making spaces feel cozy. In both cases, paint the ceiling a different shade than the walls and consider painting the top 12 inches of the wall the same color as an especially high ceiling to make it seem lower.

■ Blend unsightly objects such as pipes into the background by painting them the same color as the surface closest to them. A neutral color will make them disappear. Or go contemporary and treat them as linear accents by painting them a contrasting color.

■ Make interesting features like moldings or columns really stand out by painting them with a color that contrasts with the walls.

■ Different rooms require different moods. Decide on the mood you want the room to evoke and use the colors that fit that mood.

■ To soften the dramatic impact of bold colors or the effect of many colors in the same room, paint the ceiling and trim white. The differences create a visual rhythm and give the eye a place to rest.

■ Establish a colorful relationship between adjacent rooms to enhance the visual flow from one room to the other. Pick a key color and use it on different surfaces in each room—on the trim in one, on the walls in another, and on the ceiling in a third.

STYLE AND COLOR

When you're choosing a color scheme for your house, inside or outside, architectural style can provide a wealth of clues. Researching the color palette of various styles can greatly speed your selection. Here are some common styles.

American Colonial

In less affluent homes, earth tones made from native plants and minerals were common. In affluent homes, blue was a signature color (it was expensive), as were shades of green and pink. Red was used as an accent. On the outside, white was most common, along with blue, beige, gray, ochre, and cream. Shades of red, brown, and green accented trim and shutters.

Victorian

Victorians loved bold colors inside and out. Ruby red, forest green, and amber were paired with complementary colors to create high drama, with neutrals used as transitions in hallways and connecting rooms. Exterior color schemes varied with the location of the home. You'd find light warm colors in rural areas, with darker or lighter trim to bring out detail. In the city, deeper earth tones hid the effects of dirty air, along with schemes designed to highlight the interesting patterns of gingerbread detailing.

Arts and Crafts

This movement tended toward simplicity in design, marked by neutral ivory and beige, accented with brown, green, deep red, and blue tones derived from indigo. Exteriors tended to earth tones—brown, forest green, and red.

Art Deco

"Cool" defines Art Deco, with machine-age figures set off against pastels and blue. Cream, beige, ivory, and gray accented blues, black, green, and red. The exterior Art Deco palette most often followed the same schemes as interior designs.

Southwestern

The colors of the desert—pink, yellow, tan, and beige—dominate this style, with accent colors equally natural—deep blue from the sky, dark red from the surrounding soils, and terra-cotta.

Dark colors and earthtones are popular for homes in rural settings because they convey a rustic look. Depending upon the type of siding, the house can be either stained or painted. Here the trim is also dark for a monochrome effect.

Painting a house white is a time-honored custom. Dark-painted shutters on this house add accents and break up the expanse of white. This traditional look fits easily into most neighborhoods and suits most architectural styles.

California

West Coast colors are generally soft and muted—shades of yellow, beige, cream, tan, and peach—accented with brown, rust red, earth colors, and sage.

Rustic, forest, or mountain lodge

The style of homes that fit this category are either log cabins or houses with architectural motifs borrowing from Craftsman style. Natural stone, brick, and wood create a harmonious unity between the landscape and the home. Thus you'll find the colors of the outdoors repeated in the decor of mountain homes—brown, tan, beige, and sage green, accented with earthy red, sky blue, and forest green.

Midwestern

Farmhouses were almost universally white, though now and then you would find off-white cream colors, as well as medium yellow. Wine red and dark forest green accented door frames, window trim, and shutters—a throwback to East Coast color schemes brought to the prairie.

Miami Deco

This style is a variation of the Art Deco style, with a bit of the tropical thrown in. Pink predominates, as do shades of peach, yellow, green, and sea blue. Reflecting its location, coral is a common accent, as are orange and lime green.

Bungalows are often painted dark colors, but pale yellow siding and white trim give this one a fresh look that still fits the style. The light colors set off the stonework nicely.

Natural-finish interior woodwork is a hallmark of the Arts and Crafts style. Paint colors like these greens often reflect nature. A wood molding separates the dark lower wall from the lighter color above.

Desertlike beige is a fitting color for the Southwestern-style architecture of this room. The color suggests adobe walls, and the light color balances the dark tile floor.

Victorian houses and other styles rich in architectural detail are great candidates for polychrome—multicolor—painting. Designing the scheme and applying the many colors is laborious, but the result can be striking.

A GALLERY OF INTERIOR DESIGN

Great design schemes are contagious and inspiring. The color schemes and design ideas shown on the following pages reflect the styles and tastes of the individual homeowners. That means few of the rooms shown would probably be exactly right for you or your home in their entirety, but bits and pieces surely would be. And the underlying principles and ideas can help you develop your own color scheme.

Look to the walls first and notice how they function relative to the rest of the room. Are they design elements in their own right or are they the background for the furnishings and other elements?

Look next at the colors that have been used and their relationship to one another. Think about the color schemes in relation to the principles discussed on pages 6–7 and see how they fit the color wheel. You will probably see several kinds of color combinations in each room.

Consider where the same or similar color schemes might work in your home. This will give you a sense of the numerous possibilities for expressing yourself.

Taupe walls lend elegance to this room. The dark walls recede, bringing the fireplace surround and furnishings to the forefront.

Colors in the rug repeat in the chair covers, walls, and window shades to make a lively dining room. The two-tone walls with a lighter color on top make the room seem larger.

White woodwork and carpeting are calming influences against the strong red walls in this room. Red patterns in the bedspread and rug add visual texture while continuing the color scheme.

Bright reds and greens can be frenetic together, but muted reds and greens combine to create a relaxing mood in this bedroom.

The red wall focuses attention on the seat in these built-in bookcases. Any bold color used sparingly can create a focal point.

A GALLERY OF INTERIOR DESIGN *continued*

The ceiling is a distinctive style element in this room. To enhance the dramatic effect, the vertical surfaces in the recessed ceiling are painted the wall color while the ceiling surfaces are bright white for maximum contrast.

STANLEY PRO TIP: **Discover your style**

People often take their surroundings for granted. But if you want to discover your own color style, it helps to pay closer attention.

First look through magazines, books, catalogs, and Internet interior design sites. Then—no matter where you are—make a point of paying attention to the things around you. When you visit friends or neighbors, notice the colors in each room and whether they suit the purpose of the room. Make a mental note of what you like and what you don't. Do the same thing in houses on display at home shows or even furnished houses that are up for sale.

You can sharpen your eye for color and design at the movies too. Movie sets represent the highest level of design expertise. They're created by experts, and there's nothing on a set, and no color chosen, without a specific purpose in mind.

As you pursue your color studies, jot down ideas that appeal to you, and keep a file of photos clipped from magazines and newspapers. You'll find colors you particularly respond to. Note whether they're light or dark, intense or muted. Consider what kind of rooms make you the most comfortable—for example, traditional or ultra-modern?

Collect your notes and write down some general characteristics about the color scheme you think is best for your rooms.

Don't decorate to please anyone except you and your family. Take your time when selecting colors. Bring color chips home and when you believe you're close to a decision, buy a little paint (you can buy test-size quantities of many paints) and try it out on a test board (see page 10). Even if you find you're slightly off the mark in your first choice, it's likely that the right color will be very close to what you selected.

The panels in this coffered ceiling are painted the color of the walls. Contrasting white beams focus attention on the ceiling design.

Wall and ceiling color work alongside the furnishings, flooring, and trim color to establish the overall character of a room. The same or similar wall color can create distinct effects in different rooms. White trim and light-color carpeting help make this yellow room bright and cheerful.

Black trim and dark wood flooring make this yellow room warm and inviting. Wood beams contrast against the white ceiling, adding design interest.

A GALLERY OF INTERIOR DESIGN *continued*

Stripes of tints and shades of a neutral color subtly add visual interest to this wall. Paint the wall the lightest color first, then mask off the equal-width stripes. You could paint stripes of different colors or vary the stripes' widths. Draw and color a scaled layout to make sure you like the scheme before you paint the wall.

A ceiling is usually painted white or some other light color to make it seem higher and to brighten the room. Here the deep color on the walls and upholstery is carried onto the ceiling, making a dark, relaxing room. Though dark, the ceiling doesn't seem oppressively low because it is no darker than the walls.

Mixing options

Not all paints are created equal. Here's a quick review of some differences.

■ **Factory finish:** These are paints straight off the shelf from the manufacturer without the inclusion of any tinting or additives by the local paint outlet. Factory finishes are mixed in large quantities so you're pretty much assured that the color will be the same from can to can. They're also more resistant to fading.

■ **Standard mixes:** These are the paints that match the color cards in the store. They're not mixed until you choose them, but when they are, the proportions are strictly specified by the factory formulas. These are the most common paints, but since anything added locally can result in slight variations, boxing the paint (see page 52) before applying it to the walls is a good idea.

■ **Custom colors:** These are colors mixed by the local paint outlet to match specific requirements of the customer. Suppose, for example, you want to match the color of your carpet. Bring a color swatch from a surplus piece, and using computerized laser techniques, the staff can analyze the composition of the color and mix paint to match. Since these are considered special-order paints in most stores, expect to pay a little more for the time and expertise.

■ **Accents:** These are factory-prepared paints in pure, solid hues, rich in pigment. These paints are very durable and withstand fading better than other paints so they're excellent for sun-filled rooms. Their intensities are powerful, so use them in moderation.

■ **Specialty mixes:** This is a catch-all category that includes a variety of paints made to produce different surface textures—crackles, suedes, pebbles, chalkboards, and light stuccos, among others.

Instead of painting every room white or beige, you can paint different rooms different colors. Here a lavender dining room adjoins a red living room. Select colors that go with other decorating elements to make a pleasing color scheme.

In a room where art or furnishings are dominant elements rather than just accessories, create a gallery by downplaying the walls and ceiling. Here the light blue wall provides a background for wall art and modern furnishings yet keep the room from seeming too stark, which might be the case with white walls.

A deep color makes a good display wall for light-color objects, such as the mirror and collection of plates in this dining room. The dark wall recedes visually to highlight the items hanging on it.

Paint can call attention to a room's design features. With a light-color surround, this fireplace could be lost between the windows. Painting it green turns it into a focal point.

A GALLERY OF EXTERIOR DESIGN

Choosing exterior colors might seem like it would be easier than picking interior colors. But it can be just as hard because there are so many parts to paint—siding, windows and doors, trim, gutters and downspouts, perhaps some shutters and porch railings. You might treat some of these elements as accents, and some might need different kinds of paint. Approaching an exterior paint job systematically is the best way to avoid confusion.

First consider the style of your home. If it fits a specific historical style or design, you could make your color selection based on historic colors for the style. You might have to conform to certain standards set by historic guidelines or neighborhood groups.

Next take a look at your neighborhood, especially homes on either side of you. That will reduce your choices somewhat because you may not want the same color as a neighbor's house, and you want a color that won't clash with it either. Other houses on the block may give you some inspiration.

Give some attention to the elements of the exterior and decide what you want to paint and what you don't. You won't paint the roof, of course, but what about the eaves and fascia? The shutters and trim might need paint, along with the doors and windows.

Decide whether you want the house to stand out from or blend into the surroundings. Do you want to downplay the trim or highlight it? Choose the main color for the house first, then pick the accent colors. If you want the gutters to disappear, paint them the same color as the main body of the house. The reverse is usually true for the front door; it should be the focal point of the front of the house.

White will call attention to details and will work well with most styles and other colors. Just like inside, use gloss white on the trim and flat white on the walls. Light colors tend to change with the lighting conditions and help blend various elements together. Midtones add warmth and make good understated accents. Dark shades recede and help the house blend into the background. Choose accent colors that highlight architectural features. Test the colors with a test board (page 10) or by painting small swatches on the house.

White trim contrasts with the siding for this classic small-town Americana look. Attention to detail—the red front door and window sashes—adds interest. The shingle siding in the main gable is unpainted. White gutters and downspouts are inconspicuous.

Subtle sage green siding, white trim, and black shutters lend a calm, comfortable look to this ranch-style house. Light colors were once most popular for exteriors because they showed sun fading less. With modern paints, fading is less of a concern.

Dark green trim and stained wood siding give this home the look of a rustic lodge in the mountains. The brown and green color scheme reflects nature and links the home to its surroundings.

Breaking from conventional color schemes makes your house distinctive. Instead of a more-common blue-gray, this house is a deeper blue. White trim highlights the main color to create a bright, bold look.

Surprising colors can enliven an otherwise humdrum house. The multicolor scheme on this lakeside retreat communicates fun and an escape from the ordinary. A color scheme like this probably wouldn't fit into a suburban neighborhood—which is the point of using it here.

A GALLERY OF EXTERIOR DESIGN *continued*

Similar values of different colors create a balanced color scheme that gives this bungalow an understated look. A lighter or darker accent color could add intensity.

Scale of values

No matter what your color scheme, you'll find that even widely different colors will work well together if they have the same relative value. A value scale can help you make decisions about color schemes.

The scale runs from white to black in ten increments that show different proportions of black. The shades correspond to the relative lightness or darkness of a color. Pure yellow, for instance, is light and has a higher value than pure blue. But you can choose shades of yellow (darker) to match tints of blue (lighter), and everything will work just fine.

Conversely, you can keep the values different when you want to bring in contrasts. Strong greens and blues will often create color clashes, but a pastel of one and dark shade of another will complement each other.

VALUE SCALE
White
10% Black
20% Black
30% Black
40% Black
50% Black
60% Black
70% Black
80% Black
90% Black
Solid Black

The main colors in this paint scheme are a lighter and darker value of a yellow-green. The complementary trim color is similar in value to the darker main color.

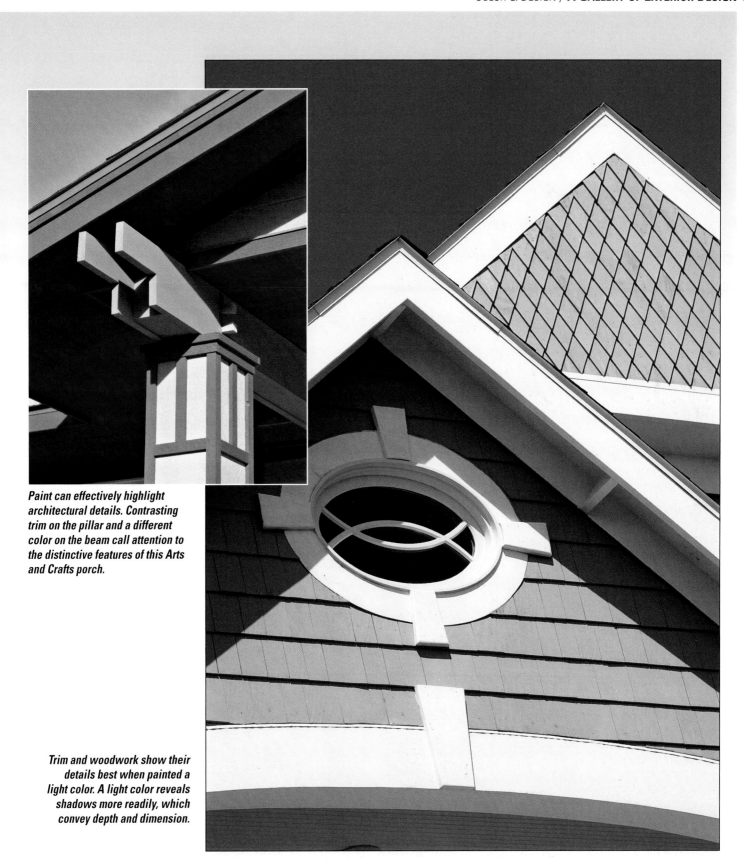

Paint can effectively highlight architectural details. Contrasting trim on the pillar and a different color on the beam call attention to the distinctive features of this Arts and Crafts porch.

Trim and woodwork show their details best when painted a light color. A light color reveals shadows more readily, which convey depth and dimension.

FURNITURE, TRIM, AND ACCESSORIES

Just as paint can change the character of a room, it can also alter the personality of furniture, trim, and accessories, transforming some objects from just functional to exciting and decorative.

Trim helps frame windows and doors and gives them definition. Crown moldings and chair rails help define the style of a room and separate spaces. Furnishings become colorful design elements. Bookcases, shelving, built-ins, and cabinets are all candidates for paint.

With modern coatings, you can paint just about anything. That makes it easy to individualize the items around your home.

When you paint the kitchen, include the cabinets in the color scheme. Painting the existing cabinets saves a lot of time and money over replacing or refinishing them, and you can achieve a singular effect that fits your style.

Fences, arbors, and other yard and garden structures are often left unfinished. But painting them can help them last longer and look better. If you want a natural wood look, apply a clear exterior finish.

New or old furniture made of wicker, twigs, or similar materials takes on a fresh new look when painted a bright color. Spray application is usually the best way to paint something like this chair.

Wood outdoor furniture such as these Adirondack chairs must be protected from the elements. Paint affords that protection and at the same time adds some color and style to this patio. It's easy to freshen the patio by repainting the furniture—whether it's made of wood, metal, or plastic.

A little paint can turn a find from a secondhand store into a distinctive piece of furniture. Paint it with bright colors to be an accent piece or, as shown here, to match the color scheme of the room.

To make a focal point without painting an entire wall, paint part of a wall. A pair of yellow panels accents this wall quickly and easily. Make sure the base paint is dry, then mask off the accent areas and roll on the paint.

HIRING A PRO

Undertaking a paint job always calls for some forethought beyond color selection and decorative themes. Painting a room (or rooms) is not difficult. In fact, it's just about the perfect do-it-yourself home improvement project. Nevertheless it is a job that places demands on your time, budget, and skills. So before you haul out the brushes, paint cans, and ladders, ask yourself a few questions.

■ How much preparation will I need to do and will I have the time to do it?

■ Am I up to the hard parts of the job, such as climbing ladders and moving furniture?

■ Do I have the patience to learn a new skill, and can I accept that my initial progress might be slow and somewhat frustrating?

■ Will I be able to live with a room left unfinished if I am called away or when I have to return to work after the weekend?

■ Are there aspects of the job I can do but simply don't enjoy? Are there parts of the work I can do myself and parts I want to contract out?

If your answers to these questions make you decide to contract all or some of the job, go about gathering bids and hiring a contractor methodically.

First talk with friends and neighbors and get their recommendations about contractors they have used. Take a look at the work done for people you know so you can make sure the quality of the work meets your standards.

Then contact at least three of the top contractors to discuss the work you want to have done. Meet with each of them individually to look at the job and discuss the specific job details.

Interview contractors

■ For each surface (including trim, stucco, aluminum siding, walls, and so forth), ask what will be done to prepare it, to prime it (including what type and brand of primer), and to apply the finish coat (including the type and brand of the paint, how it will be applied, its quality, and the number of coats).

Make sure the contractor will use a top-quality paint. A quality acrylic latex paint may cost more initially, but its durability will save money in the long run.

■ For exterior work, ask what will be done to protect landscape plants. For interior work, find out how furniture will be protected and moved.

■ Ask when the contractor can start the job and how long it will take. You should also know what remedy will be available if the job is not completed on time.

■ Discuss the warranty on the work, how long it is, whether it covers both labor and materials, what kind of failures are covered (peeling, cracking, fading), and what will be done to correct such failures.

■ Make sure the contractor is bonded and insured. Bonding will replace your costs if the contractor fails to complete the job. Insurance will cover any injury to any of the workers. Without such insurance, you may be liable for such injuries. Insurance may also cover damage done to your property.

■ Ask each contractor for the names and contact information for previous customers. Call some of the references; ask if you can see the contractor's work.

■ Get written estimates from at least three contractors. Be wary of any bids that are significantly higher or lower than the others. Bids from reputable contractors are usually fairly close to each other for the same work. The estimate should break down material and labor costs and show payment terms.

Before you make your final choice, consider the contractor's demeanor. He or she should be responsive, punctual, and businesslike when returning phone calls or arriving for an appointment. The contractor should take time to answer your questions and explain details of the job.

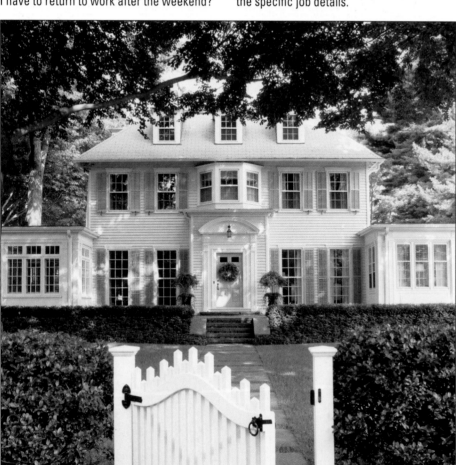

Before you decide to paint your own house, stand back and assess the job. A tall house with a substantial amount of trim to prepare, places that could be difficult to reach, and landscaping right where you would need to put ladders might be better left to experienced professional painters.

Hire a contractor

Once you've selected a professional painter, that contractor should submit a formal written contract for the work (unless the bid or estimate was already in contractual form). The document should spell out everything you've discussed with the contractor about your job. It should specify these things:

■ the work to be done

■ the materials to be used

■ the starting and completion dates and remedies for failure to stay on schedule

■ methods for resolving disputes

■ procedures for making changes (change orders are alterations to the contract to which both parties agree)

■ evidence of insurance and bonding, and licensing if required by local ordinance

Before you make final payment, inspect the job with the contractor, making notes about anything that needs correction (proper coverage, cleanup, and so forth). The contractor should correct the problems before you make final payment.

Painting a house is a big job, but the work is not necessarily difficult. Preparation of the surfaces before painting is time-consuming but essential. You must be able to climb up and down ladders to paint any house, even if you're painting only the trim.

Interior painting is generally easier than exterior painting. Because you will be close to the painted surfaces and will see them often, preparation and careful application are important. Masking the floor while painting the baseboard is just one way to ensure a top-quality paint job.

Allow plenty of time if you decide to paint your house yourself. Even with helpers, you won't be able to work as fast as a professional painting crew. Essential tasks such as moving planters and porch furniture and protecting plantings near the house add to the time and effort.

ABOUT PAINT & PAINTING

A technical definition of paint would be something like this: A combination of emulsified pigments suspended in a liquid, applied to a surface as decoration or protection.

Paint is simple in theory—after all, cave dwellers invented paint some 30,000 years ago and evidence of their work still shows on the walls of their rocky dwellings. It's doubtful, however, that cave dwellers gave much consideration to formulating their paints with precision.

Even though paint has been around for a long time and its essential definition hasn't changed much over the years, its colors, ingredients, and methods of manufacture have undergone extraordinary changes—a little at a time.

Early colors were ground from iron oxides, then from natural sources—plants, soils, bugs, and seashells. It took about 25,000 years for the first synthetic pigment to appear, and the Egyptians did that with finely ground blue glass. Ready-mixed paints for the consumer didn't show up until the 1880s when paint manufacturers figured out how to keep pigments suspended in linseed oil.

Of course, along with each major change in what went into the paint were changes in how it was applied. Fingers and hands (still employed for decorative effects) were augmented with flat sticks, then brushes, then sprayers, rollers, powered rollers, paint pads, and more kinds of sprayers.

The remarkable thing about paint and painting today is how little attention they often receive. Yet without paint, the world would be a drab place. And everything from the Golden Gate Bridge to a child's chair would succumb to rot and rust because paint provides primary protection against the environment.

Applying the right coating using the right tools and techniques is not a complicated endeavor—today's paint and painting products are designed to make the job easy. This chapter will show you what makes a good paint, how to clean and prepare the surface for painting, the tools you can use, and techniques that will help you make sure your paint job looks good and lasts a long time.

High-quality paint properly applied provides long-lasting beauty and protection for any surface.

CHAPTER PREVIEW

The chemistry of paint
page 30

The case for quality
page 32

Picking the perfect paint
page 34

Primers and sealers
page 36

Texture and speciality paints
page 38

Problems and cures— interior paint
page 40

There are many paints and tools for paint application. This chapter will help you determine what you need to use for your project.

Problems and cures— exterior paint
page 42

Painting preparation at a glance
page 44

Brushes and paint pads
page 46

Rollers
page 48

Sprayers and other tools
page 50

Good painting practices
page 52

Cleaning up
page 58

Maintaining painted surfaces
page 60

THE CHEMISTRY OF PAINT

Although different types and grades of paint often exhibit different qualities as you apply them and after they are dry, all paints generally contain four ingredients.

■ **Pigments** provide color and helps hide the surface underneath *(prime pigments)*. *Extender pigments* increase the bulk of the mix without increasing the cost.

For white paint, titanium dioxide (TiO_2) is the most common prime pigment. It provides exceptional whiteness and hiding power and exhibits a greater tendency toward chalking in exterior paints. Organic color pigments include the brighter colors. Inorganic color pigments such as red iron oxide, brown oxide, ochers, and umbers, are not as bright as organic colors but are the most durable exterior pigments.

Some commonly used extender pigments are clay, which provides hiding and stain resistance, silica and silicates, which increase scrub and abrasion resistance and control sheen, and zinc oxide, which increases resistance to mildew, corrosion, and staining.

■ **Binders** hold the particles of pigment together and creates the integral film that adheres to a properly prepared surface.

Oil-base binders can be organic oils such as linseed oil (squeezed from flax seed and refined), tung oil (from fruit of the chinawood tree), and soya oil (from soybeans), or modified oils called alkyds. Alkyds dry harder and faster than organic oils. Some coatings, chiefly exterior primers, combine oils and alkyds for increased flexibility. The term "oil-base" is commonly used to refer to both oil and alkyd coatings.

The binder in *latex-base paint* is a plastic-like, milky-white liquid dispersed as microscopic particles in water. It is reminiscent of (but not related to) natural latex from the rubber tree.

Pigment and binder are called the solids of the paint. They remain on the surface when the solvent evaporates.

■ **Solvents** (also called the carrier or vehicle) make up the liquid constituent of the paint. The liquid carries the pigment and binder and makes it possible to flow them onto the surface being painted. As the liquid evaporates, the binders and pigments coalesce into a continuous protective film.

Water is the solvent for latex paints. For most oil-base and alkyd paints, the solvent is a petroleum distillate. Shellac-base primers and varnishes use denatured alcohol as a solvent. Clear and pigmented lacquers use another petrochemical product, usually lacquer thinner.

Project Guide: Bedroom • Living Room • Dining Room • Home Office
Recommended for: Drywall • Wallboard • Plaster • Wood • Masonry • Metal
Previously painted surfaces • Most Wallpapers*
*Test metallic wallpapers: if bleeding occurs, apply a sealer or remove paper.

TO ACHIEVE DESIRED COLOR, COLORANT MUST BE ADDED BEFORE APPLICATION

This interior flat paint has excellent covering power. It dries to a smooth, even finish that maintains a warm appearance in your room. It hides minor surface imperfections and touch-ups blend easily. The surface can be washed with common household cleaners. 20 year warranty is your assurance of exceptional durability and performance.

PREPARATION: Clean and dry all surfaces to remove any dirt, dust, grease, wax, loose or peeling paint. Dull glossy surfaces by sanding or using a surface conditioner. Patch all cracks and holes with a patching compound; sand and prime before painting.

• Prime unpainted wood, metal, drywall or plaster with the appropriate **primer.**

RECOMMENDED TOOLS: Apply with a quality 1/4" – 3/8" nap roller, a nylon or polyester brush or a paint pad.

APPLICATION: Thinning of this product is usually not necessary. If required, use only water, up to one pint per gallon of this product. Some bright, deep and accent colors may require multiple coats to achieve the desired effect. Allow to dry thoroughly between coats.

1. Stir paint thoroughly with a lifting motion to insure uniform color.
2. Prepare roller by dampening it slightly with water.
3. Brush or edge a 3" or 4" border on wall around all edges.
4. Roll the remainder of the walls working in small areas with zigzag strokes. Upward, downward, up diagonal and down again. To even out texture, roll over area with parallel strokes. Do not roll or brush excessively. Move from dry areas to wet.
5. Paint woodwork last using even strokes, painting away from the wet edge.

CLEAN-UP AND CARE FOR THE PAINTED SURFACE: Clean hands and tools with warm, soapy water. Wipe up spills immediately with damp cloth. Painted surfaces may be washed after 30 days with mild household cleaner and soft sponge. Avoid using harsh, abrasive cleaners.

WARNING! CAUSES EYE, SKIN AND RESPIRATORY TRACT IRRITATION. MAY BE HARMFUL IF SWALLOWED. CONTAINS CRYSTALLINE SILICA WHICH CAN CAUSE LUNG CANCER AND OTHER LUNG DAMAGE IF INHALED. WHEN TINTED, CONTAINS ETHYLENE GLYCOL WHICH CAN CAUSE SEVERE KIDNEY DAMAGE WHEN INGESTED AND HAS BEEN SHOWN TO CAUSE BIRTH DEFECTS IN LABORATORY ANIMALS. USE ONLY WITH ADEQUATE VENTILATION. KEEP OUT OF THE REACH OF CHILDREN. This product contains a chemical known to the state of California to cause cancer. For emergency information call (800) 545-2643. For additional safety information, refer to the Material Safety Data Sheet for this product. If sanding is done, wear a dust mask to avoid breathing of sanding dust. Do not breathe vapors or spray mist. Ensure fresh air entry during application and drying. If you experience eye watering, headaches, or dizziness, leave the area. If properly used, a respirator may offer additional protection. Obtain professional advice before using. Close container after each use. FIRST AID: In case of skin contact, wash thoroughly with soap and water. If any product remains, gently rub petroleum jelly, vegetable or mineral/baby oil onto skin, then wash again with soap and water. Repeated applications may be needed. Remove contaminated clothing. For eye contact flush immediately with large amounts of water, for at least 15 minutes. **Obtain emergency medical treatment.** If swallowed, **obtain medical treatment immediately.** If inhalation causes physical discomfort, remove to fresh air. If discomfort persists or any breathing difficulty occurs, **get medical help.** **KEEP FROM FREEZING.** CCPL4-1100

L.C. 205110

The label tells the tale. Look at the label on the paint can carefully and you'll find a wealth of information—some of which can affect your decision about whether to buy it or not. Labels will vary in content from manufacturer to manufacturer, but most provide advice on what surfaces the paint is designed for, how to prepare the surface, how to apply the paint, and an estimate of how much area the contents of the can will cover. Some labels will also provide supplementary information, such as thinning proportions for use in spray equipment. "Warnings" or "cautions" contain information about health and safety issues associated with use of the paint.

Additives are ingredients that bring specific properties to the paint, such as mildew resistance, reduced foaming, good flow, and even leveling. *Thickeners* control viscosity and how well the paint flows when applied. They reduce paint spattering when you use a roller to apply it. *Surfactants* stabilize the paint so it will not separate or become too thick to use. They also help wet the surface being painted so the paint won't crawl (move about) when it is applied. *Biocides* keep bacteria from growing in the paint, and *mildewcides* discourage mildew from growing on the paint after it has been applied. *Defoamers* break bubbles as they are formed in the paint—especially important when rolling paint. *Cosolvents* are liquids additional to water that aid the binder in forming a good film, help the liquid paint resist damage if frozen, and enhance brushing properties, including flow and open time (the time the paint can be applied and worked before it sets). Cosolvents are generally volatile organic compounds (VOCs), which are increasingly subject to controls today.

Latex vs. oil

In the early days of water-base paint chemistry, the quality of the coatings was often inconsistent. Professional painters weren't always sure they'd get a good batch. But improved science and quality control now enable manufacturers to produce water-base paints that virtually match the durability of oil-base paints.

But many paint professionals—both dealers and appliers—still feel that oil-base primers bond better with raw wood and that oil-base color coats out-perform their water-base counterparts for durability, especially in demanding applications like trim and high-traffic rooms. Decide for yourself whether improved longevity is worth the inconvenience of solvent cleanup.

Watching paint dry

If you really could watch what happens as latex paint dries, you'd see the gradual formation of a tough film.

In freshly applied paint, the particles of pigment and binder are dispersed widely in the liquid. The film starts to form when the water begins to evaporate. During this process, the particles of pigment and binder come closer together. As the last molecules of liquid evaporate, capillary action draws the binder particles together with great force, causing them to fuse with the pigment into a continuous film.

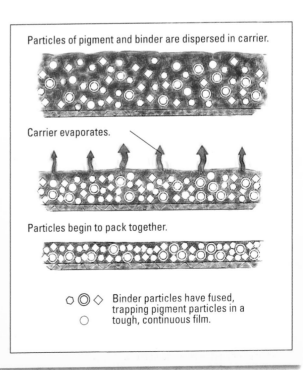

Particles of pigment and binder are dispersed in carrier.

Carrier evaporates.

Particles begin to pack together.

Binder particles have fused, trapping pigment particles in a tough, continuous film.

THE CASE FOR QUALITY

Why do some exterior paints look fresh and almost new after a decade of service while others start peeling and flaking within a couple of years? Or why do some interior paints still exhibit a rich, deep color long after the kids have grown up while others look worn, scuffed, and ready for a recoat soon after you've applied them? There's no secret in the answer—it's the quality of the paint.

Whatever you're painting, it's important to use the best paint you can afford—even if that means stretching the project budget a bit. Top-quality paints are designed to produce the best-looking and longest-lasting results. They provide a smoother, more uniform appearance and can last more than twice as long as cheaper paints. In the long run, that saves money because you don't have to repaint as often.

High-quality paint goes on faster and with less effort because it hides better and flows out evenly. That means less brushing, rolling, and retouching. It also means you can apply fewer coats to get an attractive and uniform appearance. And if you're rolling, a high-quality paint will save you cleanup time because it doesn't spatter as readily.

For exterior work, a properly prepared surface coated with high-quality paint will also require less maintenance between paint jobs. You probably won't have to clean off mildew or worry about excessive chalking, peeling, or cracking.

Likewise with interior work, a top-quality paint not only lasts longer, it also resists dirt and stains and stands up to cleaning better than lower-line paint.

But how do you determine which paints are high-quality? It's easy if you know a few things to look for when you shop for paint.

A solid case

When paint dries, the proportion of solids (pigments and binders) to the liquid solvent determines how thick the dried paint film will be. Paint with higher solids content will dry to a thicker film. In general, a thicker film hides better and is more durable. Look on the can label or ask your supplier for the specification sheet (all paints should have one). The proportion of solids to solvent (carrier) can be expressed by weight or volume. The weight of solids to solvent is

QUALITY INTERIOR PAINT RESISTS STICKING ON DOOR AND WINDOW JAMBS

Acrylic gloss paint   **Economy gloss paint**

QUALITY INTERIOR PAINT FLOWS SMOOTHLY

Quality paint   **Economy paint**

QUALITY INTERIOR PAINT CLEANS EASIER

Lipstick

Crayon

Quality paint   **Economy paint**

AFTER HAND-WASHING WITH DETERGENT

QUALITY EXTERIOR PAINT RESISTS COLOR FADING

Acrylic paint   **Economy paint**

SOUTH-FACING EXPOSURE, 4 YEARS

QUALITY EXTERIOR PAINT LASTS LONGER

Acrylic paint   **Economy paint**

NORTH-FACING EXPOSURE ON CONCRETE, 5 YEARS

QUALITY EXTERIOR PAINT RESISTS CRACKING

Quality paint   **Economy paint**

SOUTH-FACING EXPOSURE, TWO COATS, 2 YEARS

usually higher than the volume of solids to solvent; volume is a better indicator of performance. Latex paints generally range from 25 to about 40 percent solids by volume, depending on type and quality. Alkyd and oil-base paints can exceed 50 percent volume solids. A higher solids percentage is better.

Be wary of high-solid paints that don't cost much. The low cost can mean inexpensive solids make up the bulk of the paint, and that spells a shorter life span for all your work.

Better binders

Latex paint can be formulated with all-acrylic binder, vinyl binder, or vinyl-acrylic binder. All-acrylic binder is more weather-resistant and durable. If the label doesn't say "100% acrylic" or "All acrylic," check the ingredients or spec sheet to see if the paint contains acrylic polymer.

About application

Application methods count too. Even with a high-quality, high-solid paint, thinning for any reason other than spraying is not recommended because it reduces the proportion of solids in the paint layer and thus makes it thinner when it dries.

Also make sure you're applying the right paint for the surface. Most water-base exterior paints can be used on wood and hardboard siding and trim, vinyl and aluminum siding, and most masonry.

On stucco or concrete block prone to cracking, however, use an elastomeric paint. It's more flexible than standard coatings and leaves a durable film that's twice as thick (about 5 mil). These paints actually bridge gaps in masonry surfaces and can be painted over with a high-quality latex paint.

In some climates, a paint will perform better if it is formulated to stand up to specific conditions associated with that climate. For example, a paint with more mildewcide would be desirable in the Southeast, where humid conditions favor the growth of mold and mildew. In the Northwest, your painting efforts might be better rewarded by applying a paint with a high solid content to fend off the rain.

Last, check out the paint warranty. You may not actually consider the warranty period to be the exact life of the paint, but you can usually assume that paint with a longer warranty is higher-quality paint.

Low- and medium-grade paints often have less of the same ingredients as quality paints. They won't cover as well but may work in rooms that need infrequent painting.

A high-quality paint spreads easily and covers completely.

STANLEY PRO TIP: **Interior vs. exterior paints**

Interior and exterior paints are formulated with different properties for different uses. Don't use exterior paint indoors because it seems tougher. Some high-grade exterior paints can be worse indoors than a low-quality interior paint.

Interior paints are formulated for:	Exterior paints are formulated for:
Stain resistance	Color retention
Scrubbability	Flexible expansion and contraction
Splatter resistance	Resistance to mildew and tannin bleed
Lack of yellowing	High adhesion—less chance of blistering, peeling
Good hiding ability	Resistance to dirt
Easy touch-up	Resistance to peeling
Resistance to alkaline cleaners	Resistance to fading
Burnish and block resistance—won't get shiny when rubbed; won't stick to other surfaces	Resistance to alkalis

PICKING THE PERFECT PAINT

Once you have dealt with the color and quality factors, there's one more consideration when picking paint for a surface—its sheen. Sheen is a measure of how much light reflects back from the paint—in short, how shiny it is. Although sheen is controlled by quantity of the paint's pigments and additives, what's important to your choices is that certain sheens look better and clean easier on certain surfaces.

Sheens

Most paints fall into one of four sheen categories—flat, satin, semigloss, and gloss. Manufacturers may choose descriptive names such as matte or eggshell, so avoid surprises by checking actual samples when comparing paints. Sheen affects not only the appearance of a painted surface, but also its durability. The higher the sheen, the harder the paint.

But don't assume all glossy paints display the same reflectivity. Sheens are not standardized from brand to brand. One company's satin may be glossier than another brand's. Here's how the sheen of a paint can affect your choices.

Flat paints are pretty much nonreflective, with a matte finish that's good for hiding imperfections—bumps, dents, patches, and nailheads. These paints show marks and scuffs, however, and the soft surface stains easily. Newer scrubbable flat paints are tougher and easier to clean.

Satin paints display a light luster with a soft texture. They are more durable than flat paints and can be used for trim that won't get much abuse, especially when you want to set the trim apart from a flat-painted wall.

Semigloss paint has a higher gloss and tougher skin than satin paint, so it stands up to use and cleans more readily. However, a semigloss paint has just enough shine to begin to show imperfections in the surface.

Gloss paints are the hardest—and hardiest—of all. This sheen is sometimes considered enamel and can take abuse and some rough scrubbing. Its high gloss makes imperfections clearly visible.

The sheen of a paint may also alter the perception of its color. For example, the same tint of white may look whiter in a glossy enamel than in a flat wall paint. That's because more of the color is reflected, even though the color itself is the same. To make sure you have the paint sheen you want, take home samples and paint them on test boards (see page 10).

Traditionally, different paint sheens have been favored for various surfaces.

Paint for ceilings

Ceilings don't suffer the abrasion other surfaces endure, but cooking vapors, airborne grease, smoke, pollution, and plain old dirt gradually make a ceiling dingy and dull. A flat or semigloss sheen is a good choice for ceilings because it hides imperfections well. Paints formulated specifically for ceilings are thicker so they are less spatter prone, are nonyellowing, and dry faster.

Paint for walls

Many homebuilders apply flat paints to walls to help disguise less-than-perfect drywall finishing. But flat paint quickly shows wear. Attempts to clean away dirty marks often result in creating a larger smudge.

A satin finish is more forgiving, with substantially upgraded durability and without

Varnish and stain

Varnish is a clear, tough coating applied to wood, primarily as a protection. You'll find both water-base and oil-base varnishes in sheens ranging from satin to high gloss. Most varnishes do not alter the color of the wood appreciably; they may add a warmer tone. Color-tinted varnishes are available, but they do not change the color of the wood as much as stains.

Stains—either liquid or gel—color the wood but let the grain show through (except for heavy-bodied stains, which are much like paint and are used primarily on exterior surfaces). Since they are absorbed by the wood, stains don't impart a sheen.

You can purchase premixed pigmented stains, or mix your own from powders and oils, alcohol, or water, controlling the level of staining by altering the proportion of the dye or by increasing the number of coats. (See pages 186–187.)

Choosing the right paints for interior surfaces

Choosing the right paint for the surface requires balancing sheen with durability and easy cleanup. Here are the usual paints used on various surfaces around the house:

Type of surface	What paint to use	Advantages
Ceilings	Flat	Doesn't reflect light, provides uniform sheen
Walls in living rooms, halls, and bedrooms	Satin	Resists stains, cleans easily, rich appearance
Walls in bathrooms and kitchens	Satin or semigloss Gloss	Resists stains, easier to clean than flat paint Durable and very easy to clean
Kitchen cabinets	Semigloss Gloss	Resists stains, easier to clean than flat paint Durable and very easy to clean
Woodwork and trim	Semigloss Gloss	Resists stains, easier to clean than flat paint Durable and very easy to clean

excessive shine. Paint made for bathrooms and kitchens contains extra mildewcides and is moisture and peel resistant. Ask your dealer about child's-room paints. Formulated for hard use, they can be perfect in other demanding locations, such as kitchens, baths, laundry rooms, and hallways. And for a kitchen, you can even apply a semigloss or gloss finish on the walls to make them easier to wipe clean.

Paint for trim

Doors, windows, and moldings typically take a higher sheen than walls because they get more physical contact and need a tougher surface. Besides, a glossy surface accentuates the woodwork and makes it stand out from the walls. That contrast between trim and walls adds interest to your design scheme. Choose trim paint that's at least one step glossier than the walls.

Flat paint can enhance the intimacy of a room by softly diffusing light instead of reflecting it brightly. Flat paint also appears neutral—a quality that makes it effective on background walls—and helps hide flaws.

Flat paints produce a nonreflective matte finish that's good for hiding imperfections—bumps, dents, patches, and nailheads.

Satin finishes have a slight luster with a soft texture. They are more reflective and more durable than flat paints.

Semigloss paints have a higher gloss and harder surface than satins, so they stand up to use and clean more easily.

Gloss paints give the hardest and brightest finish. They are durable and easy to clean but also reveal surface imperfections.

PRIMERS AND SEALERS

Primers and sealers provide an extra measure of assurance that the paint you use will adhere to its surface. In effect, primers and sealers are preparatory products that give the surface tooth that the paint can grip.

■ **Primers** are formulated to adhere to the substrate and create a uniform surface for the finish coat. Primers stick to the surface; finish coats stick to the primer. Primers penetrate unpainted surfaces, smoothing out any porosity. Primers for wood, whether they are latex or oil-base, contain specialized ingredients that topcoats don't necessarily have, or have in lesser amounts. Stain-inhibiting tannin blockers or preservatives that are found in primers, for instance, are designed to soak into raw wood and seal it so the tannins don't bleed through and stain the finish paint. Primers for other surfaces have similarly specialized ingredients. Latex primers are best for unfinished drywall.

On raw interior wood, oil-base primers may be a better choice because of their surface penetration. On the exterior, a latex primer will last longer because it's more flexible, expanding and contracting with changes in temperature instead of cracking. There are a number of different kinds of primers—oil-base, shellac-base, water-base—and each has its own specialty. Ask your retailer for a recommendation on which product to use on the surface you're painting.

■ **Sealers,** closely related to primers, are formulated to make a porous surface non-porous. They are also used to cover knots and mildew to keep them from showing through the finish coats. You'll find oil-base sealers, as well as products with reactive resins and epoxies. Most of these products clean up with strong petroleum solvents.

Choosing the right primer or sealer
Primers and sealers come in an array of formulations. It's important to choose the right one for your job.

Exterior applications
■ **New unpainted wood:** If the wood species won't leech tannins into the paint, use either a quality acrylic latex or an oil-base exterior wood primer. For woods that will stain the paint, apply an oil-base stain-blocking primer. Prime and paint bare wood within two weeks of installation to prevent the wood fibers from deteriorating and reducing adhesion.

Specialty primers for metals and other surfaces are discussed on pages 158–171.

■ **Weathered, unpainted wood:** Sand the wood thoroughly before priming to remove deteriorated wood fibers, which will compromise primer adhesion. Remove the dust, then apply a quality latex or oil-base primer shortly after preparing the surface.

■ **Painted wood:** Scrape all loose paint and feather-sand rough edges. Sand bare spots, remove all chalking with a damp cloth, and let the surface dry. If you can't remove all the chalk, apply an oil-base primer. If the old paint is sound and adhering well, priming can be beneficial but is not necessary.

■ **Masonry:** On new masonry, or older porous surfaces, use a latex masonry sealer or primer. On previously painted masonry, you need to seal only spots where the old paint has been removed during surface preparation or by weathering.

■ **Aluminum or galvanized iron:** Remove any white, powdery oxide using a nonmetallic scouring pad or abrasive. Then apply a corrosion-inhibitive metal primer to all exposed bare metal.

■ **Ferrous metals:** Wire-brush any rust, rinse, let dry, and apply two coats of a latex or oil-base rust-inhibitive primer.

Interior applications

Most interior primers are designed for specific applications and come in both latex and oil-base formulations. You may prefer latex products because the reduced odors are an advantage when working indoors.

■ **Drywall primers:** While these products are called primers, they actually serve as pigmented sealers over drywall to give the topcoat of paint a smooth surface to adhere to. This results in a uniform appearance. They also enhance the hiding ability of the finish coat by providing additional tinting in the undercoat.

■ **Stain-blocking primers:** These primers stop bleed-through of such stain-producing agents as dirt, ink, crayon marks, smoke residue, grease, mildew, and water stains. Both latex and oil-base products are available, but oil-base products are more effective for blocking water stains.

■ **Vapor barrier primers:** These primers are useful in bathrooms, kitchens, and other rooms that can harbor moisture. In rooms without plastic vapor barriers in the walls, these primers help minimize the passage

Shellac-base stain-blocking primers are heavily tinted to keep mildew from bleeding through the paint. Always wash mildewed areas thoroughly with a mild bleach solution, allowing the solution to remain on the surface for 20 minutes. Let the area dry before priming it.

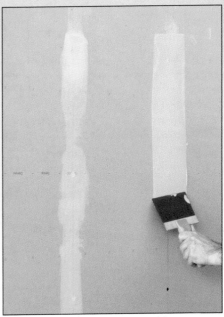

Drywall and drywall joint compound soak up paint fast, and if you've invested in a high-quality paint, you want your investment on the wall, not in it. Prime all drywall joint compound and let the primer dry. Then prime the entire surface of the wall.

of the moisture through the walls to the exterior, thereby reducing the likelihood the moisture will push the paint off the outside walls. Because they retain humidity, they also help keep indoor rooms more comfortable in winter.

■ **Latex enamel undercoaters:** Using these primers under semigloss or gloss paint helps ensure that the topcoat of paint will develop its maximum gloss and have a uniform look. For best appearance, some manufacturers recommend a light sanding on the undercoat before applying the paint.

■ **Bonding primers:** These primers are designed for slick surfaces such as glass, ceramic tile, and synthetic laminates. Sand the surface first with fine (220-grit) aluminum oxide sandpaper to improve adhesion.

■ **Concrete primer/sealer:** Use this product to reduce the dust on interior concrete floors and to smooth the porous surface.

STANLEY PRO TIP

Do you really need a primer?

Many homeowners, in a rush to complete a project, skip the primer and go right to the color coats. This shortcut often backfires because it may take an extra coat of color to get complete coverage. Because primer is cheaper than paint, that represents both wasted time and money.

Primer is specially formulated to bond to raw wood and to seal porous surfaces such as drywall. Primer typically dries rapidly so you apply the finish coat sooner. So a good primer saves time, effort, and money. Consider tinting your primer to the color of your paint so the paint covers better. Your paint retailer can tint the primer.

TEXTURE AND SPECIALTY PAINTS

Texture paint will put some pizzazz into a plain painted wall. These paints provide an easy way to get both color and texture on the walls at the same time. And they have the added benefit of covering up problem walls or ceilings—uneven surfaces, rough spots, and other flaws. You can apply texture to an entire surface or paint selectively to create patterned borders, adding a textural element at little cost.

Texture paints come in different forms. The most common is paint that has a light texture medium such as sand or other fine aggregate added. There are also texture additives that can be mixed in to most latex or oil-base paints. One such additive is an antiskid material for floors and stairs.

To paint a texture surface, apply two coats of oil-base sealer, let it dry, then apply the texture paint.

In their initial application, texture paints go on about the same way as any other paint—cut in the edges with a brush (pages 127–128) and finish the remainder of the surface with a roller. (Don't spray texture paint; the texture particles will clog and damage the sprayer.)

When cutting in, load up the brush heavily and frequently. Otherwise the brushing will thin out the texture and result in a noticeable unevenness at the edges of the wall or ceiling. Roll the paint on in long, even strokes, keeping the thickness even to maintain consistent texture.

Use a thick-napped roller to create a stippled surface. For a deeper texture, use a looped roller cover specifically designed for this purpose. The nap is stiffer than others and pulls the paint up behind it as you roll.

When using a stipple roller, avoid overlapping previously painted sections or the stipple pattern will appear interrupted at the overlaps. An advantage of texture paint is that you can stop with the roller, or, as the accompanying photos show, experiment with other tools to create other patterns.

If you have never employed this technique or product before, experiment on a large piece of scrap plywood, drywall, or hardboard. This will give you a chance to judge the final appearance of the surface and hone your techniques so your application will be easy and consistent.

A roller with a 1¼-inch nap stipples the surface.

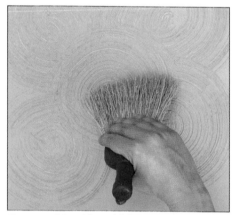

Create swirls with a whisk broom.

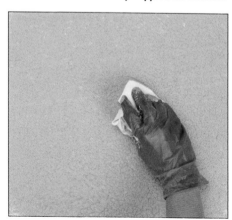

Pat crumpled paper to create a raised pattern.

Knock off the points of the texture (when almost dry) with a drywall knife.

Specialty paints

Modern technology has created so many products that there's virtually nothing you can't paint and there's a paint made for almost every purpose.

■ **Ceiling paints** are formulated for spatter-free application. Some even go on displaying one color and then dry white. This eliminates the problems inherent in painting a ceiling—if you're painting white on white, you often can't see where the new paint begins and the old paint ends. Some brands even boast a dry-up time of 30 minutes.

■ **Kitchen and bath paints** are also formulated to keep spattering to a minimum and cleaning easy, but their chief claim to fame is that they contain an extra dose of mildewcide to stop this annoying growth in these usually humid rooms.

■ **Elastomeric wall coatings (EWCs)** are specifically designed to paint over small cracks in masonry surfaces.

The key to success for these paints lies in the flexibility of their binders. Masonry cracks expand and contract at a greater rate than other materials, and standard latex paints are too rigid to handle these changes. EWCs actually stretch and bridge thin cracks. In addition a properly applied EWC can be top-coated with exterior acrylic latex paint in a flat, satin, or semigloss finish.

Before applying an EWC to a wall, repair any cracks more than 1/8-inch across with a high-quality acrylic or siliconized caulk; not even an EWC can bridge gaps that wide. EWCs should also be applied in much thicker coats than other paints for best results. Where a gallon of latex paint may cover approximately 400 to 500 square feet of surface, a gallon of EWC will cover only 40 to 50 square feet.

■ **High-temperature paints** are made in several colors and different grades that will withstand different temperatures, some up to 1,200°F. They see wide applications in commercial enterprises, but some are formulated for consumer uses, like repainting the barbecue grill or touching up the wood stove, radiator, or supplementary gas heater. They are commonly available in aerosol spray cans.

■ **Epoxy paints,** an alternative term for epoxy polymers, are a tough plasticlike material employed as a coating, especially for interior floor surfaces. Most epoxy paints are prepared by combining two components on-site, just before application. Some epoxy materials contain very high or 100 percent solids; some are two-component water-base acrylic-epoxy; and some are one-package water-base products. Two-component epoxy systems generally do not stand up and maintain color in exterior applications as well as two-component urethane systems.

Epoxy chemistry and the number of products produced for different purposes and at different prices is an extremely complex subject, and there are some surfaces to which epoxy won't stick. Research your choices thoroughly before purchasing an epoxy product.

■ **Rust encapsulators** are formulated to be brushed or sprayed onto rusty steel and iron. These products are useful where sandblasting or other rust-removal methods are impractical. (They can also be used over new metal or rusty metal that has been cleaned.) The hard, nonporous coat prevents further rusting. Moisture and humidity help the coating cure, but the surface should be dry for application. Some rust encapsulators are UV sensitive and require a topcoat.

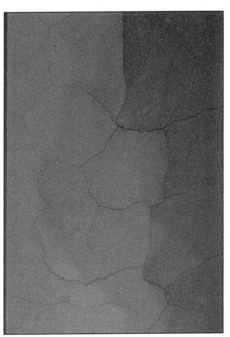

Elastomeric wall coatings form a thick, flexible film that bridges narrow cracks in masonry surfaces caused by expansion and contraction. They maintain a fresh "just-painted" appearance and can be finish-coated with a high-quality exterior latex paint.

Many high-temperature paints for at-home use are available in spray cans at your local paint distributor or auto parts store. They can quickly transform the appearance of an aging barbecue or woodstove. Be sure to remove all rust and flaking paint before applying high-temperature paints.

PROBLEMS AND CURES—INTERIOR PAINT

Sometimes you'll encounter problems in the existing surface that you must fix before repainting. Some of the problems are the result of poor-quality paint. Others are the consequence of inadequate preparation or poor application techniques. Some of the most common problems are shown here, along with an explanation of their causes (so you can avoid repeating them) and solutions (so you can fix them before applying your new paint).

Sagging can be caused by:
- Applying the paint too heavily
- Painting in humid or cool weather
- Thinning the paint
- Spraying with the spray head too close

Solution:
- Before repainting—Sand all glossy surfaces. Sand sags flat and reapply a new coat of paint.
- During application—Do not thin the paint or overapply it. Two coats at the recommended spread rate are better than one heavy coat. Avoid cool or humid conditions. If the paint sags as you apply it, immediately brush it out or reroll it evenly.

Blistering can be caused by:
- Applying oil-base paint over a damp or wet surface
- Outside moisture seeping in through the interior walls
- Exposing latex paint to high humidity or moisture shortly after paint has dried

Solution:
- Remove any source of moisture, if possible. Repair loose caulking. Remove blisters by scraping and sanding, prime bare spots, and repaint with a quality acrylic latex interior paint.

Burnishing can be caused by:
- Using flat paint in high-traffic areas
- Frequent washing and spot cleaning
- Objects rubbing against the walls
- Low-grade paint

Solution:
- Paint heavy-wear areas that require regular cleaning with a scrubbable latex wall paint. In high-traffic areas, choose a

SAGGING:
Downward drooping of the paint immediately after application.

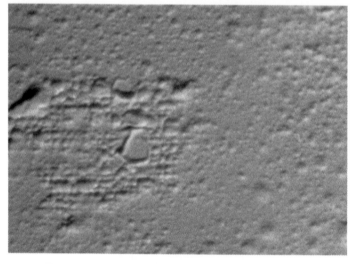

BLISTERING:
Bubbling and lifting of the paint.

BURNISHING:
Increase in gloss or sheen when paint is rubbed or scrubbed.

CRACKING AND FLAKING:
The splitting of a dry paint film through at least one coat.

BLOCKING:
Undesirable sticking of two painted surfaces.

ROLLER MARKS OR STIPPLE:
Unintentional textured pattern left in the paint by the roller.

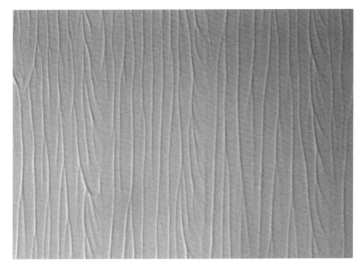

semigloss or gloss rather than a flat sheen. Clean painted surfaces with a soft cloth or sponge and nonabrasive cleansers.

Cracking and flaking can be caused by:
■ Low-quality paint with inadequate adhesion and flexibility
■ Over thinning or overspreading the paint
■ Improper surface preparation, or failure to prime the surface
■ Excessive hardening and embrittlement of alkyd paint as the paint ages

Solution:
■ Remove loose and flaking paint with a scraper, sand and feather the edges. Fill deep cracks in multiple layers of paint. Prime bare wood with a top-quality primer and paint with a high-quality finish coat.

Blocking can be caused by:
■ Closing doors or windows before the paint is dry
■ Low-quality semigloss or gloss paint

Solution:
■ Use top-quality semigloss or gloss acrylic latex paint.
■ Apply talcum powder to mating surfaces to relieve persistent blocking.

Roller marks or stipple can be caused by:
■ Using a low-quality roller cover or one with the wrong nap
■ Low-grade paint
■ Incorrect rolling technique

Solution:
■ Use a high-quality short-nap roller cover and high-quality paint whose higher solids content rolls on and levels more evenly.
■ Dampen roller covers before loading with latex paint; shake out excess water.
■ Don't let paint build up at roller ends. Begin rolling at a corner near the ceiling and work down the wall in 3-foot-square sections. Spread the paint, beginning with an upward stroke to minimize spatter; then, without lifting the roller from the surface, bring the roller back with a downstroke. Finish the section with light, parallel strokes.

PROBLEMS AND CURES—EXTERIOR PAINT

Exterior paints can exhibit more problems than interior paints because they are subjected to the sun, wind, and weather. Here are some of the most common.

Alligatoring can be caused by:
■ Applying alkyd enamel over a more flexible latex primer
■ Applying the top coat before the primer dries
■ Oil-base paints aging and undergoing temperature fluctuations

Solution:
■ Remove old paint with a scraper or heat gun. Sand the surface and prime it with high-quality latex or oil-base primer, then finish with a top-quality exterior latex paint.

Chalking can be caused by:
■ Low-grade, highly pigmented paint
■ Using interior paint on an outdoor surface

Solution:
■ Scrub off as much of the chalky residue as possible with a stiff bristle brush and rinse thoroughly.
■ If noticeable chalk is still present, apply high-quality oil-base or acrylic latex primer, then repaint with a quality exterior coating.
■ If little or no chalk remains and the old paint is sound, no priming is necessary.

Paint incompatibility can be caused by:
■ Painting latex paint over more than three or four coats of oil-base paint

Solution:
■ Completely remove the flaking paint and sand and spot-prime where necessary. Repaint with a top-quality latex exterior or oil-base paint.

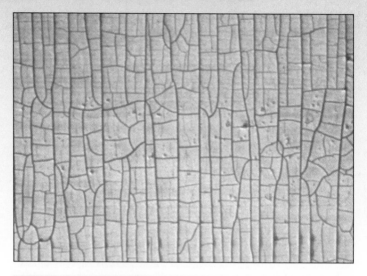

ALLIGATORING: *Cracking in the surface of the paint that resembles the scales of an alligator.*

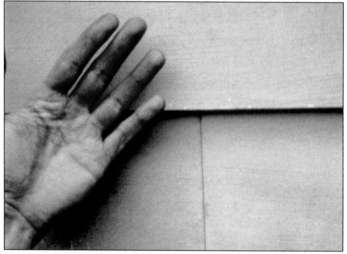

CHALKING: *Formation of fine powder on the surface of the paint. Some chalking is a desirable way for paint to wear, but excessive chalking can erode the paint.*

PAINT INCOMPATIBILITY: *Poor adhesion where latex paint is applied over many old coats of oil-base paint.*

PEELING:
Loss of paint due to poor adhesion.

CRACKING AND FLAKING:
Splitting of a dry paint film through at least one coat, which will lead to complete failure of the paint.

LAPPING:
Appearance of a denser color or lighter gloss where wet and dry layers overlap.

Peeling can be caused by:
■ Moisture seepage through uncaulked joints, worn caulk, leaks in roof or walls, or leaks through interior walls to the exterior
■ Poor surface preparation
■ Low-quality paint
■ Applying oil-base paint on a wet surface
■ Earlier blistering of paint (see page 40)

Solution:
■ Try to eliminate the source of moisture.
■ Remove all loose paint with scraper, sand rough edges, prime, and repaint with a high-quality acrylic latex exterior paint.

Cracking and flaking can be caused by:
■ Low-quality paint with poor flexibility
■ Thinning or spreading the paint too thin
■ Poor surface preparation, especially omitting primer on bare wood
■ Painting in cool or windy conditions, which can make latex paint dry too fast

Solution:
■ If cracking stops above the substrate, remove loose or flaking paint with a scraper, feather-sand the edges, prime any bare spots, and repaint.
■ If you can see the substrate through the cracks, remove all of the paint, then prime and repaint with a high-quality exterior latex.

Lapping can be caused by:
■ Failure to maintain a wet edge when applying paint

Solution:
■ Paint from unpainted to painted surface.
■ Plan for interruptions at a natural break, such as a window, door, or corner. Alkyd paints generally hold a wet edge longer than latex paints.

PAINTING PREPARATION AT A GLANCE

1. New unpainted wood
Prime with high-quality acrylic latex or oil-base exterior wood primer. Use a stain-blocking primer for woods like cedar and redwood whose tannins will bleed through the finish coat.

2. Weathered unpainted wood
Sand weathered wood to renew the surface for better adhesion. Prime as new unpainted wood.

3. Previously painted wood
Primer is usually not necessary unless the paint chalks heavily or is peeled to bare wood. However, even a sound surface can benefit from a high-quality primer, which will provide maximum adhesion, uniformity, and mildew resistance.

4. Stucco and other masonry
On new and porous surfaces, apply masonry primer. Over old paint, spot prime only where paint is removed to the substrate during surface preparation.

5. Ferrous metals
Wire-brush rusted areas on pipes or other steel or iron. Then wash, rinse, and let dry. Apply acrylic latex or oil-base rust-inhibitive primer before painting.

6. Aluminum, galvanized iron
Remove oxidation with a synthetic scrub pad and wash the surface. Apply metal primer to all bare metal.

7. High-humidity areas
Use high-adhesion interior primer on walls and ceilings in humid rooms, such as bathrooms, kitchens, and laundries.

8. Slick, glossy surfaces
For maximum adhesion, sand the surface first with fine (220-grit) aluminum oxide sandpaper. Use bonding primer on glass, ceramic tile, and plastic laminates. (But do not paint countertops.)

9. Unpainted drywall
Prime unpainted drywall with latex drywall primer, then finish coat with latex wall paint. (If stains are present, use a stain-blocking primer.)

10. Stained walls
Clean the surface. Apply stain-blocking primer on walls with stubborn dirt, ink and crayon marks, smoke residue, grease, or water stains.

11. Semigloss or gloss paint
Prime with enamel undercoater to ensure the paint will attain its maximum gloss. Some enamel undercoaters call for light sanding after application.

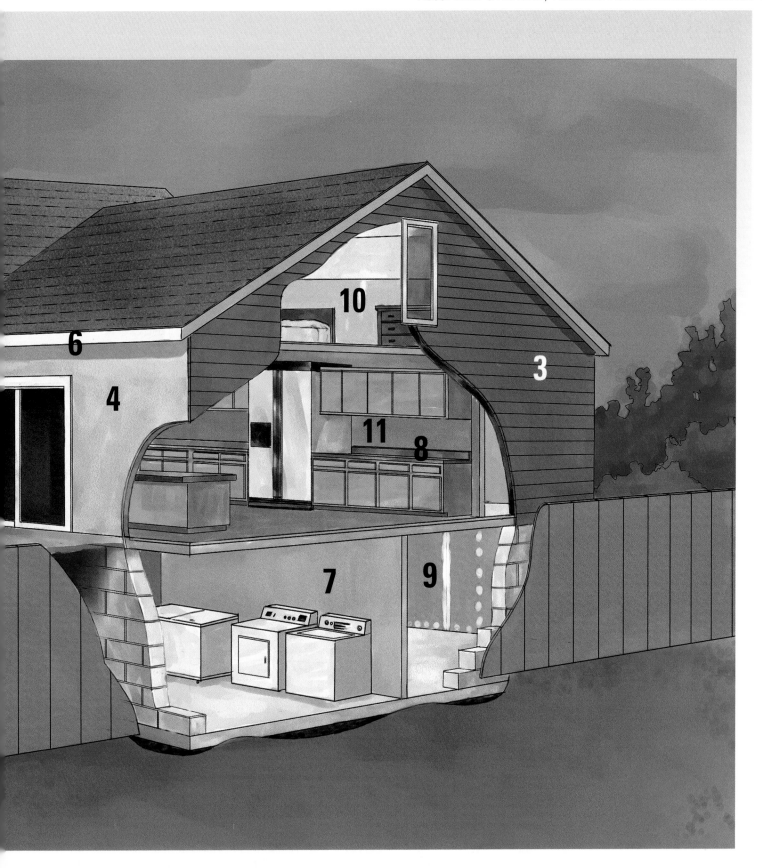

BRUSHES AND PAINT PADS

What has been said about the use of high-quality primers and paints also goes for the tools you use to apply them. Applying a coat of expensive top coat with a bargain-basement brush undermines your effort. High-quality brushes and paint pads not only get the paint on the wall more evenly and with less effort, they will produce more-durable and better-looking results.

Quality brushes apply paint in a thicker, smoother film, which results in maximum hiding and a uniform sheen. Conversely, lower-quality brushes often leave ridges in the paint where dirt can collect and mildew can grow. Paint with brushmarks in it can fail earlier in the thin spots.

Brushes

Brushes are categorized by the material used in the bristles.

Natural-bristle brushes, made from boar's hair, should be used only when applying oil-base paints. Their natural oils let paint flow out smoothly. If you use a natural-bristle brush with a latex paint, the bristles, which are hollow, will soak up a large amount of the water in the paint and will quickly become limp and unmanageable.

Synthetic-bristle brushes, made from nylon, polyester, or a nylon-polyester mix, can be used to apply all latex paints, and many can also be used with alkyd coatings. Nylon will retain its shape longer when you're faced with a large paint job requiring latex paint. Some synthetic brushes have hollow bristles; they are made solely for the application of oil-base paints, not latex.

Paintbrushes have more jobs to do than simply get the paint on the wall. The best brushes will do these things:

■ give you the best paint pickup (paint loads quickly and evenly)
■ provide the best transfer (put as much paint on the wall with one stroke as possible, and do it smoothly)

INSPECTING A BRUSH

Fan bristles to check density, stiffness, and end flagging.

Look for a well-shaped handle large enough to grip comfortably.

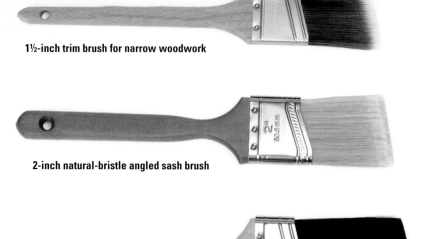

1½-inch trim brush for narrow woodwork

2-inch natural-bristle angled sash brush

3-inch synthetic-bristle brush

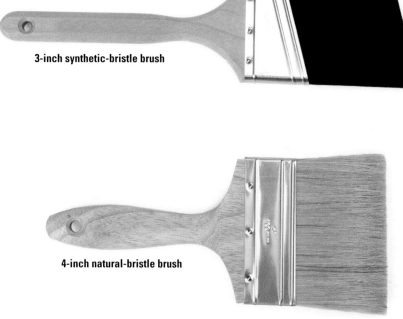

4-inch natural-bristle brush

■ level effortlessly (leave a smooth film without brush marks)

■ cut in sharply (create a sharp straight paint line)

Quality brushes have split or flagged ends that are flexible, qualities which help produce a smoother finish. The bristles are tapered, with those in the center slightly longer than those at the edge. There should be a divider at the heel of the bristles to provide a reservoir for the paint. Quality brushes feature bristles at least half as long as they are wide (for example, the bristles on a 2-inch-wide brush should be at least 3 inches long).

A bare wood handle, rather than plastic or painted wood, will give you a better, more comfortable grip (which you'll be grateful for after cuttingin the edges of a wall for an hour). A quality brush should be bound with a rust-resistant metal ferrule that is nailed on, not just crimped to the handle.

You can get by with just one brush when painting, but a collection of several sizes will serve you better. A 4-inch brush with bristles ¾ to 1 inch thick is good for general exterior painting; a 3-inch brush will do for most interior painting. Use a 2-inch brush to cut in corners for interior work. And get a 1- to 2½-inch angled sash brush for interior and exterior trim, window frames, and moldings.

Paint pads

Some paint pads are made of a plastic foam and are often cut in blocks or cut to resemble a paintbrush. Others are made of nylon fabric attached to a foam pad on a plastic plate that snaps in and out of a plastic handle. The pad can be removed from the handle for cleaning and reuse.

The pile of the nylon pad is similar to a roller cover and is about as thick. Paint pads come in different textures and are replaceable. Some professional painters like pads for cutting in at the ceiling line.

Paint pads can be used to apply latex or oil-base paints, stains, and floor finishes. They are not recommended for primers because they do not enable the penetration that brushes do.

Paint pads have one distinct advantage over brushes or rollers: They allow you to get to hard-to-reach spaces, such as corners and behind radiators, where neither brushes nor rollers will fit. Lamb's wool pads are ideal for applying exterior stains because they hold a lot of stain, are relatively dripless, and can be used on rough and textured surfaces.

Pads vary in size from 1 inch square to about 4×9 inches. Some models have wheel guides that are handy when painting against an adjoining wall, trim, or ceiling. Many pads come with their own paint tray and lid.

Disposable foam brushes are good for small paint jobs like trimming window muntins. They are especially good for laying down water-base paint and varnish because they level the coating without brush marks. Although they are made to be disposable, some can be cleaned carefully and reused a few times.

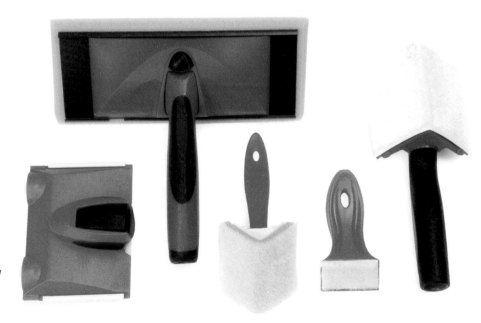

Paint pads come in a variety of sizes and shapes and are outfitted with different kinds of handles. The longest lasting are those with a nylon pad attached firmly to a plastic plate. Some of the larger models are made to attach to extension poles, although controlling the paint line is more difficult when working at a distance.

ROLLERS

Rollers have been around since the early 1940s and have become the standard applicator for interior painting because they can put a lot of paint on a lot of wall in a short time. You can spread about three times as much paint on a surface with a roller as with a brush in the same amount of time.

Rollers come in various widths—7½ and 9 inches are standard, with the 9-inch model suitable for most interior wall and ceiling jobs. Wider rollers (14 to 18 inches) make painting go quickly in large rooms, but the extra weight can be more tiring. Smaller rollers come in handy for trim and corner work. You'll also find a variety of power rollers—self-feeding rollers with a continuous supply of pressure-fed paint or manual-fill types for very large paint jobs.

Roller nap or pile

The cover material on a roller is called the nap or pile. Use synthetic covers (usually made of polyester) when applying latex paints, and covers with natural fibers (usually lamb's wool or mohair) for oil-base paints.

When using oil-base paints, check the cover core to make sure it won't be weakened by the solvents in the paint. The wrong roller cover core could be softened significantly during the paint job.

Roller covers come with varying nap lengths.

In general, smoother surfaces require a shorter nap; rougher surfaces require a longer nap. And the higher the gloss level of the paint, the shorter the nap.

■ On drywall, smooth plaster, wood, or metal, use ⅛- to ¼-inch nap.
■ On light-textured stucco, concrete, or rough wood, use ⅜- to ½-inch nap.

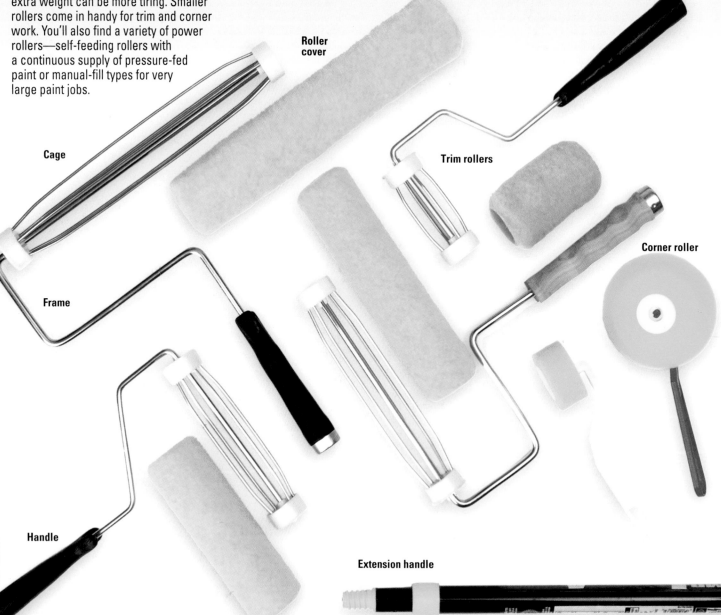

Roller cover

Cage

Trim rollers

Frame

Corner roller

Handle

Extension handle

■ On heavy-textured stucco, concrete block, or brick, use ⅜- to 1-inch nap.

Quality construction

A quality roller cover will produce the best results. As with brushes, there are several ways to identify a quality roller:

■ Make sure the roller cover has no obvious seams, which can cause streaks in the applied paint.

■ Pull lightly on the pile. It should have few loose fibers.

■ A roller cover must hold its shape. Squeeze the roller cover (off the frame) to get an idea of how resilient it is. This will also let you know whether it has a consistency throughout or whether it has irregularities across its surface.

■ With the cover on the frame, the roller should feel balanced and fit comfortably in your hand.

■ The handle and frame should be stout to ensure strength and durability. Economy handles and frames often bend easily.

■ Roller frames come in a variety of styles. U-shape frames are generally sturdier.

■ When choosing frames, be sure to select those that are sealed on the ends to help keep the paint on the roller.

■ A quality roller cage holds its shape and transfers pressure evenly across the roller cover. Cages with more spokes are stronger and provide more support than models with only a few spokes.

Before starting, be sure the roller cover fits snugly on the roller handle cage. If loose, pull the cage spokes apart for a tighter fit.

With many new homes featuring two-story foyers and family rooms, an extension handle is a great asset. For rolling ceilings or high walls, 18- to 25-foot extension poles are available at paint stores or home centers.

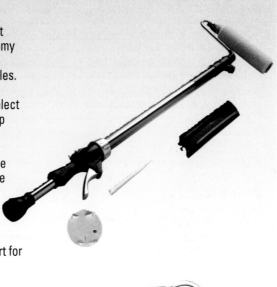

Textured roller

Power rollers apply paint with little effort. The paint is pumped through the roller, so there's no overspray or dripping. Power rollers offer fingertip control of the paint supply. Once you get the hang of it, you can cover a room quickly. Handle extensions allow you to paint high walls and ceilings.

Short
¼" nap

Medium
¾" nap

Long
1¼" nap

SPRAYERS AND OTHER TOOLS

Spray painting is the fastest way to cover large areas—spraying can be as much as four times faster than brushing and twice as fast as rolling. Sprayers put paint easily on hard-to-reach surfaces, such as soffits and lattices, and deeply textured materials such as stucco—areas that a brush or roller can leave untouched.

With spray equipment, you can paint objects with irregular or complex shapes, and because sprayed paint does not show brush marks or roller stipple, it results in a uniform appearance.

One inherent drawback however, is that the smooth surface resulting from spraying can be difficult to touch up, and some painters insist that sprayed applications be back-rolled so that the job can be touched up, if necessary. And no matter how powerful, no sprayer can overcome the effects of winds or even gentle breezes. Dead calm is the best weather for spraying outdoors.

There are several major types of sprayers—conventional, airless, and high volume low pressure (HVLP).

Conventional spraying

Conventional spraying uses compressed air supplied by a hose to atomize and propel paint, supplied to the gun from a cup or through another hose. The design of the spray gun nozzle controls the spray pattern.

Internal mix guns require less air pressure and less air volume. That makes less overspray and a thicker coat of paint.

External mix guns are popular because they control the spray pattern better and there is less wear on the gun.

Cup sprayers are ideal for small jobs. The cup is attached to the spray gun and usually holds 1 to 2 quarts of paint. Paint is fed either with a gravity or siphon feed system.

Conventional spray equipment can apply many types of paint, from thin lacquer to heavier latex paint. However, conventional spraying requires thinning of heavier paints, which can ultimately result in a failed coating. For that reason, paint manufacturers often discourage thinning for spraying by providing little or no information on how much to thin the paint. Conventional spraying also produces a great quantity of overspray, which increases the amount of

paint needed to cover the surface.

Airless spraying

Airless spraying is popular because:
■ Its high pressure (1,500 psi or more) alleviates the need for thinning most paints.
■ Overspray is minimized.
■ It applies paint more quickly than any other method.

An airless spray gun looks like a conventional spray gun except there is only one hose connected to it—the paint supply hose. There is no air-supply hose because the paint is pushed through the paint hose by a pump.

Airless spraying puts paint on at least twice as fast as conventional spraying and produces less overspray. Airless units are also more portable, less cumbersome, and easier to clean.

When spraying, maintain a distance of about 12 to 14 inches between the spray gun and the surface. Holding the gun too close results in sags and runs; too far away applies a coat that's too thin.

An airless system has only two settings: on and off. You can't vary the paint flow with the gun control. You have to keep the gun moving at a speed that is comfortable and provides proper coverage.

OSHA requires the mandatory use of a tip guard to help prevent a major injury—the high pressures of this system can actually inject paint into flesh, which can cause serious harm and even be lethal.

High volume, low pressure spraying

High volume low pressure (HVLP) spraying describes a system that uses a large quantity of air at only 10 psi to push paint through the spray head and atomize it. The result is a very fine mist that produces a minimal amount of overspray.

Because more paint reaches the surface, HVLP is ideal for interior applications, confined areas (such as closets), trim, doors, frames, cabinets, shutters, and other fine finish work. HVLP is not typically used for large areas because paint goes on at a much slower rate than with airless spraying.

Many HVLP sprayers cannot handle heavy paints with high solids unless they are thinned, which can compromise the quality of the coating. A larger compressor can often provide a suitable compromise.

Most manufacturers offer a variety of nozzles for special applications and the option of using compressed air with an HVLP gun or an accessory kit that converts a pressure tank for use with HVLP systems.

HVLP spraying techniques are similar to those for conventional spraying but with the gun held 6 to 8 inches from the surface. You should overlap sprayed areas by 50 percent.

HVLP is as fast as or faster than conventional spraying but slower than airless spraying. You can adjust the speed at which the unit applies paint by changing the nozzle size. The larger the nozzle, the faster the application.

General application tips

No matter what kind of sprayer you use, here are some general practices that will ensure a consistent and safe application:
■ Test the sprayer and your technique on a large piece of cardboard. Adjust the spray head and pressure to get a uniform pattern with a minimum amount of pressure.
■ To achieve a smooth, even coat, keep the gun moving across the surface in a succession of overlapping strips. Move the sprayer in a smooth motion and at a consistent pace. Release the trigger at the end of each stroke, and then pull it again as you begin to reverse direction.

■ Spray straight at the surface; avoid swinging your arm or hand in an arc.
■ Once you have begun to work, do not leave the sprayer idle for more than 20 minutes or the paint will begin to harden.
■ When you have finished painting for the day or are taking a break of some length, clean the paint from the unit, carefully following the manufacturer's instructions.
■ To avoid mishaps or injury, always wear protective clothing and gloves, as well as goggles. **Never point the sprayer head at your body or anyone else's.** The powerful jet of paint from a sprayer can force paint through your skin. If that happens, get immediate medical attention.
■ Before you clean a power sprayer, turn off and unplug the unit. Then pull the trigger to release the remaining pressure in the hose.
■ Make sure to set the safety lock on the spray gun when you are not spraying.

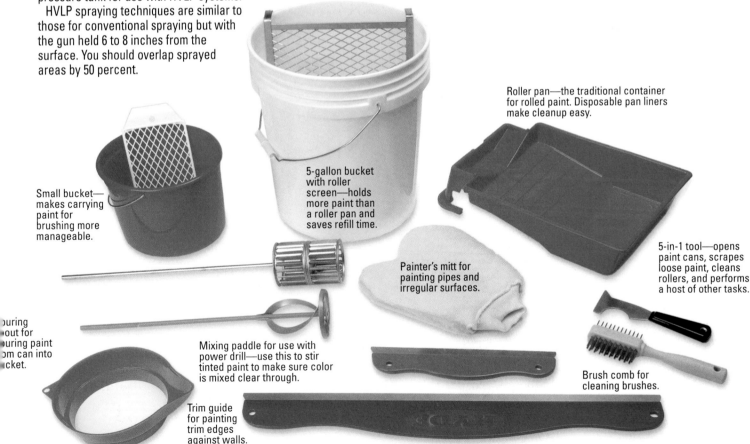

Small bucket—makes carrying paint for brushing more manageable.

5-gallon bucket with roller screen—holds more paint than a roller pan and saves refill time.

Roller pan—the traditional container for rolled paint. Disposable pan liners make cleanup easy.

5-in-1 tool—opens paint cans, scrapes loose paint, cleans rollers, and performs a host of other tasks.

Painter's mitt for painting pipes and irregular surfaces.

Pouring spout for pouring paint from can into bucket.

Mixing paddle for use with power drill—use this to stir tinted paint to make sure color is mixed clear through.

Trim guide for painting trim edges against walls.

Brush comb for cleaning brushes.

GOOD PAINTING PRACTICES

Painting can be easy and enjoyable if you follow a few time-proven procedures.

Before you start, buy all the paint for a room at the same time, and have it shaken at the home center. If you use it within a week, just stir it lightly. If you have to wait more than a week, take it back for shaking or mix it with a paint-mixing propeller affixed to an electric drill (run the drill at a slow speed). To reduce spattering, stick the shaft through a foam plastic picnic plate before inserting it in the drill chuck.

Always paint from a small plastic bucket, not the paint can. That way, you can keep the lid on the can so the paint stays fresh. Don't pour more than a couple inches of paint in the bucket. That means less weight to carry and you won't overfill the brush as easily. Before dipping a brush into paint, dampen it with water (for latex paints) or paint thinner or mineral spirits (for oil-base or alkyd paints). Blot excess solvent from the brush so it is just damp. Priming the brush this way keeps the paint on the surface of the bristles and makes cleanup easier.

Prep and pour

1 Use a 5-in-1 tool, not a straight screwdriver, to pry up the can lid around its circumference. (A screwdriver will put crimps and dimples in the lid, compromising the seal and letting air in.)

2 If the paint was mixed and shaken at the store within the past week, stir it lightly. You can use a flat wooden stirring paddle (usually free at the paint store), but one with holes will move through the paint without causing it to spill over the edge of the can.

Additives go with the flow

If brush marks on your painted projects bother you, consider a paint additive that improves flow-out without affecting the durability of the finish. One such product for oil-base finishes is Penetrol. Its companion product, Floetrol, is for water-base paint.

These products also work well when you're rolling paint onto walls or ceilings. The improved paint consistency reduces spatters and the appearance of roller marks.

The label provides general guidelines for the amount of additive needed, which varies with the type of paint and the application temperature. It takes some experimenting to get the feel of these products.

STANLEY PRO TIP

Box the paint

Whenever you buy two or more containers of the same paint, take a few minutes to mix them together in a larger container, such as a 5-gallon bucket. Doing so ensures consistent color throughout your project. This is absolutely essential when you're using colors custom-mixed at the store. It's also a good idea with factory-mixed tints because the paint you've purchased may have been manufactured in different

batches and the color could vary. Professional painters call this procedure "boxing the paint."

No matter how you apply it, paint goes on better when temperatures and humidity are average for your climate.

Loading the brush

3 Carefully lift the paint can with one hand on either side (you get better control of the pour this way) and pour paint into your small bucket. Put about 2 or 3 inches in the bucket. That way you reduce your chances of overloading the brush. (An overloaded brush keeps paint in the ferrule of the brush instead of applying it to the wall.)

Dip a primed brush into the paint only one-third to one-half the length of the bristles. Work the paint into the brush by pressing the bristles against the sides of the container. Tap the brush lightly against the inside of the bucket and lift it clear. Do not scrape the sides of the brush against the top edge of the bucket. That removes paint that belongs on the surface you're painting.

WHAT IF…
You're using old paint?

Paint that is more than a year old may have lumps in it that will interfere with application. First stir the paint up from the bottom until it's as free of lumps as possible. Then box the paint (see opposite), straining it through a nylon paint strainer or cheesecloth. If the paint has developed a skin on top, cut around the skin with an old kitchen knife and remove it.

Keep the lid clean

1 Nothing creates more potential for mess than a wet paint can lid—someone will probably step on it and track paint across the floor. When you remove the lid, slide it into a plastic freezer bag and seal the closure. That will protect the lid and give you a clean edge to lift it off with the next time you need to remove it.

2 Punch holes with a 6d or 8d nail at 1-inch intervals around the well the lid fits into. The holes will allow excess paint (from pouring it into a smaller bucket) to drain back into the can and not harden in the well. Dried paint in the well prevents the lid from sealing tightly. This will help keep the paint fresh for its next use.

Painting with a brush

1 Load the brush with the proper amount of paint (see page 53), and start your application in one corner of the wall. Holding the brush between your thumb and fingers, and keeping it at about a 30-degree angle to the wall, unload the paint from the brush with an upstroke, from 16 to 20 inches long. Flex the brush slightly so it releases the paint on the surface. (Whenever possible, paint with vertical strokes—they will tire you less than horizontal strokes.)

2 Immediately set the paint on the surface with a downstroke, applying slightly less pressure than the first stroke, and holding the brush at a slightly steeper angle to spread the paint evenly. Flexing your wrist as you work will help you fall into a natural rhythm, and you will not tire as easily.

STANLEY PRO TIP: **Holding a brush**

To apply paint to flat surfaces, it's most comfortable to grip the brush between your thumb and fingers in a relaxed grip, as shown above. This gives you control of the paint flow and won't tire your hand.

When painting trim, hold the brush like you'd hold a pen, with the handle resting against the bottom joint of your thumb.

Don't grip the brush with a fist around the handle. This grip will throw paint spatters. Keep the brush in front of your eyes when possible—you'll have better control.

Painting trim

It takes a little practice to lay paint with a bead line next to an adjacent surface with a different color. But you can forgo the bead line by masking the walls and using a paint guard as shown. Always paint in the direction of the grain, applying it in three strokes and keeping a wet edge.

3 With slight pressure on the brush, smooth the applied paint with a light upstroke. While you're finishing this stroke, lift the brush slightly to feather the end of the paint line. Resist the temptation to overbrush latex paint. A few strokes is all you need to produce a level coat. Overbrushing will thin the coat and invite lapping and other problems when the paint dries.

4 Some painters apply paint working from an unpainted area to a painted area. Others apply paint from the painted area. Whichever method you choose, work in 2- to 4-foot sections, and always finish with a light stroke into the edge of the last painted section, then with one long continuous stroke to eliminate overlap lines and brush marks. Latex paint starts to dry fairly quickly, so adjust your application accordingly. Oil-base paints have a longer open time.

Using a paint pad

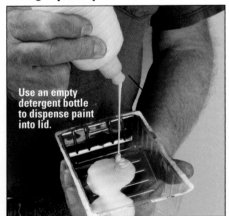

Use an empty detergent bottle to dispense paint into lid.

Masking tape makes a convenient handle.

1 The packaging for many paint pads doubles as a paint tray. Pour paint through a funnel into an empty detergent bottle. Filling the tray from the bottle will make the job less messy. Pour about ¼ inch of paint into the tray.

2 Set the paint pad flat into the paint and wiggle it a little to load its bristles. Remove excess paint by scraping it gently across the edge of the tray. Leave the bristles full but not dripping with paint.

3 Place the pad flat on the surface, with the side or guide wheel against the adjoining edge. Unload the paint from the pad with one stroke and if necessary to remove bristle marks, run the pad gently back in the opposite direction. Lift the pad at the end of this stroke to blend it into a previously painted section.

Painting with a roller

First stroke, unload roller.

Second stroke, set the paint.

Third stroke, smooth the paint.

1 Load the roller with paint in a roller pan or bucket equipped with a roller screen. Starting at the bottom of the wall, apply the paint with a smooth upstroke, keeping the pressure consistent. Roll in one continuous stroke but not so fast as to spatter the paint.

2 Without lifting the roller, set the paint on the surface with a continuous downstroke. Keep consistent pressure on the roller.

3 With a light upstroke, smooth the paint, with slightly more pressure on the end of the roller in the direction you're painting. This minimizes bead lines. Repeat the steps until you've painted one roller-width to the top of the wall. Start again at the bottom and paint to the top till you've covered the wall.

LOAD THE ROLLER
Prepare the tray and roller

Rub the roller cover to remove loose nap. If the nap is excessive, replace the cover. Moisten the cover with water (for latex paints) or paint thinner, then blot it dry. Pour an inch of paint into the pan and roll the cover into it, spreading it on the rake at the top of the pan. Roll a new roller cover on scrap to remove any trapped air bubbles.

Removing bead lines

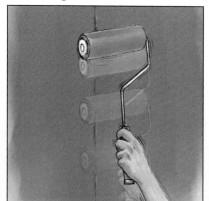

After you've covered about 8 feet of the wall from top to bottom, lay off the section (blend the paint and level any bead marks) by lightly rolling an unloaded roller in continuous vertical strokes from bottom to top. As you reach the end of the upstroke, lift the roller up and off the surface. Don't overwork the paint.

STANLEY PRO TIP

Cutting corners

Cutting in the edges of a wall is an easy task with a corner roller. This tool will work only when adjoining surfaces are the same color, and it's best when two painters are on the job. That way, one can paint one wall, keeping a wet edge on it while the other paints the other wall to avoid lap marks caused by painting over dried paint.

Painting with a sprayer

1 Some sprayers come with a cup to test the viscosity of the paint (to make sure it will spray correctly). Follow the manufacturer's instructions to test and thin the paint to the proper specifications.

2 Load the paint into the sprayer reservoir and make test patterns on a scrap board, adjusting the nozzle (or changing nozzle sizes) to get the proper paint flow and application speed that results in the right coverage (not too thick or thin).

3 Start the paint flow off the edge of the surface you're painting and move the gun at an even speed in overlapping passes. Release the trigger only after the gun has passed the opposite edge of the painted surface. Apply paint in several thin coats.

Good spraying technique

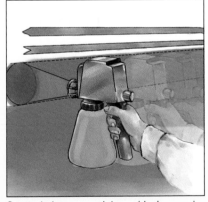

One technique essential to achieving good results when using spray equipment is to keep the spray head the same distance from the work across its entire surface. It may be wise to practice a bit to resist the natural temptation to swing the gun in an arc, which applies the paint unevenly.

WHAT IF…
You're spraying corners

Spraying corners requires a slightly different technique from that used to spray flat surfaces. Always spray the corners first.

If you're spraying an outside corner (above left), stand directly in front of the corner and apply the paint in short horizontal strokes. This will put a thin coating of paint on the adjacent

walls, but painting the walls will even it out. Don't wrap the spray pattern around the corner on either wall.

If you're spraying an inside corner (above right), move the sprayer in one continuous stroke from top to bottom, releasing the trigger at the end of the pass to avoid paint buildup at the bottom.

CLEANING UP

Quality painting tools are expensive, so it pays to keep your brushes, rollers, and spray equipment in good condition. The first step in tool maintenance is preconditioning them before use. The second step is cleaning them thoroughly afterward.

Precondition natural-bristle brushes by spraying a small amount of nonsilicone spray lubricant on them and working the lubricant into the bristles. This helps keep the natural oils from drying out.

Precondition synthetic bristles by dunking the brush in liquid fabric softener and rinsing. Fabric softener is a surfactant, which makes water-base emulsions (such as latex paints) flow more easily.

All frequently used brushes will profit from periodic reconditioning. Some painters stop to clean their brushes and rollers once every couple of hours. This removes paint that has inevitably begun to set up in brushes and rollers from exposure to the air in the room.

When you've completed the cleanup, dry the brushes and rollers with paper towels and dispose of the towels properly.

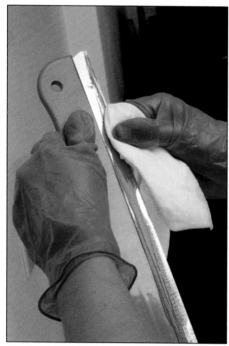

To clean a trim guard, saturate an old rag with the solvent appropriate to the paint and wipe the surfaces clean. Soak rags with petroleum-base solvents in water and hang out to dry.

Cleaning brushes

1 Remove excess paint from a brush by scraping it with the edge of a 5-in-1 tool or a brush-comb made specifically for this purpose. If you don't have a metal brush-comb, you can use an old comb with wide teeth or break out every other tooth from a narrow-toothed comb.

2 Mix ½ cup of liquid fabric softener in a gallon of warm water, and soak the brush in this solution for about 15 minutes. Do not use hot water, which can soften the temper of the bristles and ruin the brush. Swish the brush around in the solution periodically.

Cleaning oil-base paint from brushes

Oil-base paints require petroleum solvents, but cleaning a brush solely with mineral spirits leaves the bristles stiff. Use this three-jar method.

Fill one large jar two-thirds full with mineral spirits, a second jar with a 50-50 mix of mineral spirits and denatured alcohol, and a third with full-strength denatured alcohol.

Scrape off excess paint as shown in step 1 above, swish the brush in jar No. 1 for about 15 seconds, then spin out the excess. Repeat the process in each solution, let the brushes dry, then recondition them as discussed above left. Store them in their original wrappers.

1
Mineral spirits

2
Mineral spirits and denatured alcohol (50-50)

3
Denatured alcohol

Cleaning rollers

3 Set up a 5-gallon bucket by lining it with a trash bag and cutting a hole in the top. Snap the top on in a couple of places (just to keep it in place) and attach your brush to a brush spinner. Lower the brush into the bucket and spin it dry, then dry any excess with paper towels.

Brush spinner

Cut hole in lid of 5-gallon bucket.

1 Even when you think a roller cover has exhausted its paint supply, you'll be surprised at how much paint it still holds. Scrape this excess out of the cover with the curved side of a 5-in-1 tool. Let the excess fall into the roller tray and dump the paint into the original paint can.

2 Soak the roller cover in a fabric-softener solution (see step 2, opposite) and rescrape the cover periodically. Remove the cover from the cage and rinse it in water, squeezing the diluted paint into a work sink or bucket. Repeat as necessary.

STANLEY PRO TIP

Taking a break

When you take a break from your paint job, wrap your brushes and rollers in plastic bags, squeeze the air out, and seal the bags. This keeps the air from setting the paint and you can pick up right where you left off without restoring the brushes.

Storing paint

Storing paint means finding a way to keep the air out of the container. The easiest way to accomplish this is to add a gasket between the cover and the can. If you originally enclosed your wet can lid in a plastic storage bag, you can use that or you can cut a circle from a heavy-duty trash bag. Spray vegetable oil on one side of the bag and set it on the can, with the lid on top of the plastic. Drape an old rag on top of the can and tap the lid to seat it in the well. Store the can upside down to prevent a skin from forming on the paint and in a room where the temperature consistently stays at about 50 degrees.

MAINTAINING PAINTED SURFACES

Even though properly applied, high-quality paint will protect and beautify your home for years, paint has a number of enemies that can spoil both its appearance and its longevity. Like any aspect of home improvement, painted surfaces need periodic attention and maintenance.

You should check painted surfaces twice a year so you catch problems early and thus minimize paint failures. In addition to assessing and treating dirt, chalking, mildew, and efflorescence, look for cracking or checking, blistering, peeling, serious fading, loss of gloss, and signs of rusting—and treat these conditions immediately.

Eliminating mold and mildew

For all their protective qualities, all paints, especially flat paints, oil-base paints, and economy formulations, can provide a great growth medium for mold and mildew. These fungi love damp and shaded conditions, so on the exterior, check northern exposures thoroughly. On the inside, check laundry rooms, bathrooms, and basements.

Wherever you find these conditions, household bleach is the solution. Protect plantings, grass, and interior floors with plastic and scrub the affected paint with a 3-to-1 water-bleach mix and a stiff scrub brush. Work the solution into the surface 1 foot beyond the affected area and let it set for 20 minutes, keeping it wet as it sits. Then rinse the area thoroughly.

Dealing with dirt

Most dirt on exterior paints is airborne and can be removed with a pressure washer as shown below. Dirt on interior paint is usually in the form of handprints around switches and knobs; splashes in kitchen and bathrooms; marks on hallways and corridors; or "soot" above lamps and other heat sources.

Removing dirt before it accumulates not only keeps the paint looking tidy, it prohibits dirt from permanently embedding itself in the paint film.

Check for dirt and assume you'll find it near cooking areas and at all places at hand height. Always begin cleaning with a mild detergent and a sponge or soft cloth and work up to harsher cleaners only when necessary. Alkaline cleaners can dull the sheen of glossy paints. Abrasive cleaners will burnish nearly any paint, and will dull the gloss of satin, semigloss, and gloss products. Rinse the surfaces thoroughly to keep residual cleaner from interfering with the adhesion of new paint.

Removing chalked paint

Accumulated dirt can darken paint and provide nutrients for mildew. Weathering can cause release of chalky pigment, fading the colors. Both dirt and chalk can be removed by scrubbing or power washing.

Scrubbing is best done with a mild detergent and a scrub brush, followed by thorough rinsing. Harsh, alkaline cleaners, such as TSP, can reduce the gloss of alkyd paints and of some latex paints. Power wash with plain water, without cleaning agents. Use care to not lift the paint or to damage the substrate.

Removing efflorescence

Efflorescence is a film of white, powdery salts carried out to the surface of masonry by water within the substrate.

Remove any buildup of efflorescence with a stiff wire brush; wear eye and skin protection and a dust mask. If possible, identify and eliminate the water causing the efflorescence. Where necessary, prime with a latex masonry primer, and repaint.

Touchy touch-ups

Just when you've finished artfully touching up a damaged surface, and after the paint has dried, you take another look at your handiwork only to find that the area you've touched up looks glaringly different from the rest of the wall. Touch-ups can look lighter or darker than the original color, they can have a different sheen, and they can stick out from the surface, depending on how much paint you apply.

To minimize these effects:

■ Apply an appropriate primer, especially if you have removed some paint from the area.
■ Tint your touch-up paint—this may mean taking a chip of the old paint to your supplier to match a faded color.
■ When spraying, backroll the final coat to create a less uniform surface that will hide later touch-ups more easily.
■ Apply the touch-up paint in a thin coat with a foam brush. Dab the brush to mimic the texture of the rolled surface.

Crayon marks

Soften up crayon marks with a hair dryer and blot up the marks with a heavy-duty paper towel or soft rag. Keep the dryer close enough to the wall to soften the crayon but not the paint. You can also try to soften the crayon by running a warm iron over an old rag placed over the area.

Keeping track

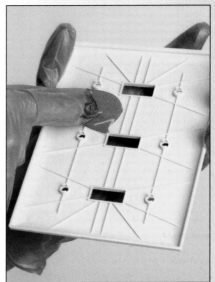

Many times you'll have to repaint a cleaned or repaired area, and you'll need to know the color of the original paint. To keep track of the colors in each room, dab the paint on the back of a switchplate. Note the brand and name of the paint on tape and put it on the back of the switchplate too.

Unsticking painted edges

Painted surfaces usually stick together because they come into contact before the paint dries. Dark colors stick more than light ones, and glossier paints stick more than flats. Allow ample drying time before putting a painted area back into service. If surfaces stick, rub them with talcum powder. Plasticizers in window and door gaskets can soften latex paint and cause sticking, so avoid painting the gasket.

Scrubbing paint stains

Fast action is the best way to ensure that stains don't evolve from a temporary blemish to a permanent mark in the paint film. In time, chemicals in the stain can bond with those in the paint and become tougher to get out.

You can kill mildew with a bleach solution, but try hydrogen peroxide first. It's milder and might not fade the color of your paint.

To clean dirt from gloss paints, use a mild detergent and increase its concentration only if the stain proves stubborn.

Use a diluted deglossing agent to clean grease from kitchen surfaces. Increase the concentration of deglosser if results aren't immediate.

Remove rust with a solution of ½ cup epsom salts to 1 cup of water. Rinse all cleaned areas thoroughly.

PAINTING EXTERIORS

Painting the exterior of your house is part science, part art. Because the house might have many different surfaces, you'll have to be familiar with a variety of preparation methods as well as a number of paint products and application techniques. On top of that, you'll need to consider upcoming weather and organize your work based on the local forecast as well as the path of the sun during the workday. And the exterior of your house probably represents the largest surface you'll ever work on, so you'll need to do much of the work from ladders or work platforms. All this requires planning, preparation, and patience.

It's no surprise that preparation of the surfaces you're painting is the key to success. In fact preparation will consume approximately 80 percent of the total time you'll devote to the project. But this time will pay off in the long run. Paint on a well-prepared surface can last for decades.

Moreover if you use quality products to begin with, you don't actually have to complete the job all at the same time. Quality primers and paints will adhere securely to the surface and won't fade rapidly, so you can paint one or two walls this year and another set of surfaces next year without worrying that it will look like you've used different colors. Just be sure not to stop in the middle of a wall.

Dealing with lead-based paint

Prior to 1978, lead was a major ingredient in paints, but legislation that year banned its use in paint because it is a carcinogen. Because you may be scraping, sanding, or otherwise removing paint in preparation for the new coating, you should ascertain, if possible, when that paint was applied. If that's not possible, contact the Environmental Protection Agency (EPA) or your local health department for instructions on how to proceed where lead paint may be present.

To further acquaint you with the hazards associated with lead-based paint, request a copy of the most recent literature from the EPA. It will provide information about how to test for the presence of lead paint, steps to take to minimize your exposure to lead where lead-based paint may be present, how to remove it safely, and in-place management of lead-based paint.

Preparation is the key to a long-lasting, paint job. With quality products and proper preparation, your paint will last for decades.

CHAPTER PREVIEW

Planning and estimating
page 64

Getting the site ready
page 66

Preparing siding
page 68

Preparing masonry surfaces
page 72

Ladders and scaffolding
page 74

Ladder jacks and accessories
page 78

Setting up scaffolding
page 79

Painting soffits and siding
page 82

Painting windows and doors
page 86

Painting masonry and other surfaces
page 90

Finishing cedar shingles and siding
page 92

Finishing fences and gates
page 94

Selecting finishes for a deck or porch
page 96

Preparing and painting decks and porches
page 98

Applying a clear deck finish
page 100

PLANNING AND ESTIMATING

Existing stonework, brickwork, or roofing on your home will remain the same, so choose colors that work in harmony with them. Stay true to the style of your home and neighborhood.

A fresh coat of paint is the least expensive method available to renew and protect the exterior of your home. It might also be the largest exterior renovation job you'll do. It can be a gratifying endeavor if you approach it with forethought.

Deciding on Saturday morning that you're going to paint the house that weekend, then picking up some paint before lunch is not a good way to approach the project. You'll be better off with some careful planning. Having a good plan will place the job within the reach of your skills, time, and budget.

Scheme with colors first

Your first objective, of course, is to choose the exterior color scheme, and your choices should result from a consideration of several factors—the architectural style of your home, the design of other houses in the neighborhood, the possible necessity of conforming to historic-preservation ordinances or neighborhood covenants, and, of course, your personal taste. See pages 12–13 and 20–23 for information about choosing exterior colors.

Inventory materials and conditions

With color choices made, it's time to look at the materials used on your house and any conditions that need remedial attention before the paint goes on.

Walk around the house with a notepad or take photos of each side of the house, along with close-ups of significant details. Print 8×10 photos and use a permanent marker to make notes on them. Measure each side of the house and note the measurements on the photos. Then inventory the materials that are on the exterior. You may be surprised at the number of different surfaces on your home. Note them on the photos—you'll need

HOW MUCH PAINT WILL YOU NEED?

1. Multiply the length of a wall by the height of a wall to find total wall area.

2. Multiply the width of a window or door by the height of a window or door to find the area of one window or door.

3. Add the areas of all windows and doors to find the total window and door area.

4. Subtract the total window and door area from the total wall area to find the wall area to be painted.

5. For triangular areas, multiply the height by the length and divide by 2 to find the area.

6. Add the area of triangle to the wall area calculated in step 4 to find the total area to be painted. Add areas of all walls together.

To estimate the number of gallons you need, divide the total area by the coverage of a gallon (see "Coverages," right). Multiply by 2 if you plan to apply two coats. Buy about 10 percent extra paint to allow for spillage and future touch-ups.

Height

Length

Height of house wall

Length of house wall

Nothing is more irritating than getting close to the end of a paint job and running out of paint. Besides having to stop, clean your painting tools, and make a run to the paint store, you also risk getting a slightly different color than the one you've already applied. And if you stop the job in the middle of a wall, you'll get lap marks where the new paint begins and the old paint has dried.

To avoid this annoyance—as well as the costly problem of having too much paint left over after the job—estimate carefully. All it takes is some simple math for figuring the areas of various sections of your house and adjusting your computations for those parts (such as windows and doors) that either won't get painted, or will be treated as trim and painted a different color.

this information because different materials may require different kinds of paint. Almost any surface can be painted, including aluminum or vinyl siding.

Then go back and look critically at potential problem areas and make notes on the photos. If surfaces are peeling, you'll need to scrape, sand, and prime. Chalking paint will require power washing. Areas with rot will need replacement. And you'll have to do away with mold and mildew.

Look closely around windows and doors, where the framing meets the siding. You will probably have to recaulk gaps where different surfaces meet. And don't forget the gutters and downspouts. They're notorious for showing signs of deterioration.

Make a list and a plan
The notes you make will form the basis for a materials list and an organizational plan.

First list quantities of preparation materials, such as caulk, sandpaper, cleaning agents, and replacement siding you'll need. Then calculate the quantity of paint you'll need, as well as brushes, rollers, and other tools. If the job calls for rental equipment, such as ladders, scaffolds, ladder jacks, or spray equipment, put them on the list too.

Break up the tasks—caulking, replacing siding, scraping, sanding, and priming—into manageable time periods and write them on a calendar.

Buy your supplies and materials a couple of days before you intend to start any phase of the work, and list the tasks in the right order—remove mold and mildew, clean dirt and chalking, replace or repair siding, repair and prime loose paint, cut in the new paint around the edges of a wall and fill in, paint doors, windows, and trim. Then add "watch the weather report" to your list.

Watching the weather
Nothing can foul up your plans faster than the weather. Here's what to watch for in the weather report when painting exteriors:

■ Don't paint when air and surface temps are below 50°F or will drop below that within 24 hours—60° to 80°F is better.

■ Don't paint if the air temperature is less than 5°F higher than the dew point or if the humidity is greater than 90 percent and the temperature is predicted to drop. These conditions lead to condensation—moisture formation on the surface. Don't start painting if there's moisture on the house.

■ Don't paint when the forecast calls for rain in the next 24 hours.

■ Don't paint in direct sunlight. It causes the paint to blister.

STANLEY PRO TIP

Coverages

Manufacturers generally estimate a gallon of paint will cover 400 square feet. Under ideal conditions, this may prove true, but in real practice, it's rare. You'll generally find most paints will cover about 300 square feet of surface in one properly applied coat.

Paint coverage is affected by the surface you're painting. Previously painted surfaces of a similar color usually take less paint than unpainted surfaces. Brick will soak up paint, and stucco is even more absorbent. If you are unsure of coverage, you can paint one wall before buying all the paint and use the coverage rate on that wall to determine how much more you will need.

To simplify your area computations (opposite page), use these generalizations: 15 square feet for a window and 21 square feet for a door.

How much time will it take?

These estimates will give you a rough idea of the amount of time various surfaces will require. Estimates apply to homeowners with moderate skills and some prior painting experience.

Surface	Application method	Time needed to paint
Exterior walls	Roller and brush, clapboard or other smooth siding	1 hour/75–150 square feet
	Roller and brush, medium-textured stucco	1 hour/200 square feet
	Roller and brush, shingles or new siding	1 hour/80–130 square feet
Windows	Brush, double-hung, single pane	25 minutes
	Brush, double-hung, 6 light over single pane	45 minutes
	Brush, double-hung, 6 light over 6 light	75 minutes
Doors	Roller, slab	20 minutes
	Brush, paneled	40 minutes
	Brush, louvered	60 minutes

GETTING THE SITE READY

Preparing the exterior of a house for painting starts with the site itself, not the surface—that comes later. The goal is to remove or cover anything you don't want to put paint on, and to clear away as many things as possible that might impede or interrupt your progress. This is relatively easy, but you might find yourself surprised at how much stuff is in your yard.

Here are some of the objects you might need to move out of your work area: potted plants on the deck or patio, hanging plants, barbecue grill, patio furniture, birdbaths, statues and other yard decorations, doormats, garden hoses, and lawn tools.

Tour your yard and move such items far enough away that they won't get spattered or hit by overspray and won't be in your way as you work along a wall.

Then go around with screwdrivers, pliers, and wrenches and remove items that are fastened to the house—outdoor light fixtures and electric outlets (shut off the power first, put wire nuts on the bare wire ends, and push the wires back into the outlet box), window boxes (even if you're going to paint them), decorative accents, address numbers or plates, flagpole holder, doorknobs, hooks, brackets, and hangers.

Lastly, mask or tape anything you don't want to or can't remove—door handles and hinges, locksets, the porch, deck, or patio surface, and all window and door trim. You can mask door hardware and other small objects with the careful application of tape. Don't leave plastic sheets or tarps loose on the deck or patio surface; tape them down to keep them from moving or tripping you.

If you're painting the siding or foundation to ground level, dig a 3- or 4-inch-deep trench around the house to expose the surface below the soil. This will ensure you won't leave any spots unpainted.

When you're going about these tasks, do one thing at a time and follow an order.
- Remove the portable items.
- Remove all attached items.
- Cover what you can't remove.

Being orderly reduces your chances of missing something and having to interrupt your painting to take care of it.

A primary goal of site preparation is to clear a path for you and your equipment, removing objects that will interfere with the application of paint. This includes outdoor light fixtures, hanging baskets, basket brackets, planting boxes, and any hooks used to support decorative or functional items.

STANLEY PRO TIP: **Every last little thing**

Painting the outside of your house is much easier if you don't have to paint around light switches, outdoor lighting fixtures, doorbell plates, address signs, hinges, locks and handles, and other obstructions.

You can mask these things carefully to keep them from being painted, but the easiest thing to do is to remove them before you start painting. A common problem, however, is that the mounting screws and other necessary hardware become separated from the fixture. Then when you're done painting, you spend an inordinate amount of time searching for them, perhaps having to buy new hardware that may not quite fit the style of the original.

Avoid this hunt for hardware by taping the screws and any other removable parts to the assembly itself. Use blue painter's tape—as much as you need to keep the whole collection firmly together. If there's a lot, put it all in a plastic bag and tape that to the fixture. Then

store all the handles, hinges, and fixtures you removed in one place so you can find them quickly and reinstall them all at the same time.

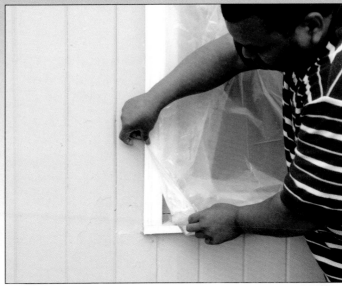

Paint and plants don't mix. Many paints can be toxic to plants, and spatters, even of those that aren't, deface the plants. Protect the plants by draping a lightweight, light-color tarp (an old sheet will do perfectly) over them. Do not use dark plastic sheets and do not apply the covering until you're ready to start working directly above the plants—heat trapped by the tarp or sheet will harm them. Mist the plants before protecting them and remove the covering immediately after you're done painting.

Mask anything you don't want to put paint on. Use blue painter's tape (it comes off easily). Seal down the edge by running a putty knife or plastic spatula along the edge you're masking so paint doesn't seep under it. When masking long sections, unroll a length of tape that will span the section and anchor it tightly at one end. Keep tension on the tape with one hand and position it tight to the corner with the other, working in lengths of about 1 foot. Press it in place as you go. Remove the tape while the paint is still wet so it won't pull dried paint up with it.

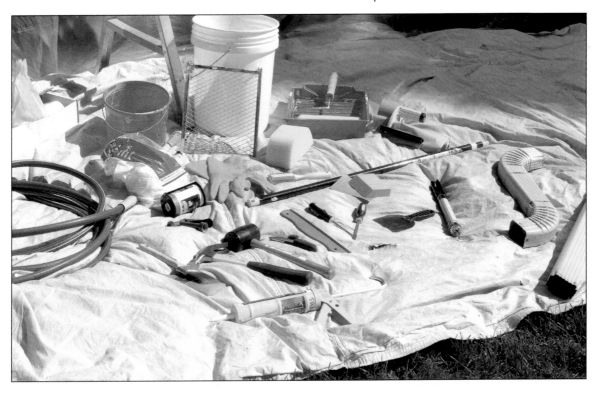

Protect your air conditioner, electric and gas meters, and other fixtures by wrapping and taping them with plastic. When you have completed all the site preparation, spread a drop cloth or plastic sheeting close to the project to create a staging area for tools and supplies. Always return tools to this area so you don't have to hunt for them. Remove the sheeting as soon as you're done with this side—and at night—so it doesn't kill the grass.

PREPARING SIDING

No matter what kind of siding you have on your house, perform a general inspection before you prepare it for painting. Look for mold, mildew, damaged siding, and wet or dry rot.

Once you've inspected the siding, preparation follows the same general order—remove mold and mildew, wash away dirt and chalking, repair or replace damaged siding, remove loose paint, and spot-prime the affected area.

To get the best finish on glossy surfaces, scuff sand them using a sanding block, pole sander, or sanding pads and 120- to 150-grit sandpaper. Do not oversand; just scuff the surface lightly to provide a roughened tooth for the new paint.

Water is the chief enemy of both wood and paint, so caulking gaps is important. Apply a top-quality all-acrylic or siliconized acrylic caulk to inside and outside corners, joints, seams, and other gaps where water could penetrate the wood's exterior. These caulks will adhere to a wide range of materials, even when they are wet.

Preparing wood siding

1 Starting at the eaves and soffits, wash the surface with water only. Use a pressure washer equipped with a fan nozzle and adjust the pressure for cleaning wood surfaces. Do not hold the tip too close to the wood. A power washer can poke holes in wood and break windows.

2 Working from the top of the wall to the bottom, direct the water downward. Spraying head-on can damage the siding, and aiming the spray upward can drive water behind the siding and lift it from the wall. Turn the water off to release pressure before disconnecting the hoses.

Removing mildew

1 Mask, cover, or otherwise protect plants, surfaces, or objects that could be damaged by the cleaning solution. Dampen grass, plants, and other vegetation with water. Wet the mildewed area with water using a pump sprayer, a garden hose, or a pressure washer.

2 Mix a cleaning solution of three parts water and one part household bleach in a pump sprayer and apply it liberally. Scrub the mildewed area with a stiff brush, reapplying the solution to keep the area wet for 20 minutes.

3 Using a pressure washer or hard spray from a garden hose, rinse the area thoroughly with water. Take up any protective coverings from adjacent surfaces and rinse vegetation with a light spray from the hose. Let the surface dry thoroughly.

3 Using a 5-in-1 tool or scraper held almost flat against the surface, scrape away loose paint down to the bare wood. To avoid gouging the surface, work parallel to the grain of the wood as much as possible. On carved millwork, use contoured scrapers available at your home center or paint store.

4 Using a 5-in-1 tool or stiff scraper, widen cracks to just under ¼ inch. This will remove debris in the crack and create a recess for patching compound. Remove loose paint with 80-grit sandpaper and take up any dust with a brush and water-dampened rag.

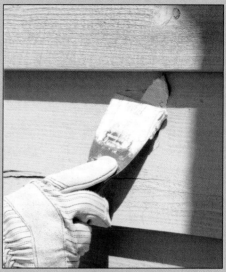

5 Apply a thin layer of exterior patching compound to all scraped and cracked areas, feathering the compound to create a level surface. Allow the compound to dry thoroughly. If the compound shrinks, sand it lightly and apply another thin layer.

6 Sand patched areas with 100-grit sandpaper to make the compound level with the existing paint. This leveling process will help hide the repair when you apply the primer. Remove dust with a wide brush or damp cloth.

7 Apply an exterior stain-blocking primer on all repaired areas and all bare wood. This prevents wood tannins from discoloring the paint. On cedar, redwood, and mahogany, use an oil-base primer and apply it in dry weather at the recommended spread rate. Finish-coat the surface within a week.

WHAT IF...
I have a lot of paint to remove?

You may have to remove most or all of the paint from neglected surfaces before repainting. To make this job less of a chore and to save time, use a power stripper, an aggressive disk sander made specifically for paint removal. Do not use a stripping head with flapping metal tines.

Replacing damaged fascia

1 Remove the guttering and trim, taking care it doesn't bend. Keep metal guttering away from power lines. Pry the damaged fascia from the rafter ends with a pry bar and pull out nails that stay in the rafters. Fasten a new length of rafter alongside the old one if the old rafter shows signs of rot.

2 Measure the opening spanned by the old fascia and cut new fascia to that length less ⅛ inch. Do not measure the old fascia—its length may not be accurate, due to weathering. Prime the front, back, and ends of the new board. Nail or screw the replacement to the rafter ends.

3 Replace moldings and trim, and set and fill all nailheads. Paint the fascia in accordance with your work plan. Reinstall the gutters after the paint dries.

Replacing board and batten siding

 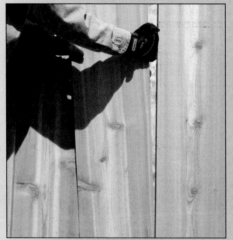 

1 Pry off the battens on both sides of the damaged boards with a flat pry bar. If water has damaged the sheathing, remove enough boards and battens so you can cut out the sheathing with a circular saw set to the thickness of the sheathing.

2 Cut and replace the sheathing and cut replacements for the damaged boards, less ¼ inch for expansion. Prime the faces and edges of the replacements and let them dry. Fit them in place.

3 Nail the replacement boards in place and caulk the joints between the new and old boards. Prime and replace the battens in the same fashion. Repaint the entire section with high-quality exterior latex paint.

Repairing damaged aluminum siding

  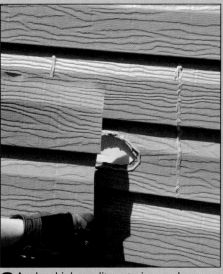

1 Using aviation snips and a sharp utility knife, cut out the damaged section. You can either follow the contour of the section as shown here or mark off and cut a larger rectangular section. Do not cut along siding seams. Using a piece of scrap 1×4, flatten all the edges of the cutout.

2 Cut a length of the same siding material about 2 inches longer than the hole. Trim off the fastener strip along the top of the replacement patch and file the edges smooth. Leave the bottom lip of the patch intact and unbent.

3 Apply a high-quality exterior-grade construction adhesive around the damaged area and to the siding where the edges of the patch will fall. Slide the patch under the course of siding above and tap the bottom edge to lock it. Press the patch firmly to adhere the patch to the adhesive.

Preparing vinyl and aluminum siding

1 Scrub mildewed areas with a stiff brush and a 3-to-1 mix of water and bleach solution. Keep the area wet for 20 minutes. Scrub corroded areas with a synthetic cleaning pad or sanding sponge.

2 Power wash the entire wall, including all scrubbed areas. Prime bare metal with a corrosion-inhibitive latex primer and prime excessively chalked areas with exterior alkyd primer.

WHAT IF...
I'm painting aluminum or vinyl windows?

To prepare aluminum and vinyl windows, you must remove whatever will interfere with the bonding of the paint. Scrub off the oxidation from aluminum windows with a metallic scouring pad or 120-grit sanding sponge.

Vinyl windows might exhibit some oxidation, but the main problem will be their gloss finish.

Remove both by scuff-sanding with 220-grit sandpaper or a sanding sponge.

Prime aluminum with a water-base corrosion-inhibiting primer. Paint both aluminum and vinyl with two coats of a high-quality acrylic latex exterior paint.

PREPARING MASONRY SURFACES

Masonry surfaces suffer some of the same categorical damage as other surfaces. They often display cracks or damages that require patching.

Patching damaged masonry can prove more difficult than repairing wood siding because even the best masonry repairs are visible, if only slightly. Although it's almost impossible to match the texture and color, getting a tight seal between the patch and the original surface is what really matters. Cracks and holes in stucco let water into the walls and will cause problems far worse than a mismatched patch.

When pigmenting a stucco patch, take the time to experiment with pigment proportions until you find a tint that matches the existing stucco when the patch dries.

Make necessary repairs to the underlying structure before you begin. Plan on building up your repair in layers over several days, allowing the patch to cure between applications. Thick applications will crack.

Repairing masonry mortar joints

1 If the surface of the brick is actually flaking off, the best solution is to skimcoat the entire wall with a portland-cement mortar. If it's just the mortar joints that show serious deterioration, rake out the loose mortar with a raking tool, remove the dust, and tuckpoint them.

2 Small cracks can be enlarged and filled with a masonry-repair patching compound. Whatever kind of repair you make, be sure to smooth the joints with a masonry jointing tool so the contours of the repaired joints match those of the old.

Removing efflorescence

Efflorescence, a residue of salts contained in masonry and brought to the surface by moisture in the masonry, must be removed before you paint. Scrub the affected area with a solution of 1 cup of water in 3 cups of muriatic acid. Wear protective clothing.

FLAKING OFF
Mortar is the answer

Flaking brick doesn't necessarily indicate a structural deficiency but does pose an aesthetic problem. Once flaking begins, it is almost certain to continue, even if you paint the brick. The best solution is to apply a skimcoat of mortar over the entire surface. Let it cure, then paint.

Caulking the gaps

Caulking joints keeps out moisture, snow, and rain. Here are some of the primary targets you should caulk:
- Where framing meets a wall
- At the junction of different materials
- Where the siding ends and the foundation begins
- On siding corner joints
- In any crack in masonry
- Around the edges of vents or ductwork, or in openings bored for wires or pipes

Repairing concrete block

Narrow cracks in concrete block (less than ¼ inch wide) can be filled with caulking made specifically for this purpose or painted with an elastomeric wall covering. Both products expand and contract with the block, effectively bridging the crack, and both can be painted.

Wider cracks in concrete block should be keyed (made wider at the bottom of the crack than at the surface) with a cold chisel. This helps them hold the patching mortar more effectively. Remove residual dust with a brush or vacuum.

To patch a repaired area, mist it lightly with water, using a spray mister, and fill the recess with concrete patching mortar. Let the mortar dry thoroughly before painting the repaired area.

Repairing stucco

1 Clean out the damaged area with a wire brush, removing any loose stucco pieces. Blow the dust out with compressed air.

2 Using a pointed trowel, narrow putty knife, or margin trowel, apply a thin coat of stucco patch and let it dry. Apply two more layers in the same fashion until the patch is level with the surrounding area. Do not let this coat dry before going to step 3.

3 Roughen the final coat of stucco patch until its texture matches that of the surrounding stucco. Add isolated clumps of patching material to increase the roughness of the texture.

LADDERS AND SCAFFOLDING

Ladders and scaffolds allow you to safely paint surfaces that otherwise would be difficult or impossible to reach.

Ladders come in a variety of heights, widths, and configurations. They are made from wood, fiberglass, or metal.

■ **Non-self-supporting ladders** (must lean on something)

A *straight ladder,* a single section, is indispensable for general use. Though not longer than 30 feet, it's the most common of portable ladders and combines practical height with easy maneuverability.

Extension ladders, essentially two straight ladders fitted with guides that allow one section to extend beyond the other, offer the greatest length in a general-purpose ladder. Wood ladders can't have more than two sections and must not exceed 60 feet. Metal and fiberglass ladders can have as many as three sections but must not exceed 72 feet. Individual sections of any extension ladder must not be longer than 30 feet.

■ **Self-supporting ladders**

A *standard stepladder* has flat steps and a hinged back. It is self-supporting and its height nonadjustable. Standard stepladders can't be longer than 20 feet and should be used only on surfaces that offer firm, level footing, such as floors, platforms, and slabs.

Whenever possible steady the ladder by attaching a stand-off stabilizer. This accessory comes in a range of widths. A 10-inch stand-off will allow you to work around windows, gutters, and overhangs. The device can be attached and detached quickly as you need it.

SAFETY FIRST
Using a ladder safely

Ladders make painting easier but must always be used with safety in mind.

■ Inspect every ladder before use. Make sure the rungs are secure and are free of dirt and paint buildup.

■ When extending or retracting an extension ladder, hold the rope firmly; if it slips, the upper section can fall on your fingers.

■ With an extension or straight ladder, make sure that the tops of both rails make solid contact with the wall and that both legs are placed firmly on the floor or ground.

■ Foam boots or pads on the tops of an extension or straight ladder can keep it from sliding and protect the walls.

■ Make sure the spreader bar of a stepladder is fully extended and locked before you use it.

■ Set the base of a straight or extension ladder 1 foot from the wall for every 3 feet of ladder height.

■ On the ladder, keep your hips between the rails for good balance.

■ Do not push or pull too hard on a scraper while on a ladder.

■ Always wear rubber-soled or nonslip shoes on a ladder.

■ Avoid working in wet or windy weather. Do not climb a wet ladder.

■ Keep all ladders away from power lines.

■ Place plywood under the legs of a ladder to ensure solid footing.

■ A ladder (or scaffolding) can be secured by tying it to a sturdy portion of the house or to a large eyebolt in the wall or fascia board.

A *two-way stepladder* features a set of steps on each side. With them, one person can work from either side or two people can work from the ladder at the same time.

A *platform ladder* is made with a large stable platform from which you can work at the highest standing level, which can't exceed 20 feet.

Scaffolds are assembled platforms, with or without wheels, that allow one or more painters to work at increased heights— comfortably, safely, and efficiently. Scaffold height can be increased by fitting additional sections to the frame. Scaffolds offer a primary feature not available in ladders—

their working area is both wider and deeper, allowing for greater coverage before a move is required.

You can construct a platform or working scaffold using ladders, ladder jacks, and planks (see page 78).

Choosing a ladder

1. Select the height

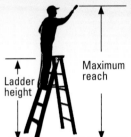

Stepladders

Ladder height	Max. reach
4'	8'
6'	10'
7'	11'
8'	12'
10'	14'
12'	16'
14'	18'
16'	20'

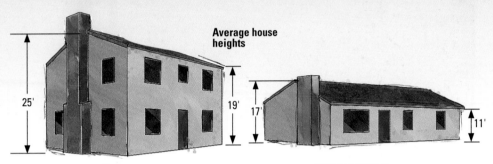

Average house heights

25' — TWO-STORY HOME

19' / 17' — 11' — ONE-STORY HOME

Choose a ladder size that will let you reach high enough to comfortably paint the maximum height of the walls of your house.

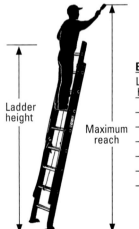

Extension ladders

Ladder height	Max. reach	Height to top support point
16'	15'	9' max.
20'	19'	9' to 13'
24'	23'	13' to 17'
28'	27'	17' to 21'
32'	31'	21' to 25'
36'	34'	25' to 28'
40'	37'	28' to 31'

Support points for extension ladders reflect section overlap, ladder angle, and 3-inch extension above the roof line.

SUPPORT POINTS

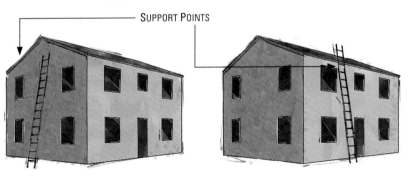

2. Choose the weight load

300 lbs.

Look for label on ladder that lists maximum weight load.

3. Choose the material

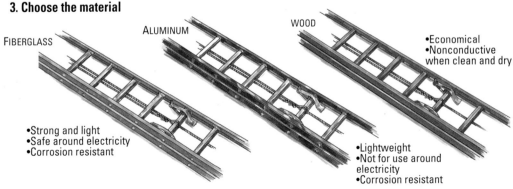

FIBERGLASS
- Strong and light
- Safe around electricity
- Corrosion resistant

ALUMINUM

WOOD
- Economical
- Nonconductive when clean and dry

- Lightweight
- Not for use around electricity
- Corrosion resistant

Raising a ladder

1 Start with the ladder flat on the ground and make sure the extension section is on the bottom. Station a helper at the end of the ladder with a foot placed against the bottom of each leg. Grab the other end of the ladder, lift it above your head, and support it by holding the third or fourth rung. If you don't have a helper, set the bottom legs against the foundation of the house and raise the ladder using the procedures shown in this and the remaining steps.

2 Take a step forward and move your hands to the next rung down, raising the ladder as you move forward. Continue moving forward, pushing the ladder toward an upright position and moving your hands from rung to rung. When the ladder is close enough, have your helper grab a rung so both of you are supporting the ladder as it approaches vertical.

Protecting the surfaces

Even a well-supported ladder may prove slightly unsteady as it approaches its maximum usable height. You can add to the stability of the ladder by placing ladder boots on each rail top. These rubber accessories help keep the ladder from slipping sideways and protect the side of the house from scrapes and gouges.

STANLEY   PRO TIP: **The 3-to-1 rule and other safety tips**

Raising a tall ladder can be tricky, and once you have it in place, you'll need to take a couple of precautions to make sure you have positioned it safely.

Your first step should be to check the ladder at ground level. Make sure the legs are on a level surface; on uneven surfaces, slide wide, thick wood shims under the legs to level them. If the ground is soft, which can cause one or both feet to sink, raise the ladder slightly and have a helper slide a 2×4-foot sheet of ⅝-inch plywood under the feet.

Make sure the ladder is positioned so the distance from the building to the feet equals one-third the height of the ladder. If the surface slopes away from the house, put a 2×4 behind the ladder feet and drive 2×4 stakes into the ground to secure it.

Use ladder boots or wrap and tape rags to the top of the rails to keep them from slipping or marring the siding.

3 Continue raising the ladder, one person pushing and the other pulling, until the ladder is vertical. Then place your feet against the legs of the ladder to keep it from kicking out.

4 With your feet against the legs of the ladder, ease it toward the house, with your helper supporting it from the other side and stepping his or her hands down the ladder until it rests on the wall. Keeping your feet on the legs of the ladder, have your helper push it slightly away from the house while you adjust its height. Move the ladder so the legs are 1 foot away from the wall for every 3 feet of height and make sure it's properly supported.

WHAT IF...
The ground is not level?

There is perhaps no more dangerous condition associated with using a ladder than setting it up on sloping ground. Even a 1-degree variation from vertical can send painter, paint, and ladder quickly groundward. Yet the soil around most homes is usually anything but level.

You can remedy some situations by supporting the ladder on a plywood sheet (see "The 3-to-1 Rule and Other Safety Tips," left) and shimming the legs level, but leg extensions offer a more secure solution.

These accessories bolt to the ladder legs and are adjustable along their length, creating legs of different lengths that accommodate sloping ground. Leg extensions are built in on some ladders. Add-on extensions are available from your ladder dealer.

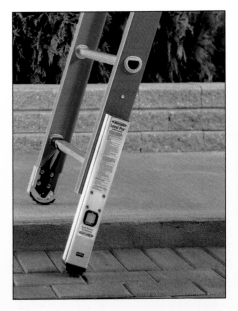

LADDER JACKS AND ACCESSORIES

Brushes, rollers, and sprayers are not the only accessories associated with a residential paint job. Manufacturers provide a host of labor- and time-saving accessories, from hooks and brackets that hold paint cans, to removable shelves on which you can stand or set tools.

Ladder jacks are perhaps the most useful accessory when it comes to making a paint job easier and faster. The jacks are essentially brackets that fasten to the sides of two ladders and support a plank or platform—in short, a smaller version of a scaffold, using ladders for legs. This assembly is easily portable and cuts down on what is the most time-consuming aspect of painting a home exterior—moving paint and equipment.

This simple scaffolding is useful when you're painting a wide section of wall or when you can't get a ladder precisely where you want it, such as the center of a second-story window. Ladder-jack scaffolds are made to support no more than two people, and the platforms should not be higher than 20 feet above ground. Always use a proper plank, typically aluminum, 10 feet long, and extending 12 inches beyond the jacks.

Ladder jacks and a scaffold plank can make painting much easier. Make sure you place the ladders no more than 8 feet apart and adjust the jacks to fit the width of the plank. Always remember you're standing on a narrow platform.

In some situations, the terrain or configuration of the house will keep you from setting up both ladders at the same angle. In such cases, you'll have to put one ladder jack on the outside of one ladder and one on the inside of another. This will compensate for the different angles and hold the plank level and parallel to the house.

Make your paint job go quickly with accessories, such as this bracket for holding a paint bucket. This bracket clamps to the ladder rail; other styles are made from heavy tempered rod stock formed into double hooks.

Some stepladders have a shelf that will hold a paint bucket and other tools. The shelf is not strong enough to stand on; even using it to rest one foot on can upset the ladder.

SETTING UP SCAFFOLDING

Framed scaffolds or pipe scaffolds offer several advantages over ladder-jack assemblies. They provide a wider platform working surface, can be moved without disassembly, and feature guardrails to keep you from falling.

Assembly is more time-consuming, however, and they come with a bigger price tag at the rental outlet.

Their main components consist of frames and crossbraces that stack to make taller units. The most common frame section is 5 feet wide and 5 feet tall with crossbraces 7 or 10 feet long. Other sizes are available.

In addition to base plates and guardrails, you should rent adjusting screws for easy leveling on uneven ground, locking casters to keep the unit from moving, and three planks that provide the work floor of the assembly. When you are computing the height you need, figure you can reach work 4 to 6 feet above the scaffold planks. Get sections tall enough to bring you to the height of the wall with two stacked units. Scaffolds higher than two sections can become unstable.

Toggle pins and pigtails

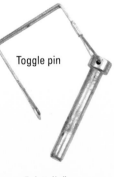

Many scaffolding designs have slight differences in their construction, but all will include some kind of mechanism that locks the pieces together. Toggle pins are common, as are "pigtails"—curved steel pins that insert into holes in the scaffold assembly. Your scaffold model may use other forms of locking mechanisms to hold the assembly together. Always make sure that connecting mechanisms are correctly engaged or in place.

Toggle pin

Scaffold "ladder"

End frame

Adjustable screw bar

1 Before you assemble your scaffolding sections, organize all the parts in one place. Then lay two end frames on the ground near the area you intend to paint. Place the ends facing each other, their ladders on the same side, and their bases about 7 feet apart (or at the final width of your crossbraces). Raise the leg of one frame and insert the long end of the adjustable screw bar into the leg. Then insert the remaining bars into the remaining legs.

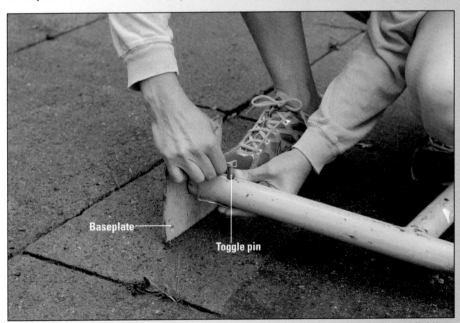

Baseplate

Toggle pin

2 Install the baseplates or casters now so you don't have to lift the assembled scaffolding later to put them in. Different scaffold models may have different methods for this assembly, but most have an open tube that slides over the base of the adjustable screw bar. Secure all baseplates or casters with pigtails, toggle pins, or the locking accessory supplied with the scaffolding. Once you slip the mechanisms into the holes, lock them in place.

3 Raise one end frame, expand one crossbrace, and slip the holes in the crossbrace arms over the pins on the frame. Lock the pins and let the crossbrace support this frame while you raise the second frame. Raise the second frame and slip the opposite ends of the crossbrace over the pins and lock them. Repeat the process by assembling the other crossbrace and locking the pins.

4 Move the scaffold into the position where you'll use it. On soft ground slide 2×10 blocks under each baseplate or wheel. Lock the wheels, and set a long straight 2×4 on the bottom bars of the end frames. Level the scaffolding with the adjusting screws.

7 Set up a workstation on your scaffold platforms either by carrying needed items up the ladder with you or by putting the items in a large bucket and hauling them up with a rope. Having all the items you need readily at hand before you start will cut your prep and painting time by a surprising amount. It's not just the painting that will go faster. Such major repairs as tuckpointing brick walls and removing large sections of paint from wood siding are much easier from a scaffold than from a ladder.

5 Grasp a scaffold plank in the middle, hoist it overhead and at an angle, and slide it on the top bar until its upper end is beyond the bar. Level the plank and position it so the hooks will engage the bars on both end frames. Then lower the plank until the hooks are on the bars. Secure the plank with the swivel locks. Repeat until you have installed all the planks.

6 Carry the guardrail parts to the platform using the ladder side of a frame. Slide the guardrail posts down over the corner posts of each frame and secure them with a pigtail, toggle pin, or bolt, as provided with your scaffold model. Install top and bottom rails between the posts.

8 Avoid working on scaffolds around electrical power lines. If power lines are present near your work area or in the path of your workflow, pay close attention and keep an eye overhead when moving the scaffolding. Don't assume the scaffolding will always move on the level. Variations in the ground surface can cause the scaffold to tip, bringing the metal frame into contact with power lines that are higher than the scaffold. If a framed scaffold assembly simply won't let you paint without danger of electrocution, you may be able to use ladder jacks to get you close to the house but away from the lines. Otherwise, individual fiberglass ladders will make your work slower but keep you safe.

PAINTING SOFFITS AND SIDING

Once you have the prep work out of the way, you are at the easy part of the job. Painting is easier than preparation—and more rewarding. When you begin to put the paint on, you begin to see the results of all your color planning and preparation.

Exterior painting is fairly straightforward from an organizational point of view. The order of the work proceeds from top to bottom. Not only does this keep spatters from marring fresh paint (if you had applied it from bottom to top), it also gets the most difficult details out of the way first.

What to do with the guttering is always a perplexing question on an outside paint job, and the answer is always "remove it." Even if you're not painting the gutters, you need to paint the fascia that supports it. Slipping the brush between the fascia and the gutters will not get the paint where you need it to protect the wood.

PRESTART CHECKLIST

☐ **TIME**
From 1 to 2 hours for every 25 linear feet, depending on the skills of the painter and the amount of ornamentation

☐ **TOOLS**
4-inch brush, 2-inch tapered sash brush, corner roller, 9-inch medium-nap roller

☐ **SKILLS**
Priming and painting trim, working from ladders or scaffolds, intermediate painting skill

☐ **PREP**
Scrape, repair, and prime damaged wood, clean surface thoroughly

☐ **MATERIALS**
High-quality primer and paint

Painting soffits and fascia

1 Raise your ladder until its rests solidly on the house below the soffit. Position the rungs so you can paint all parts of the soffit without overreaching or unnecessarily tucking your head under the soffit. Cut in the edges of open areas, then fill in between them.

2 Paint the horizontal section of the soffit first, then apply paint to the sides and faces of any corbels or other decorative elements. Don't forget to paint the backside of any vertical boards or fascia that trim the soffit. You won't see these rear surfaces, but they need the protection of the paint.

Painting eaves

1 Center the ladder on the wall and start at the peak. Paint as many boards as you can comfortably reach. Paint one board at a time, from one side to the other, in order to keep a wet edge.

Keeping the ladder centered on the wall, move it down a couple of boards and paint them from one side to the other. If you have to overreach, move the ladder to one side or the other.

Painting soffits with a roller

3 Starting at the top, apply paint to the front and bottom edge of any cornice or fascia. If you find you can't reach this area comfortably, come down from the ladder and adjust its height. If you have to reach too far, you will apply the paint unevenly. Move the ladder to successive unpainted sections.

1 If your house has been built since the 1950s or 1960s, your soffit design probably will not have much adornment, which will make painting easier. First cut in all the edges you can comfortably reach, including rafter extensions. Then brush-paint joints or seams in the soffit facing.

2 While the cut-in paint on the section is still wet, paint in the remaining areas with a roller, overlapping the roller strokes and removing any bead marks (see page 56). When one section is painted, move the ladder to the succeeding unpainted sections.

2 Lower the ladder a couple of boards and move it to one side of the wall. Paint two or three boards from that side, across the top of the ladder, and then to the other side as far as you can reach. Cut in the edge of the siding first, then fill in.

3 Keeping the ladder at the same height, move it to the unpainted side and continue painting the same two or three boards. Don't paint boards below the top of the ladder, even if you can reach them—you'll lose the wet edge.

Painting the siding

1 After scraping away loose paint and repairing damaged sections, spot-prime any bare wood with a tannin-blocking primer. Work the primer into the wood, taking care to not apply it too thin. Primer is not paint, however, so you don't need to apply it so thickly that it completely hides the surface underneath it.

2 Let the spot-primed areas dry (they will dry quickly). If the remaining surface is painted and the paint is well adhered, you can proceed directly to painting it. If the coating is in poor condition or you're working with unpainted wood, you'll have to prime it. Brush prime all the edges of each board. Don't edge-prime so large an area that the primer dries. Use a roller to fill in the face of the boards while the edges are still wet.

Make the paint flow

Paint additives can improve paint flow-out and actually improve the durability of the finish. Use Penetrol for oil-base paints, Floetrol for water-base finishes. The label provides general guidelines for the amount of additive needed, which varies with the type of paint and the application temperature. It takes some experimenting to get the feel of these products.

Masking the trim

Before you start painting lapped-siding trim, decide whether you want the edge of the trim the same color as the siding (faced off) or the same color as the face of the trim (wrapped). From an aesthetic point of view, painting the trim one color may look more attractive. Both methods require about the same effort.

If you're going to paint the edge the same color as the siding, you should mask off the face of the trim. For wrapped trim, carefully mask the siding as shown (above). Paint the face of the trim, then paint the edges while the face paint is still wet, brushing out any paint that overlaps the front edge of the trim.

3 When the primed surfaces are dry (and on surfaces for which priming wasn't necessary), apply the finish paint coat, cutting in the edges of the siding with a 3- or 4-inch brush.

4 Before the paint on the edges has dried, fill in the face of the boards with a brush or 7- or 9-inch medium-nap roller, smoothing out any bead marks but using care not to over-roll the paint or exceed the spread rate recommended by the manufacturer. If you're applying two coats, let the first coat dry as specified on the paint can label and repeat the process with the second coat.

WHAT IF...
You want to brush on the final coats?

Some painters prefer brushing the top coats because they feel that brushing makes the paint stick to the surface better. This debate has been around since rollers, and both theories have plenty of supporters.

Brushing the final coat does take a little longer. Follow the techniques for loading the brush and applying paint shown on pages 53–55. Use the same methods—the first stroke (in one horizontal direction), lays the paint on, the second (in the opposite direction) sets the paint on the surface) and the third coat (in the first direction) smooths it.

On textured wood surfaces, you may need to periodically hold your brush at almost right angles to the surface and gently work the paint into the recesses of the texture. Then finish with a smoothing stroke.

STANLEY PRO TIP

Spraying

Spraying the exterior of your home is the fastest application method, but it may require more preparation than others. Use an airless sprayer (HVLP sprayers are too slow); before you pull the trigger, make sure you've covered or masked off all surfaces you don't want to be hit by the overspray this method produces.

PAINTING WINDOWS AND DOORS

If you're in any doubt about whether the exterior of your home needs repainting, check the windows. Windows take a major beating from the elements and show damage and wear more quickly than other parts of the house.

Preparing windows is the same as for any other surface. Start the job in the morning, so the paint will dry by evening.

Wash the wood thoroughly with a scrub brush and mild cleaning agent (or TSP if you want to remove the gloss from the paint). Remove rotted framing members and clean mildew. Scrape loose paint and repair damaged wood. Spot-prime repaired areas and scuff-sand or degloss gloss paint. Reglaze any glass that is loose or glazing that is cracked or missing. You may have to soften the old glazing with a hair dryer, but don't use any hotter heat source—you're likely to crack the window. Let the new glazing compound dry for about a week. Then mask off the glass at the edge of the glazing with blue painter's tape.

PRESTART CHECKLIST

☐ **TIME**
From 30 minutes to 1 hour for a 23-inch window, depending on the skills of the painter

☐ **TOOLS**
3-inch tapered sash brush, putty knife, or glazier's tool

☐ **SKILLS**
Intermediate painting skills and basic mechanical ability, careful painting and raising and lowering sashes

☐ **PREP**
Wash, repair, and spot-prime surface

☐ **MATERIALS**
Glazing compound, primer, paint, masking tape

Painting an exterior window

1 Unlatch the window from the inside and lower the top sash till it's about 3 inches above the sill, and raise the bottom sash to about 3 inches below the top of the frame. If you prefer, you can remove the sashes, paint both sides, then reinstall them when the paint is dry.

2 In general, paint the window from the inside out; that is, start by painting the glazing and inside edge next to the glass. Be cautious at the corners next to the glass. To avoid paint buildup (and consequent drips and sags), pull the excess paint out of the corners with the tip of a relatively dry brush.

WHAT IF...
Your windows have more than one pane?

Position the sashes as recommended in step 1 above or remove them. Paint the edges next to the glass on the top frame, taking care not to leave excess paint in the corners. Then paint the face of the sashes you can reach. Repeat the process on the bottom frame.

3 Next paint the face of the sash—first the boards that don't extend from one end of the window to the other (here, the horizontal rails). Then paint the boards that extend the length of the window (here, the vertical stiles). That way you won't leave crossed brush marks. Keep paint out of the stops.

4 Return the sashes to their proper position, but leave them short of the top and bottom by about 1 inch. Then paint the parts of the sashes you couldn't reach. Next paint the edge of the window casing and the edges and front of the stops. Don't paint the tracks unless you have removed the sashes.

5 Paint the face of the casing and trim. Then, periodically move the sashes up and down while they're drying, so they won't stick in one place. If the sashes end up stuck, try tapping lightly or free them with a sash saw made for this purpose.

Reverse the position of the sashes and paint the remaining edges next to the glass on the bottom frame.

Paint the edge and faces of the window casing and the sash.

STANLEY PRO TIP

Masking the windows without tape

Some manufactures have devised a tool that masks windows without tape. Held against the glass and at the inside edge of the muntins or sash, the tool dispenses a film that keeps paint off the glass. When you're done, the dried film pulls up in an even layer.

Painting a slab door

1 Slab doors are the easiest doors to paint, but they require careful finishing to achieve a professional appearance. Remove the door if you can and set it on sawhorses. If you leave the door in place, remove all the hardware you can so it won't be in the way and won't interfere with straight roller or brush strokes. Mask off what you don't remove. Paint the door with a roller until you have an even coat on the entire surface.

2 Lay off the finish in an even layer with a 4-inch brush, working in single strokes from the bottom all the way to the top. The few brush marks left in the surface will even out as the paint dries.

STANLEY PRO TIP

Masking hinges and hardware

If you don't remove a door to paint it, you'll have to mask off the hardware. An easy way to mask hinges is to apply two coats of rubber cement, letting each one dry. After you're done painting, you can peel the rubber cement off in one continuous layer.

PAINTING A PANELED DOOR

Painting a panel

Pull paint out of corners

When you're painting paneled doors or multilight windows, you're bound to leave excess paint in the corners. To remove this excess, use a slightly dry brush and tip it into the top corner bringing it down and raising it off the surface at the bottom of the stroke.

PAINTING ORDER

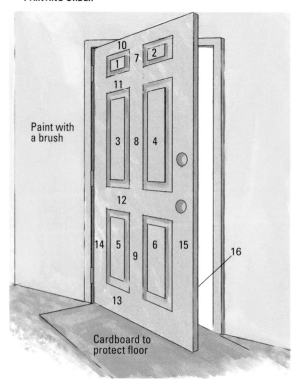

Paint with a brush

Cardboard to protect floor

Painting a paneled door

1 Remove the door if possible or wedge it at the bottom to keep it steady and mask off the hardware (see "Painting a slab door," opposite). Using a 2- or 3-inch sash brush, paint the edges of each panel. Then paint the face of the panel and remove excess paint in the corners before moving to the next panel.

2 After you've painted all the interior panels, roll the paint on the vertical center stiles (numbers 7, 8, and 9 in "Painting order," opposite). You can paint slightly beyond the joints of these panels because the next sequence of strokes will cover these overlaps. Continue rolling the paint in the sequence shown on the previous page, finishing with the long stiles that run vertically the entire height of the door and the edge. Then level the paint with a 3- or 4-inch brush in the same order, always brushing with the grain. Let the door dry, then reinstall the hardware.

Painting shutters

1 Make painting shutters easier by putting supports in the ends of the frames. Predrill each end of the frame for a pair of #10×3-inch drywall or all-purpose screws, and screw them in about an inch or so.

2 Set the shutters on sawhorses spaced so the shutters are supported by the screws, not the frame itself. Paint one side of the shutters with a spray can or brush.

3 When one side of the shutter is painted, grasp the screws at one end and flip the shutter so the other side of the shutter is supported on the screws. This way you don't have to wait till the paint on the first side dries. Paint the second side and let it dry.

PAINTING MASONRY AND OTHER SURFACES

An inventory of the different materials used on the exterior of homes could fill a book, and although painting each material proceeds generally with the same techniques, there are a few differences specific to each.

One viable option, of course, is to leave masonry surfaces unpainted, but if so, now is the time for careful inspection of exterior masonry. Tuckpointing, caulking, and repairs are essential whether you paint them or not. See pages 72–73 for various preparation steps you should take.

If you plan to paint a newly installed masonry surface, wait six weeks before painting it. This will ensure that the concrete has sufficient time to cure properly and in many cases will allow enough time for any efflorescence to appear. Efflorescence can appear later, but whenever it does, you'll need to remove it. (See page 72 for information on removing efflorescence.)

REFRESHER COURSE
Elastomeric wall coatings

Elastomeric wall coatings (EWCs) are specifically designed with flexible binders to cover small cracks in masonry surfaces. Standard latex paints are too rigid to expand and contract with masonry surfaces. EWCs actually stretch and bridge thin cracks. Properly applied EWC can be painted with exterior 100 percent acrylic latex paint in a flat, satin, or semigloss finish.

Before applying any EWC, make sure to repair any cracks more than 1/8 inch across with a high-quality acrylic or siliconized caulk; not even an EWC can bridge gaps that wide. EWCs should also be applied in much thicker layers than paints for best results. Where a gallon of latex paint may cover approximately 400 to 500 square feet of surface, a gallon of EWC will cover only 40 to 50 square feet.

Concrete block

1 Prepare concrete block by removing efflorescence and alkali deposits and fixing cracks. Then seal the surface with a masonry sealer, applied with a medium-napped roller cover. Let the sealer cure according to the manufacturer's directions.

2 Using a foam roller, paint the block with latex masonry paint or exterior acrylic latex paint in flat, satin, or semigloss finish, depending on appearance desired. Keep the coating even by rolling in one direction only.

Board and batten siding

1 Prepare the surface, then prime with a tinted latex primer (to improve hiding of the undercoat). Starting at one end of the wall, paint all three sides of two battens, cutting in the edges of the board at the same time.

2 Using the widest roller that will fit between the battens, paint the board with a roller. Continue across the surface of the wall. Paint the frieze (the horizontal board running across the top of the boards) and the kickboards too. Brush away any excess paint along the edges of the battens.

Painting smooth stucco

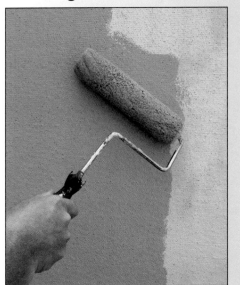

Smooth stucco is relatively easy to paint because the recesses are not deep. Seal unpainted stucco before painting. Cut in the edges and around obstacles with a wide brush first, then use a long-nap roller to apply a high-quality exterior 100 percent acrylic latex house paint.

Painting rough stucco

1 Because the recesses in rough stucco are deep, the aggregate in the surface will prevent paint from reaching much of the interior if you use a roller or brush. Spray the stucco in sections, keeping the spray head at an angle (about 30 to 45 degrees) and changing the angle at random intervals.

2 Move to the other side of the section you have just painted and repaint the section, holding the spray head at the opposite angle. Before you move on to the next section, check for complete coverage. You may have to take a couple of passes from the top and bottom for complete coverage.

Painting modern substrates

Many newer exterior products, ranging from siding material to railings, columns, windows, stairs, and decks, are made to stand up to the elements. Most of these products may be successfully painted to:
■ Alter the color
■ Change selected colors to complement trim and other elements
■ Refresh the appearance or change the degree of gloss or sheen
■ Enhance the protection of the material
Preparation steps are generally the same as for other surfaces—treating mildew, cleaning dirt and dust, removing white, powdery oxide with a nonmetallic scouring pad, and lightly sanding glossy areas with 220-grit sandpaper (but do not expose any metal substrates). Painting, likewise, is best accomplished with exterior acrylic latex paint. Apply a flat sheen on dented surfaces.

Some of the most common materials and problems include:
■ **Factory-finished aluminum materials** usually have a powder coating and a glossy finish. After years of weathering, released pigment may chalk the surface. For uniformity prime the area, including the factory finish.
■ **Vinyl and PVC materials, including polymer/wood mixtures,** can release pigment chalk after years of weathering. Avoid painting rigid vinyl, especially vinyl siding, with a dark color, because the color may absorb the sun's heat and warp the panels irreversibly. As a rule, you should not paint vinyl siding any darker than its original color. Do not attempt to paint any material if the manufacturer recommends against it.
■ **Polyester, fiberglass, and synthetic (polymeric) stone materials,** generally molded or cast with mineral fillers such as limestone, talc, or clay may also chalk after

years of weathering. For best adhesion and uniformity, apply a quality latex stain-blocking primer recommended for this material. Don't apply oil-base or shellac-base primer. For exterior furniture, use a quality exterior latex satin or semigloss product.
■ **Fiber cement siding,** a high-density material made from cement and fiber and formed into siding and soffits, is supplied factory primed, to be painted prior to or after construction. It sometimes comes with a factory-applied color finish coat. Seal all cracks and openings with a quality acrylic or siliconized acrylic sealant. Do not seal side or bottom edges unless directed by manufacturer. Remove loose paint by careful power washing with plain water. Apply a quality exterior latex stain-blocking or masonry primer recommended for this material. Apply exterior acrylic latex paint recommended for masonry surfaces.

FINISHING CEDAR SHINGLES AND SIDING

Cedar is a popular material for shingles and siding because natural oils in its heartwood (the dark red wood at the center of the tree) make it resistant to the weather and hungry insects. Even unpainted, cedar will last for years. Painting cedar, however, calls for some preparation.

Some sections of old, unpainted shingles and siding may look darker than others. This discoloration is most likely caused by a combination of excessive tannins leeching from the wood and mildew growth. You'll have to remove the mildew and prime the wood with a stain-blocking primer.

You can prime and paint new shingles as soon as you have installed them, but since weathering can quickly alter the paintability of wood, if you don't get to the job within two weeks, you'll have to recondition the wood fibers. Powerwashing old shingles is not recommended. Weathering makes them soft, and it's almost impossible to avoid gouging them and to properly dry the water forced under them.

PRESTART CHECKLIST

☐ **TIME**
Varies with age, condition, and size of siding area to be painted

☐ **TOOLS**
Large sponge, garden hose, bucket, 4-inch brush, roller, sprayer, old paintbrush, ladder, stiff scrub brush

☐ **SKILLS**
Preparing, priming, and painting shingles or siding, working on ladder

☐ **PREP**
Remove mildew, brush surface, clean surface

☐ **MATERIALS**
Household bleach, stain-blocking primer, acrylic exterior paint

Painting old shingles

1 Survey the entire area of your house, especially the lower levels, where the shingles will more likely retain water. Wherever you find mildew, sponge on a 1-to-3 bleach-water mixture, scrub it, and let it soak in for 20 minutes, keeping it wet during this period.

2 Using a garden hose with a moderate spray, rinse off the bleaching solution thoroughly. Let the area dry completely, which can take as much as two weeks.

Painting new shingles

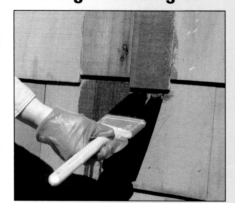

1 Within two weeks of their installation, prime the shingles with a stain-blocking primer. (If you wait longer than that, recondition the surface as shown in step 3 above.) Apply the primer with a 4-inch brush, starting along the overlap and painting a length of about 4 feet.

2 Once you have primed a section of the overlap, paint the face of the row, working the paint in all directions and between the shingles. Smooth the application with downward vertical brush strokes and repeat the process on the next section, always working toward a wet edge.

Spraying shingles

3 Recondition the entire surface to remove aged and weathered fibers in the wood. Use a stiff scrub brush, working the bristles into the overlapped edges along the bottom of each course and drawing the brush down the face of the shingle. Brush off the dust with an old 4-inch paintbrush.

4 Using a 4-inch brush, apply an oil-base stain-blocking primer. Work the brush into the overlapped edges and the recesses between the shingles. Let the primer dry and apply a high-quality acrylic latex house paint. If you roll either primer or paint, back brush so all surfaces are protected.

If you choose to spray either primer or paint on your shingles, apply the coating evenly and from different angles. Work in sections of about 20 square feet and backbrush the coating immediately so it gets worked into the shingle fibers and the recesses between them.

STAINING CEDAR SIDING

Staining cedar siding differs from application of paint and other finishes. Stains dry rapidly, and fresh stain applied over dried stain will show lap marks.

First remove any mill glaze (a hard shiny surface on one side of the siding) by sanding. If possible, stain all sides of the siding before installation. Working in tandem with a helper or working alone, stain one length of siding from end to end before moving down to the next board.

FINISHING FENCES AND GATES

A smart-looking fence in tip-top condition can greatly increase the curb appeal of your home. Wood fences and gates, however, are subject to the same effects of the weather as exterior house surfaces, plus the wear and tear of daily use.

Put your fence on a regular maintenance schedule and check the support structure first, repairing or replacing any damaged posts and rails. Grab each post at the top and put pressure on it from all sides. If it's properly seated in the ground, it should move little or not at all. Movement may signify rot at the base and the need for replacement. Do the same for the rails, and repair them if necessary. Look for mildew, especially on the lower sections of the fence, and clean it with a 1-to-3 bleach-water solution, letting the section soak for 20 minutes and keeping it wet during this period. Then scrub the area with a stiff brush, rinse it with a garden hose, and let it dry thoroughly before painting.

If your fence is in good repair, it may benefit from a yearly power washing to remove dirt. Use a fan head and low pressure to avoid gouging the wood.

PRESTART CHECKLIST

☐ **TIME**
About an hour to prep, prime, and paint a 6-foot section, depending on its condition

☐ **TOOLS**
Wide putty knife, nail set, cordless drill, paintbrushes, sandpaper

☐ **SKILLS**
Preparing wood surfaces for priming and painting, applying primer and paint

☐ **PREP**
Remove mildew, clean and repair fence

☐ **MATERIALS**
Exterior wood filler, stain-blocking primer, high-quality acrylic exterior paint

Spot-seal and prime new wood

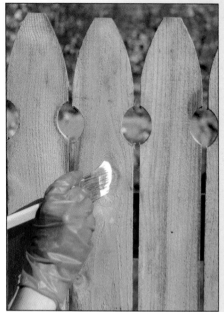 

1 On a new fence or gate, set nails and screws below the surface, fill all cracks and nail holes with an exterior-grade wood filler, and spot-seal knot holes with an exterior sealer. This will keep the knots from bleeding through the finish paint.

2 Using roller, sprayer, or a brush sized appropriately to the fencing, apply stain-blocking primer to the wood. If you use a roller or spray gun, follow the application by back brushing, working the primer into the spaces between the fence boards. Paint with a high-quality exterior acrylic paint.

In time, all unfinished woods will turn gray when exposed to the weather. Common naturally resistant species used in outdoor construction, such as redwood and cedar, weather without deteriorating. These woods can be further protected with weather-resistant finishes, and you can induce a weathered appearance with bleaching oils, a mixture of linseed oil and bleach crystals— if you don't want to wait for nature to do the work.

Rejuvenating an old gate

To rejuvenate an old gate, first make structural repairs as necessary, replacing rotted boards and squaring the gate by shoring up the frame. Scrape off any loose paint with a scraper or remove it with a heat gun and wide putty knife. Set nailheads and drive screws slightly below the surface of the wood. Fill holes with an exterior wood filler, sand, prime with a stain-blocking primer, and paint with a high-quality acrylic exterior paint.

Paint before assembly

If you're constructing a new fence or gate, prime and finish the individual parts of the structure before you assemble them. That way, you are assured of getting more complete paint coverage and better protection. Painting before assembly will reduce your maintenance chores in the long run.

Spray painting a fence

Spraying a wood fence requires the same preparation as brushing it but gets the paint on quickly. Protect vegetation and porch and deck surfaces from overspray. Back-brush the surface.

Painting chainlink

If you don't like the factory-galvanized gray of your chain-link fence, transform it with a coat of paint. On new chain link, etch the surface with household vinegar, then paint. On weathered fences, just roll the paint on both sides with a long-nap roller.

Paint with a mitt

A paint mitt can make quick work out of painting narrow boards or square or round balusters. Put the mitt on your painting hand, dip it into the paint bucket, and squeeze out some of the excess. Then grab the board with the mitt and slide down it.

SELECTING FINISHES FOR A DECK OR PORCH

Finishes do more than make the wood look good. The right finish will protect your deck and help it seem a natural extension of your landscape design.

When you're out shopping for deck finishes, or while you're still in the early planning stages, think first about the color you want—for example, brown, red, or green. Then consider what shade of that color your deck should be—dark brown, tan, pale red, or dark green. Then give some thought to what sheen (flat or glossy) will look best. Decks generally look best with a flat sheen, but a contemporary design scheme might call for something different from the norm.

Then look for information that tells you how durable the finish is and how easy it will be to apply. Generally sealers are the easiest to apply, followed by stains, with paint taking the most time and effort. Consider the species of the wood too. A clear finish is a good choice for redwood and cedar. It allows their natural colors to show through. Pressure-treated lumber usually requires staining or painting.

Sealer

Clear or lightly pigmented sealers protect the wood from water damage and don't change its color much. Look for additives that will ward off mildew, insects, and fungi. Ultraviolet (UV) blockers are a must—they reduce damage caused by the sun's rays. Pigmented sealers do all of the above, but the pigment is designed to change the color of the wood slightly. All-purpose sealers contain water repellents, preservatives, and UV blockers. You can apply sealers over or under stains and under primer and paint.

Stain

Stains are primarily formulated to transform the appearance of the wood—some slightly, some dramatically. Certain formulas are designed to offer some protection to the wood, but this is a job best done with a sealer in conjunction with a stain.

What kind of stain you use will depend on how much of the original wood tones you want to retain. Semitransparent stains allow more wood grain to show through but wear away more quickly; they are particularly suitable for highlighting wood grains. Heavy-bodied stains contain more pigments and hide the grain. All stains (both oil- or water-base products), including those not designed to penetrate the fibers of the wood, tend to retain the wood's natural look far more than paint. Apply oil-base stains on redwood and red cedar.

Stains are somewhat less expensive than paints, take less time to apply, and go on easily over rough and smooth surfaces.

Paint

Paints conceal some defects and tend to last longer and look better than stains on smooth surfaces. Exterior alkyds (oil-base products) are more costly, more difficult to clean up, and slower-drying. Water-base latex paints cost less, clean up easily, and dry quickly. Each comes in a range of colors and sheens (gloss, semigloss, and flat or matte). New, unpainted surfaces need to be primed first. Oil-base primers provide better protection on raw wood than water-base primers. Add stain blockers to stop bleed-through from redwood and cedar. A good-quality acrylic-latex top coat applied over an alkyd primer makes a durable finish.

STANLEY PRO TIP: **Enough sealant?**

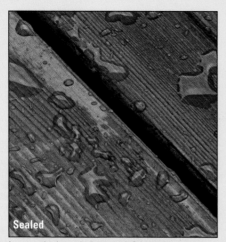

Sealed

Needs sealant

Is your deck sealed properly? In some cases the answer is obvious. Old wood with a dried-out look clearly needs a stiff dose of sealer. But boards that look OK may also be in danger of drying out. So do a quick test once or twice a year. Sprinkle a little water onto the surface. If the water beads up and does not soak in within two minutes, the board is sealed well enough. If water soaks in within 2 minutes, apply additional sealer.

The weathered look

If you like wood with a gray, weathered look, don't finish, seal, or paint the deck. Let nature weather the wood naturally. Natural weathering works best with all-heartwood grades of durable species, such as cedar, cypress, and redwood.

The aging time varies with the species and its exposure. Generally cedar and cypress weather to a light silver-gray and redwood turns dark gray. Pressure-treated lumber turns a soft gray but sometimes retains a hint of its green or brown coloring.

Safety gear

Wear rubber gloves and safety glasses or goggles when you work with finishing materials. Many stains, paints, and sealers contain solvents and other volatile organic compounds.

What will it look like?

All finishes will alter the appearance of all woods. The photos give some idea of the range of appearances different finishes will effect on the same wood (here, untreated Douglas fir). The colors and tones shown in the photos are only representative of degrees of change. Different brands and changes in the wood grain, even within the same board, produce different results.

OIL-BASE CLEAR SEALER

LATEX CLEAR SEALER

SEMITRANSPARENT STAIN

HEAVY-BODIED STAIN

PAINT

DIFFERENT FINISHES
Sample finishes first

Before applying any finish—staining or painting especially—you'll want to know how the final color will look. The only way to really be sure is to see the color when the finish is dry.

Test the final color by applying a small amount in an out-of-the-way spot on your deck. Let the finish dry to make sure it produces the color you want. Paint usually dries darker than when wet. Stains usually dry lighter.

WHAT IF...
You want to lighten the wood?

Bleaching agents change the appearance of wood by altering the chemical composition of the surface fibers. They offer a way to tone down the jarring look of a brand-new deck. They soften the raw-wood look and help the varying shades of natural wood to blend in. You get the effect of two seasons of natural weathering in one application, because like the sun, the treatments strip color from the wood fibers. Sealers stop the bleach from working, so if you plan to bleach the wood, don't seal it first. Wait two months after applying the bleach to seal the wood.

PREPARING AND PAINTING DECKS AND PORCHES

Deck coatings live a demanding life. Because they face up, their horizontal surface is subject to a heavy dose of UV light from the sun; stress from standing water, snow, and wet leaves; and wear and tear from foot traffic, furniture, and pets.

If your deck is brand new and you've used untreated wood in its construction, stain or paint it promptly after you've completed it. Let the preservatives in pressure-treated wood dry two to six weeks before finishing.

When possible, apply the finish to edges, ends, and undersides of pieces. Apply only products recommended for deck surfaces and always apply an exterior wood primer before painting.

When recoating your deck, remove all loose paint or stain. Thoroughly sand bare wood and wipe it clean. You can also powerwash it with plain water or a deck preparation treatment. Remove all mildew and rinse off all residual cleaner, bleach, dirt, and dust. Prime and finish when the deck is in the shade, and when weather extremes are not predicted with the next 24 hours.

PRESTART CHECKLIST

☐ **TIME**
From 7 to 12 hours to prepare and finish a 12×16-foot deck, plus drying time

☐ **TOOLS**
Scrapers, putty knife, sandpaper, power washer, paintbrushes or pads, rollers, or spray equipment

☐ **SKILLS**
Preparing the surface, spraying, brushing, or rolling finish

☐ **MATERIALS**
Plastic sheets or tarps, cleaning solution, primer, and paint

Preparing the surface

1 Remove loose or chipped paint or opaque stains with a paint scraper or wide putty knife, scraping the area down to bare wood. Then sand the bare wood, feathering the edges of remaining finish so they won't create ridges where you apply new finish.

2 Use a stiff-bristled brush to loosen flaking stain or dirt. Don't use a metal-bristle brush on cedar or redwood because the metal bristles can scar the soft wood.

Painting a deck or porch

When brushing the deck finish, coat the railings first, using a 3-inch trim brush to cut in and paint balusters and rails.

If using a paint pad, select the largest pad available and keep it fully loaded. That way you reduce your painting time by covering more surface area. Don't run the paint out on the surface, which will thin it and make it less durable.

3 Apply a cleaning product made specifically for decks, mixing it according to manufacturer's directions. Work the cleaner into the wood with a stiff-bristle brush, using an extension handle to make the work easier on your back.

4 To remove the cleaning agent and other residue, rinse the surface with a power washer with a fan spray nozzle. Use the low power setting to avoid damaging the wood. Let the deck dry thoroughly before applying any new finish.

Painting a deck or porch

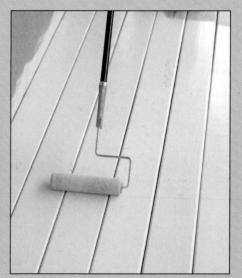

If you decide to spray paint your deck, use an HVLP unit to minimize overspray. Spray the railings first, unless the railings are to be a different color than the deck. In that case, mask off the railings and spray the deck first.

When you spray close to the house, have a helper hold up a large piece of cardboard to protect the siding from overspray.

To paint with a roller, use the widest one you can comfortably handle. Paint the deck in sections of about 6 square feet. A roller cover with $\frac{1}{2}$-inch nap will cover a deck surface efficiently.

APPLYING A CLEAR DECK FINISH

Home centers offer a wide array of deck cleaners, sealers, and finishes. Check with deck owners in your area to see which products work best and how often they need to be applied. If the deck is exposed to hot sun for extended periods, you may need to apply a fresh coat of sealer every year.

A deck that has turned gray can usually be made to look like new if you wash it and apply a protective finish. Even grayish-green pressure-treated wood can be stained to resemble cedar or redwood.

It may be worth the cost to hire a professional to finish or refinish your deck. Look through your phone directory for companies that restore, finish, and maintain a deck's appearance. Check out their prices and examine some of the decks they have worked on. Compare the cost with the time and expense it will take you to do it yourself.

PRESTART CHECKLIST

☐ **TIME**
Several hours to clean, and several hours to apply a finish the next day

☐ **TOOLS**
Scrub brush, power washer, pole sander, pump sprayer, paintbrush

☐ **SKILLS**
Attention to detail, applying a smooth coat of finish

☐ **PREP**
Ask a supplier about the best products for your wood and your climate

☐ **MATERIALS**
Deck cleaner, deck sealer, and/or finish

Preparing the surface

1 Lightly sand the deck using a pole sander, then sweep it thoroughly. Mix a batch of deck cleaner according to manufacturer's directions, apply it, and scrub with a stiff brush.

2 Use a garden hose or a power washer to rinse the cleaner completely from the deck. If you use a power washer, use a fan or 40-degree nozzle. Be careful not to hold the nozzle too close to the wood; the pressure of the spray can tear the fibers.

Finish and their uses

Choose a finish that contains all the ingredients you need: water repellent to seal out moisture; preservative to protect against mildew, wet rot, and insects; and UV blockers to stop the sun from turning the wood gray.

Finish	Uses
Clear sealers	These products use oil or waxes to keep moisture from soaking in. Some contain preservatives to keep bugs away and prevent mildew.
Semitransparent stain	Though some products claim to block UV rays without adding color to the wood, the only reliable way to avoid damage from the sun is to add at least a slight pigment. Some finishes dramatically change the color, while others are more subtle.
Resinous finish	This typically comes in two parts and is expensive. The resin gives a deck a permanent wet look. It provides superior protection against water but may need to be reapplied every year.
Solid stain, porch and deck paint	A solid stain completely changes the color of a board but allows its grain to show through. Paint covers the color and texture of a board. Oil-base products can be long-lasting; water-base products will wear away quickly.

Applying the finish

1 Allow the deck to dry completely. Use a pump sprayer to spread sealer/stain onto the deck. Cover a strip about 3 feet wide—an easy reach for brushing.

2 Immediately backbrush the surface with a 5- to 6-inch brush to spread out any puddles. Move the brush in one direction only, always with the grain.

3 For detail work, use a smaller brush. Pay attention to the edges of boards, so you don't end up with brush strokes that run across the grain.

STANLEY PRO TIP: **Prefinish when possible**

If you're building your own deck, prefinish the components if possible.

Set up the various sections in assembly line form prior to installing them. For example, lay all the deck posts on concrete blocks and apply the finish to all surfaces. Let the finish dry, then install the posts. Then set the joists up and finish them in the same way.

Prefinishing will put the protection of the finish on surfaces you can't get to once the pieces are assembled.

Apply with a roller

You can apply sealer with a paint roller instead of a pump sprayer. Work carefully to avoid blobs and streaks. Brush the wood within a couple of minutes of applying with the roller.

INTERIOR PAINTING

Most people consider painting the interior of a house easier than painting the exterior. Even though the procedures for both jobs are essentially the same—selecting colors, primers, and paints; preparing surfaces; and applying the materials—and the tools and techniques are the same, interior painting always seems less intimidating.

That's probably because the scale of an inside painting project seems more comfortable. You can probably paint the walls and ceiling in a room with a long-handled roller and perhaps a lightweight stepladder or step stool. You rarely need high scaffolding or tall extension ladders inside. And the job schedule doesn't depend on the weather. You can paint inside your house rain or shine, winter or summer.

Because you spend most of your home time inside the house and usually see the exterior only briefly, the interior is probably the part of the house you identify with most readily. The walls, ceilings, floors, and trim affect the overall design and feel of every room, and that ambience can have a significant impact on your outlook and disposition and whether or not you find a room enjoyable.

Living closer to these inside surfaces makes their attributes and flaws more immediately apparent. You'll usually notice handprints (and in a young family, maybe some writing) on the wall in the kitchen or bedroom right away, but you might not spot a scuff mark on the exterior siding for quite a while. Keeping room interiors bright and fresh-looking is the biggest part of home maintenance for many people.

Rooms are often repainted long before it would be necessary from a pure maintenance point of view. Appearance is usually the main reason to repaint—whether to change the color for a new decorating scheme or just to bring back the crisp feeling of a freshly painted room. Because appearance is so important, you should take time to prepare the surfaces and apply the paint carefully. When you live with the results every day, you may find that just doing a good enough job may not be quite good enough.

Following the advice in this chapter will help you complete a paint job that you and your family will enjoy for a long time—or until it's time to redecorate again.

CHAPTER PREVIEW

Planning and estimating
page 104

Getting the room ready
page 106

Removing wallpaper
page 108

Cleaning and sanding
page 110

Smoothing textured surfaces
page 111

Preparing and repairing walls
page 112

Preparing trim
page 116

Protecting surfaces
page 120

Ladders and work platforms
page 122

Priming tips
page 124

Painting ceilings
page 126

Painting walls
page 128

Painting interior windows
page 130

Staining and varnishing trim
page 136

Painting interior doors
page 138

Painting a basement wall
page 142

Painting a basement or garage floor
page 144

Painting a wood floor
page 146

Staining or varnishing a wood floor
page 148

Painting vinyl flooring and ceramic tile
page 150

Painting steps
page 152

Painting cabinetry
page 104

PLANNING AND ESTIMATING

Whether you're painting one room or the entire inside of your home, the job will go more smoothly if you have a plan. If you start your planning after you get to the paint store and try to finish the job the same day, you risk having a badly painted wall and some disappointment. The place to start planning is at a desk or table where you can make notes and consider all your options.

Colors come first
The first goal is to choose the color scheme for the room, and your choices should result from a consideration of several factors. First determine the purpose of the room and the mood or feeling you want to create in it. For example, the atmosphere in your bedrooms is probably best served with quiet and understated color. The kitchen, which is often the center of family activities, can be brighter and feature bold colors. A living room can be either calm or lively, depending upon how your family uses the room.

Then consider whether there are features of the architectural style of your home you want to enhance with the color scheme. An Arts and Crafts style home, for instance, takes much of its hand-hewn character from earth tones on the walls and natural wood trim, stained and varnished.

If you are starting from scratch and planning a complete makeover, including new furniture, choose colors and furniture together so they complement each other. If you're not changing the furniture, pick colors for walls that don't clash with the furnishings. These are just a few things to think about. Chapter 1 has further information on color selection.

Check conditions
With color choices out of the way, look at the condition of the walls and make notes about problems that need fixing before you start painting. Sketch the walls of each room you plan to paint and note holes that need

patching, cracks that need repair, and loose paint that needs scraping and sanding. Note other preparation steps on your sketch, such as "remove baseboards" or "replace light fixture," so you help yourself stay organized without overlooking any preparation step. Measure each room and mark the dimensions on your sketch.

From the list, make a plan
The notes you make will form the basis for a materials list and an organizational plan.

First list quantities of prep materials, such as caulk, sandpaper, cleaning agents, and replacement trim you'll need. Then calculate the amount of paint the job will require (see below), as well as brushes, rollers, and other tools. If you need rental equipment, such as ladders or spray equipment, put them on the list too. Break up the tasks—caulking, replacing trim, scraping, sanding, and priming—into manageable time frames and write them on a calendar.

How much paint do you need?

1 Multiply the length of one wall × its height to find the area of one wall.

2 Add areas of all walls together to find the total wall area.

3 Multiply the width of a window or door × its height to find the area of the window or door.

4 Add the areas of all windows and doors to find the total window and door area.

5 Subtract the total window and door area from the total wall area to find the wall area to be painted.

6 For triangular areas multiply the height × the width at the base and divide the result by 2 to find the area of the triangle.

7 Add the area of triangle to the total wall area (less windows) to find the total area to be painted.

To estimate the quantity you need, divide the total area by the coverage of a gallon (see "Coverages," opposite page). Multiply by 2 if you plan to apply two coats. Buy a little excess paint to allow for spillage and future touch-ups.

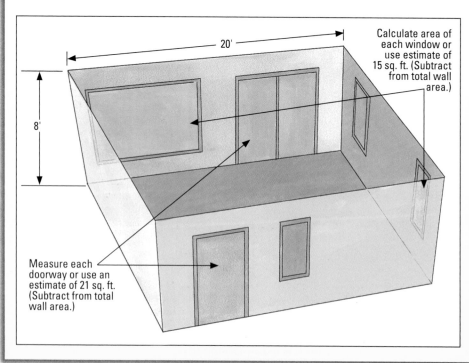

20'

8'

Calculate area of each window or use estimate of 15 sq. ft. (Subtract from total wall area.)

Measure each doorway or use an estimate of 21 sq. ft. (Subtract from total wall area.)

Buy your supplies and materials a couple of days before you intend to start any phase of the work. List (and complete) the steps in the right order—remove mold and mildew, clean dirt, replace or repair damaged trim, scrape loose paint, prime, cut in the new paint around the edges of a wall and fill in, and paint doors, windows, and trim.

Coverages

Paint manufacturers generally estimate that a gallon of paint will cover 400 square feet. That's true under ideal conditions but rare in practice. You'll generally be able to cover about 300 square feet of surface with a gallon of paint applied properly. Paint coverage is affected by the surface you're painting. For example, previously painted surfaces with a similar color can take less paint than unpainted surfaces. New drywall soaks up paint, and fresh plaster is even more absorbent.

You can paint one wall before buying all the paint and use the coverage you get to guide your purchase of the remaining paint. You may have a color variation from the first wall to the others this way. (See "Box the paint" on page 52.)

If you're planning to paint the interior of cabinets or bookcases, add their surface area to the wall area you've computed.

To simplify your computations, you can figure each window at 15 square feet and each door at 21 square feet.

Considerable information is available to make color selection as easy as possible. Your paint dealer should be able to provide paint chips, charts with color schemes, and other aids to you so you can narrow down the possibilities to final choices. Some manufacturers make stick-on paint chips that you can put on the wall and remove without causing any damage to your existing paint.

 PRO TIP

Air conditions

Humidity and temperature affect the way paint flows on and bonds to the surface. The best conditions for interior painting are moderate humidity and temperatures—late spring or early fall in most parts of the country. You can add conditioner to paint to improve its flow and run a humidifier if the air is really dry.

Green paints

With increasing concern about the effect of chemicals on the environment and human health, paints have become more environmentally and health friendly in the past few years.

Lead, chromium, and mercury have been removed from almost all consumer paints, and chlorofluorocarbons (CFCs) have been eliminated from spray-can paints. Manufacturers are also working to reduce and eliminate volatile organic compounds (VOCs)—petroleum solvents used to thin and clean up oil-base paints, small amounts of which are also used in latex paints. Many of these compounds are hazardous to people and require proper personal protection.

In addition, VOC vapors escape into the atmosphere, and in a complex chemical reaction, they produce ozone, a component of smog.

Today, most latex paints contain no more than 10 percent solvent, and many contain only 4 to 7 percent. And the solvent content of oil-base paints has dropped from 50 percent to about 20 percent. Some paint manufacturers have also developed no-VOC lines in response to demands for safer, less noxious paints. Anyone with health or environmental concerns should ask their paint supplier about these environmentally friendly paints.

Water-base paints have improved so much in recent years that many professional painters now consider them superior to oil-base paints for most uses. They exhibit greater colorfastness and better adhesion and allow the surface to breathe better. Water cleanup makes them easier to work with and releases less solvent into the environment.

GETTING THE ROOM READY

If you really want to make your paint job easy, empty the room. This, however, is often easier said than done. Many pieces of furniture are unwieldy and may be difficult to move without hiring help. And you have to find a place to put it. You may not have room elsewhere in the house. The best solution often is to move it to the center of the room and cover it with plastic or tarps.

Make any repairs necessary, especially those, like sanding damaged areas and sawing replacement trim, that will raise dust. Thoroughly vacuum or mop the floor and wipe the baseboards and woodwork clean. Cover the floor with plastic sheeting, and fasten the edges to the floor with duct tape. Lay cloth tarps over the plastic.

Turn off the power to any outlets or fixtures. Remove all light fixtures, switch and outlet plates, heat registers, towel rods—anything that you would have to paint around. Tag each item with its location and tape screws and mounting hardware to the mounting plates so all the pieces are in one place. That way you won't have to hunt for them or buy replacements when you go to reinstall them. Stuff electric wiring into the boxes to get it out of the way.

Before you take down window treatments, make sure you know how they are attached to the wall. Draw a diagram, if necessary, then put the parts in a plastic bag. As you remove small items, put them into plastic bags and label the bags by room. Tape the bags to a windowpane with masking tape—this keeps the bags off the floor and prevents the small parts from getting lost or broken.

In some cases, you can loosen the canopy of a ceiling fixture and slide it down from the ceiling and still leave the fixture in place. You can then tape the fixture with plastic trash bags for protection. Never unscrew a fixture from its box and allow it to hang by its wires.

Ceiling fans must come down. Cover outlets and switches with duct tape to shield them from paint and moisture.

Make your cleanup easier by lining a trash can with several bags. When one bag is full, remove it, and you have another ready and waiting. Then, when you've finished painting the room, toss the disposable drop cloths, disposable brushes, steel wool, and all other debris onto the plastic sheeting on the floor and roll it into a ball for easy disposal.

Masking light fixtures and outlet plates often won't keep paint off them and painting around fixtures leaves brush marks on the wall. So turn the power off and remove the fixtures. Tape the mounting screws to the back and stuff the wires into the box. You can then paint across the area without interruption.

SAFETY FIRST
Turn off the power

Before you remove light fixtures and other electrical devices from the room, turn off the power at the breaker. Put a piece of tape over the breaker so someone else in the family doesn't inadvertently turn it back on.

Create a doorway

Preparing for a paint job can create a lot of dust, and you'll want to keep it from migrating into other areas of the house. Even with a closed door, dust can escape. To help keep the dust contained, attach plastic sheeting over the doorway to act as a seal. Cut an opening in the sheet for exit and access.

1 Tape the plastic over the door, leaving a 12- to 18-inch fold in the center of the sheet. Slit the sheet vertically to make two flaps. Seal the flaps with spring clamps.

2 Set a small rug or carpet sample on the floor outside the room. It will help keep you from tracking dust with your shoes.

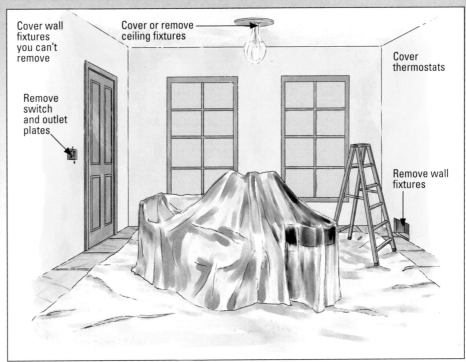

Protect switches and outlets by masking them with blue painter's tape.

"Move it" or "cover it" are the key words in preparing a room for paint. If you can't get the furniture conveniently into another room, put it in the center and cover it with plastic. This will leave you with a clear passageway along the walls.

STANLEY PRO TIP: **Deal with dust**

Blow it out: If the room has a window, open it and prop a box fan in place so it blows out. This will evacuate a lot of the airborne dust. Remove the screen or it will act as a barrier and send the dust back to the room.

Wrap the registers: Prevent the spread of dust by removing any heating, cooling, or ventilation registers in the demolition room. Wrap them in plastic wrap and replace them.

Don't hide the hardware holes

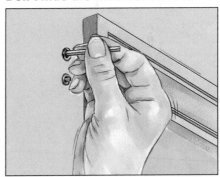

It doesn't take much paint to cover the holes made by mounting screws for curtain hardware, and if you hide the holes, you may have to go through all the original steps of locating and hanging the hardware. To eliminate this annoyance, stick matches into the holes so they stick out. Paint around them, and when you get ready to remount the screws, snap them off even with the wall. The matchsticks will keep the screws tight.

REMOVING WALLPAPER

When you remove wallpaper, take it down the same way it went up—in whole sheets, not pieces. To remove the wallpaper and adhesive without damaging the wall, you have several options—removing the paper in layers, using wallpaper removal solutions (either liquid or gel), or steaming it off.

Removing a wall covering in layers requires stripping off the vinyl top sheet, then removing the paper backing with a liquid (a commercial product or a 1-to-16 solution of vinegar/water) or gel. If your wallcovering is a fabric-backed vinyl or strippable solid-surface vinyl, you can probably remove it in layers. Gels offer the advantage of clinging to the paper while they soak in and attack the starches in the wallpaper glue. Steaming is dangerous, both to operator and the wall, especially drywall.

Whatever method you use, turn off the power, remove all outlet and switch plates, and thoroughly protect switches and outlets with duct tape to prevent water or steam from entering and causing shorts when you turn the power back on.

PRESTART CHECKLIST

☐ **TIME**
Several hours to two days, depending on the type of covering and size of the wall

☐ **TOOLS**
Screwdriver, perforation tool, spray bottle or garden sprayer, rubber gloves, plastic bucket, scraper, sponge, drop cloths, 1-inch dowel rod (as long as wallpaper section is wide)

☐ **SKILLS**
Using wallpaper-removing tools

☐ **PREP**
Remove fixtures and outlet and switch plates and cover them with duct tape

☐ **MATERIALS**
Baseboard masking, solution for removing wallpaper

Stripping a layer

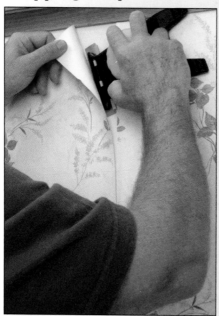 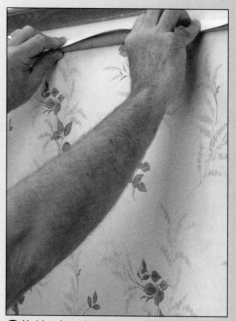

1 Begin by peeling a corner of the top edge of a sheet of wallcovering away from the wall about 2 inches to give you an edge you can hold onto. Use a stripping knife to help strip the vinyl layer away from its backing.

2 Hold a dowel against the flap of loose paper and roll the paper down around it. Continue rolling the covering about 8 to 10 inches. The dowel keeps the pressure spread evenly across the sheet of paper, which should reduce tearing.

3 Hold the paper on the dowel with both hands and pull straight down, keeping the dowel close to the wall and wrapping as you remove the paper. This should minimize tearing the covering and damaging the drywall surface. If the paper starts to tear, roll the rest of it off the wall—don't pull it. When all the top layer is off, use the methods on the next page to remove the backing and glue.

Using a liquid wallpaper remover

1 Perforate the wallcovering with a perforation tool. Its teeth penetrate the surface and the perforations will allow the solution to soak through and soften the adhesive. Start at a top corner, working down and across the wall in large circles.

2 Apply the wallpaper remover with a garden sprayer or spray mister. Spray the walls from the bottom up, working around the room in one direction. Apply the solution at least three times.

3 When the walls are saturated, smooth 7-mil plastic sheeting over the surface with a wallcovering brush or squeegee, cut the plastic to fit around the moldings, and tape it at the top. This keeps the solution from evaporating so it can dissolve the glue. Leave the plastic in place overnight.

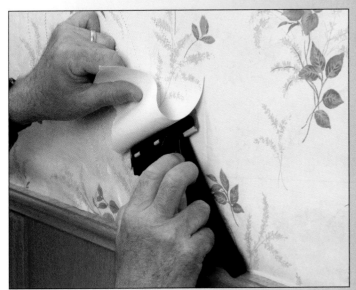

4 Test the adhesive to determine if it will release the paper. Pull back a lower corner of the plastic and gently scrape open a seam. If the covering won't come loose easily, lift the plastic away at the top of the wall and resoak the covering. Smooth the plastic back and let the solution work for an additional 6 to 12 hours.

5 When you can strip the paper easily, fold back about 4 feet of the plastic and anchor a corner with pushpins to keep the rest of the glue from re-adhering to the wall. Starting at the top, scrape off one section at a time. Keep the scraper low to avoid gouging the wall. Spray additional solution to keep the backing moist.

CLEANING AND SANDING

It takes little time for the walls in your home to accumulate a thin film of grime, grease, and dust. And walls often look clean when they are not. Dirt and grime between the wall and the new paint must come off, because they will interfere with the adhesion of your new coating. If you think your walls are clean, dampen a paper towel with a little vinegar and gently rub a small place on the wall. You're sure to see the evidence on the paper towel that doesn't show up noticeably on the wall.

Phosphate residues weaken paint bonds, so use a low-phosphate household cleaner or brew your own with ¼ cup of trisodium phosphate (TSP) in a gallon of water. Use the procedures discussed in "Good cleaning techniques," below.

Sanding walls provides a uniformly smooth surface with a slight "tooth," which helps the paint stick more securely. If you scrub flat or semigloss paints with a scrubbing strip, you have effectively wet-sanded them and won't need to go further. Glossy surfaces will need sanding with a 100-grit sanding screen.

Washing and sanding a wall

Vacuum dust from the wall. Using a sponge mop with a cleaning strip, wash the wall with a low-phosphate cleaner or TSP solution. Work in sections, scrubbing each section with the cleaning strip and rinsing immediately with a 16-to-1 solution of water and white vinegar.

Some walls need to be sanded, others don't. Flat or semigloss surfaces cleaned with a low-phosphate cleaner and scrubbing strip won't need sanding. Glossy paints will—sand them with a sanding screen and wipe down the dust. In all cases, fix cracks and patch holes before sanding.

WHAT IF…
My walls are mildewed?

1 Mask off the baseboard and the floor area below the mildewed surface. Sponge on a 1-to-3 solution of bleach and water and scrub the mildew with a sponge. Let the solution set for 20 minutes to kill the mildew, keeping it wet during this time. Rinse the area thoroughly and let it dry overnight.

2 Using a high-quality stain-blocking primer or shellac-base sealer, prime the mildewed section and let it dry. The primer/sealer will keep the residual mildew from bleeding through the finish paint coats.

Good cleaning techniques

A thorough, effective cleaning depends not only on what cleaner you use, but also how you put it on. Because it's important to not leave cleaning residue on the wall, set up two 5-gallon buckets with two sponge floor mops (one needs to have an abrasive cleaning strip). Cleaning solution goes in one bucket, the rinse (1 cup of white vinegar to 1 gallon of water) goes in the other.

Map out imaginary sections in about 8-foot widths, sponge on the cleaning solution, and let it set for a minute, but do not let it dry. Immerse your mop in the cleaning bucket and scrub the section with the sponge. Then scrub the section again with the abrasive cleaning strip. This effectively removes dirt and opens up the old paint film so it will take new paint more readily. Rinse the section as soon as you have completed the second scrubbing and continue cleaning the remainder of the room in the same fashion. Change solutions often.

SMOOTHING TEXTURED SURFACES

There was a time when textured surfaces were all the rage. Contractors loved them because they covered flaws in drywall work. Homeowners liked the added textural interest they provided to the design scheme. But textured surfaces have one major drawback—they collect a lot more dirt and are more difficult to clean than smooth walls.

If you have a textured wall or ceiling and you want to smooth it, there are several options. You can sand the surface completely smooth (which produces a tremendous amount of dust), you can sand off high spots and skim-coat the wall with drywall compound (still dusty and labor intensive), you can wet and scrape the surface (time-consuming and risks damaging the drywall), or you can install thin drywall over the old (a little more expensive but the most practical in the long run). If you choose any sanding method, rent a drywall sander. It comes with a vacuum that reduces the dust.

Smoothing a textured wall

1 Prepare the room, covering the furniture, and pole-sand the walls with 100-grit sandpaper or a sanding screen. This knocks down the high points on the wall to a more consistent level. Be careful not to gouge the texture or the drywall.

2 Vacuum dust from the wall and spot prime any damaged areas with two coats of an oil-base primer. Let the primer dry. Thin premixed joint compound with water to the consistency of mayonnaise and apply it in sections, finishing each with overlapping vertical strokes. Lightly sand when dry.

Smoothing a textured ceiling

1 Protect the floor with plastic sheets, taping them to the floor at the perimeter. Spray the texture with a solution of 1 cup of ammonia to 1 gallon of water and let it soak in for 15 minutes, keeping the section wet but not soaked.

2 Using a floor squeegee or the widest drywall knife you can find, scrape the softened texture from the ceiling. Let the surface dry, then smooth, sand, and prime damaged areas. Paint the ceiling.

STANLEY PRO TIP

New drywall = less mess

Installing new drywall creates less mess and with a helper, goes quickly. First staple 2-mil plastic over the existing surface. Then cut drywall sheets to fit and screw them to the ceiling into the studs. Use a T-brace to support the sheet until it's fastened.

PREPARING AND REPAIRING WALLS

Before you paint a wall, repair any defects and damage so you have a clean, flat, and unblemished surface for painting. Paint (especially semigloss and glossy coatings) does not hide defects in the wall surface; in fact, it usually makes them more noticeable.

First, remove any wallpaper or covering (see pages 108–109). Then use drywall compound to skim-coat any gouges or other damage created in the removal process. Let the compound dry and sand it when you sand the rest of the wall (see page 110). Push on the wall to test whether the drywall has pulled away from the studs. If the wall gives in any places, drive screws into the studs to re-anchor it. Skim-coat the screws, also. Then repair any holes in the wall.

You don't actually have to remove sinks and other fixtures to paint the walls, but if you get them out of your way, your paint job will proceed much more smoothly and the surface will look much more attractive.

PRESTART CHECKLIST

☐ **TIME**
About 20 to 30 minutes per square yard

☐ **TOOLS**
Level, hammer, cold chisel, framing square, margin and mason's trowels, dry-cutting saw (for plaster)

☐ **SKILLS**
Cutting with utility knife, driving fasteners with cordless drill, troweling patching compound

☐ **MATERIALS**
Drywall, 1×3 lumber, 1-inch drywall screws, drywall tape, 2×4 lumber

Repairing damaged drywall

1 Use a framing square to mark a rectangular area around a hole. Score the drywall on the lines, then cut through it with a drywall saw or utility knife. Pry out the damaged area or knock it into the wall recess.

2 Cut 1×3 boards about 6 inches longer than the area to be patched. Insert the boards into the recess and cinch them on one side to the rear of the drywall with 1-inch screws. Repeat for the other side. These cleats will keep the drywall patch from falling into the wall.

WHAT IF...
You want to remove the sink or toilet?

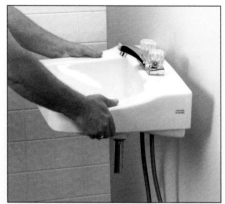

To remove a sink, shut the water off, loosen the nuts that connect the water-supply lines, and remove the lines. Set a bucket under the trap to catch any water released as you remove it. Loosen the slip-nut fittings on both ends of the trap with groove-joint pliers and pull the trap off the tailpiece below the sink bowl. Dump the trap water in the bucket and remove the sink-mounting bolts and any legs that support the sink. Grasp the sink with both hands and pull it up and off the brackets. If the sink won't come away, try loosening the wall-bracket bolts a couple of turns, then pull the sink off the brackets. Remove the brackets.

Popped nails

3 Cut a drywall patch of the same thickness as the rest of the wall and to the dimensions of the repair area. Place it in the recess against the cleats. Use 1-inch screws to fasten the patch to the cleats. Tape the joint around the patch with fiberglass-mesh drywall tape.

4 Finish the joints by applying a thin coat of drywall compound around the perimeter. Let this coat dry and apply a second coat with a wide drywall knife, feathering the edges until the surface is level with the surrounding wall. Prime this area when you spot-prime minor damage.

Over the course of time, drywall nails may come loose from the studs in the wall. Before you prime or paint, look carefully for popped nails. Reset the nails with a hammer, adding an additional fastener just above or below them. Then level the depressions with drywall compound.

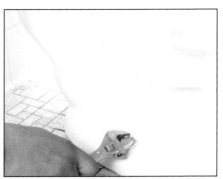

1 To remove a toilet, pour a quart of bleach into the tank, flush, and let it refill. Close the supply valve and reflush, holding the handle down until the tank empties. Push the water out of the trap with a plunger and stuff the bowl with rags. Disconnect the water-supply line with a wrench or groove-joint pliers.

2 Pry off the anchor bolt caps. Remove the anchor bolts with an adjustable wrench or groove-joint pliers. If the bolts spin, snap, or won't come off, cut them with a hacksaw. Even if you have to cut the bolts, you can still remove the toilet and replace the bolts when you reinstall it.

3 The bottom of the toilet trap fits snugly over a wax ring in a flange in the floor. Rock the toilet back and forth as you lift it off the floor. Low-capacity toilets may be light enough for you to lift by yourself, but older toilets can weigh up to 60 pounds. Get help to avoid risk of injury. Lift the toilet off the floor and carry it to another room. Remove the wax ring and dispose of it.

Repairing holes in plaster

1 Cut damaged pieces from the hole with a wide cold chisel. Plaster is held together with a fibrous binder, so there may be small pieces clinging to the edge of the hole. Remove them and, if possible, angle the edges of the hole so they are wider next to the lath than at the surface.

2 Brush out the area or vacuum it. Using a spray bottle, moisten the edges of the hole and the lath with water. Don't soak the area; a moderate misting is sufficient.

3 Apply patching plaster to the damaged area with a wide putty knife, forcing the material slightly into the lath. If the thickness of the plaster is more than ½ inch, apply a thin coat first, let it dry, and apply another coat. Thick patches tend to crack if applied all at once.

Repairing an outside corner

Using a wide cold chisel, pry out the loose plaster. Clean the edges thoroughly, making sure to remove small pieces still attached to the binding material. Tack a 2×4 batten on one wall flush with the corner. Moisten the damaged area with water and apply patching plaster in two applications, allowing one coat to dry before applying the other. Let the compound dry, move the batten to the other wall, and repeat the process. Sand smooth when dry.

Repairing cracked plaster

1 If the crack is a hairline crack, clean it out with the edge of a putty knife or can opener and dust out the crack with an old paintbrush. Moisten the crack and apply spackling compound.

For wide cracks, use a can opener to scrape plaster from the rear of the edge, making it wider at its bottom than on the surface. This will help hold the patching compound more securely. Clean out the crack and vacuum or dust it with an old paintbrush.

2 Use a spray bottle to moisten the interior of the crack and pack joint compound or thinset into the recess with a wide putty knife or drywall knife. Press the compound into the recessed edges. When you have filled the crack, draw the putty knife across the surface to smooth it. Allow the compound to dry and reapply if necessary. Sand any rough or high spots smooth with medium-grit sandpaper.

Repairing large damaged areas in plaster

1 Outline a rectangle larger than the damaged area and score the outline with a utility knife. Use a wide cold chisel to remove the plaster, working from the scored line to the center. Work in small sections; tap gently to avoid cracking the remaining wall. Measure the thickness of the plaster at the edge of the cutout area and, if necessary, attach ¼-inch plywood strips to the lath so a ¼-inch drywall patch will be flush with the surface.

2 Cut a drywall patch to the dimensions of the cutout and apply a ¼-inch bead of construction adhesive to the shims or lath. Press the patch into the area. Starting at the corners, drive 1-inch drywall screws around the perimeter of the patch. Space the remaining screws about 6 inches apart. Tape the joints with fiber-mesh drywall tape and spread a thin, level coat of drywall compound over the tape. Sand level when dry.

WHAT IF…
The wall is sound but not flat?

Fill minor depressions with drywall compound in several coats, letting each coat dry before applying the next one. Mark the perimeter of the depression with a carpenter's pencil and apply the compound with a mason's trowel. When dry, recheck the area with a level.

If a wall is seriously out of plumb, you'll notice it first at the corners. Apply a skim coat of drywall compound along the corner to bring adjacent surfaces plumb. Let the compound dry and sand it smooth.

STANLEY PRO TIP

Finding studs in walls

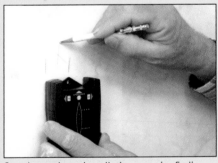

Certain repairs or installations require finding studs behind a finished wall. Electronic stud finders make the job easy. Be sure to mark both edges of each stud.

If you don't have a stud finder, probe the wall by tapping a long finishing nail through the wallboard until you find both edges of one stud. Mark its center. The remaining studs should be found at 16- or 24-inch intervals.

PREPARING TRIM

Door and window trim, as well as baseboards, cornices, moldings, and chair rails, make a major design contribution to the style of a room.

Whether finished with paint or stain, trim must be properly prepared. This normally means setting nailheads below the surface of the wood, filling and sanding holes, cleaning, and repairing or replacing damaged wood. It can also require the removal of old paint or varnish to provide a fresh surface for the finish.

Whether you finish your trim before or after painting the walls, it's best to have all the preparation work completed on both the trim and the walls before finishing either surface.

Be sure to wear protective glasses when stripping and a dust mask when sanding. Chemical strippers can contain toxic fumes, so ventilate the room adequately before applying the stripping solution. Rubber gloves are also a must to keep the chemicals from burning your hands.

Refinishing clear-finished wood trim like this would require extra preparation and care. The trim should be masked off when painting the walls to prevent spattering, which could be difficult to remove from the wood.

SAFETY FIRST
Testing for lead

Lead is a hazardous material used as an ingredient in paints before the late 1970s. In 1978 legislation banned its use, but your house could still contain lead paint. There are prescribed precautionary steps you should employ in the removal of lead paint, but in some cases you'll need to call a professional to stabilize or remove these materials.

The best ways to abate lead-paint hazards in your house include:

■ **Paint removal:** Scrape paint from peeling walls and woodwork with a broad knife. Wear a respirator as you work. You can apply chemical paint strippers to soften the paint. If you dry-scrape the paint, mist the surface with a spray bottle to reduce hazardous dust. Clean up dust and particles with a wet mop—vacuuming it spreads lead dust. Sanding, sandblasting, and similar methods aren't recommended because of the dust hazard. And softening paint with a heat gun could create toxic fumes.

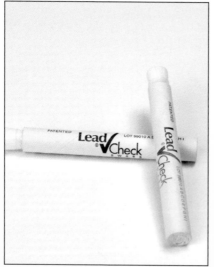

■ **Encapsulation:** Instead of removing the paint, isolate it or seal it off. Apply new drywall over an existing wall or float the wall with wallboard compound.
■ **Surface replacement:** Remove and replace woodwork and moldings that have been painted with lead paint.

Filling nail holes

Use the right size nail set to push nailheads below the surface of the wood. Set the point of the nail set in the recess of the nail head and tap sharply with a hammer.

Removing gloss

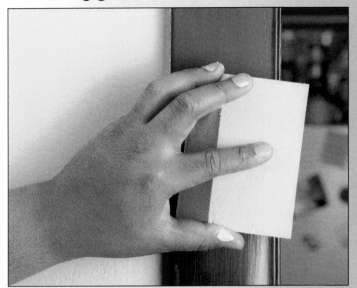

1 New paint or clear finish will not adhere well to gloss paints. Scuff-sand all glossy surfaces with 150-grit sandpaper. Use a sanding block or palm sander on flat surfaces or a contour sander on curved surfaces.

2 After scuff sanding, the surface will contain microscopic dust particles left in the grooves by the sandpaper. Pull these particles off the surface with a soft cloth dampened in mineral spirits or water. Don't use a tack cloth; it can leave a residue that will interfere with the paint bond.

If you will ultimately paint the surface, slightly overfill the nail holes with interior wood filler. Sand it smooth when dry.

For clear finishes, buy different colors of putty and use the one that most closely matches the finished tone of the wood.

STANLEY PRO TIP

Kitchen spatulas smooth putty

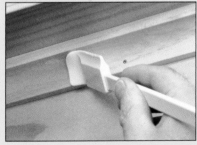

The usual putty-application procedure involves rubbing your finger over the hole. But if you've installed several rooms full of trim, you can easily rub your fingertip raw before completing the job. Also your finger can dip into the hole, creating a slight depression. Use an ordinary kitchen spatula as a solution. It's firm enough to wipe away excess putty and leave a smooth surface. It also conforms to curved surfaces, speeding your work.

Patching trim for painting

1 Wash the surface of the trim with a TSP solution (see page 110) or a low-phosphate household cleaner. Rinse thoroughly with a vinegar/water solution and let the trim dry. Use a stiff putty knife to scrape loose paint to the bare wood.

2 Apply high-quality latex wood patch in nail holes, dents, and other damaged areas. Overfill the area slightly to accommodate its tendency to shrink. Let the filler dry.

3 Sand the repaired area smooth with 150-grit sandpaper. If the filler has shrunk below the surface of the wood, reapply another layer, and sand it after it's dry.

Preparing stained and varnished trim

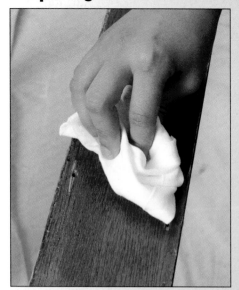  

1 Clean varnished surfaces with a soft cloth and odorless mineral spirits. Scuff-sand the entire surface with 150-grit sandpaper.

2 Apply stainable wood patch whose color matches the surface closely. Level the patch and sand it smooth when dry.

3 Restain the patched area to match the finished surface. Apply the finish coat.

Removing paint with chemical strippers

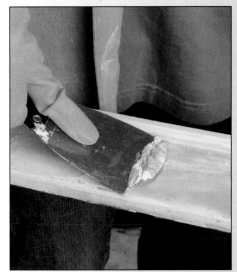 

1 Apply a thick coat of stripper to the surface with an old natural-bristle paintbrush (many strippers will melt nylon bristles). Brush in only one direction to avoid lifting the stripper off the surface. Let the stripper work for about 20 minutes, then remove it and the paint with a scraper.

2 Reapply stripper where paint is still adhered and repeat the process. Remove small flecks of paint with a coarse abrasive pad, cleaning it with water or mineral spirits, depending on the stripper you've used. Finally, clean the surface with a fine abrasive pad dipped in denatured alcohol.

Using a heat gun

Pull the trigger of the gun and let it come to its working temperature. Hold the gun with its tip at an angle and just close enough that it softens the paint without burning it (and the wood underneath). When the paint bubbles, back the gun away from the surface slightly and scrape the paint.

Sanding surfaces

For large or small flat surfaces, a palm sander or random orbit sander is a great timesaver when sanding walls or woodwork.

Contoured surfaces are difficult to sand with rectangular sanding blocks because they can gouge the wood. Use flexible sanding blocks or sanding sponges to smooth these curved surfaces.

PROTECTING SURFACES

Paint can get on a surface any number of ways—intentionally or accidentally, from spatters, spills, and drips. When all the cleaning, sanding, and repair work is done, your last preparation step is to make sure to protect any surface you don't want painted.

Protecting surfaces is generally accomplished by masking them off. It takes a bit of time, but it's a lot easier and takes a lot less time than trying to remove paint from a place it doesn't belong—and from which it may not come off. So don't rush this process.

Painting a room starts with the ceiling, but if you are not painting the walls, you should drape them as shown here. If you are painting the walls, you generally won't have to protect them, even if the wall color will be different than the color of the ceiling. The wall may receive some spatters (minimized by the use of a quality ceiling paint), but you can get at spatters with a quick swipe of a dampened cloth. When masking surfaces, use blue painter's tape. It goes on and comes off more quickly than the old-style masking tape. Remove the tape before the paint dries.

Protecting the walls

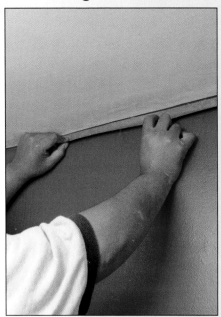

1 Starting at one corner, stick one end of the 2-inch painter's tape to the wall, carefully pull away about 10 feet of tape from the roll and tear it. Tack this end to the wall so it doesn't stick to itself. Press the top half of the tape into the corner where the ceiling meets the wall.

2 Unfold a sheet of clear plastic so you can work with it, and starting at either corner, slip the top edge of the plastic under the loose flap of the tape. Press the tape to the plastic and continue along the wall, letting the sheet drape down to protect the surface.

WHAT IF…
I need to cover only the baseboards?

If baseboards are stained and varnished, will be painted a different color, or won't be removed for replacement, you should mask them to keep ceiling- and wall-paint spatters off them. For this job, use masking film or masking paper applied with a dispenser. Start at one end of the baseboard and press the tape firmly on the top edge for about a foot. Gradually pull the dispenser away from the corner, exposing more film and tacking it as you go. Let the film drape down over the baseboard or tape its edge to the floor.

Masking the edges of the floor

To protect the floor from spatters and drips, first lay protective plastic sheeting on the entire surface, from one end of the room to the other. If the baseboards are not to be masked, simply tape the edges of the plastic to the floor. For masked baseboards, apply masking film or paper from a dispenser as shown, and tape the edge to the plastic sheets on the floor.

Masking window and door trim

1 Starting at any corner of the trim, carefully stick 2-inch painter's tape on the trim where it meets the wall. Work the tape in 4- or 5-foot lengths so it doesn't fall back and stick to itself.

2 Run a spatula or other hard plastic tool quickly along the corner edge of the tape, pressing it solidly against the trim. This will keep paint from seeping under the edge of the tape.

3 Unfold a plastic sheet and work its top edge under the flap of the tape along the top of the window. Then fold the tape down to hold the plastic. Repeat the process on the sides of the window to create a mask for the entire surface.

Protective gear

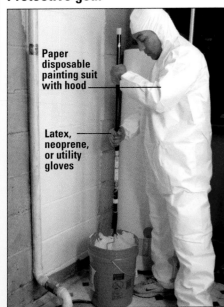

Paper disposable painting suit with hood

Latex, neoprene, or utility gloves

Protecting yourself from unwanted paint is as important as masking surfaces in a room. Wear paper disposable overalls and a paper cap, gloves, and old shoes or boots. Wear eye protection and a dust mask or respirator as preparation work demands.

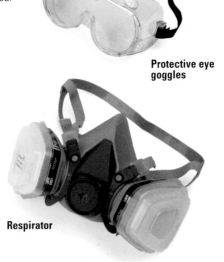

Protective eye goggles

Dust mask

Respirator

LADDERS AND WORK PLATFORMS

Ladders are almost indispensible when painting an interior room. They let you get close to surfaces beyond your normal reach so you can apply paint evenly and comfortably. Even if you use a roller with an extension handle, you'll need a ladder to put you close enough to the ceiling to cut the corners in with a brush.

Ladders come in a wide array of sizes and materials—wood, fiberglass, and aluminum. You'll find a 5-foot stepladder well suited, not only for interior paint jobs, but also for other general home-maintenance projects. Ladders are also manufactured with various degrees of quality. Purchase the best ladder you can afford, and make sure it's rated to support both your weight and the weight of tools and materials you'll be using on it. Look for sturdy hinges that lock securely when you extend them, nonslip pads on the legs, and steps wide enough that your feet fit comfortably. And if the ladder wobbles or bends when you extend it, don't buy it.

If you want a ladder strictly for painting, get a platform model. Its top step, which you can stand on, lets you face the wall you're painting without obstruction, and its size makes it easy to move.

SAFETY FIRST
Know the limits

No matter what material they are made of, ladders carry a label that will help you decide which model you need. Look for the weight rating, climbing and use instructions, applications, and procedures for storage.

A single ladder will get you through most paint jobs, but you'll need a work platform to paint stairwells and high walls. Construct your platform with two ladders and a scaffolding plank, which you can rent. Make sure the ladders are rated for your weight and the weight of the platform and materials and that the steps on both are at the same height from the floor. Set up the ladders parallel to the wall with their steps facing each other and lay the plank on the steps. The plank should overlap the steps by at least 12 inches. If the plank sags when you stand on it, move the ladders closer together.

MAKE PAINTING CONVENIENT

Use two step stools and a scaffold plank to create a portable work platform you can quickly move from place to place. Make sure the step stool height will put the top of the wall and ceiling you're painting comfortably within your reach.

Before using a stepladder, open it fully and push down firmly on the hinge locks.

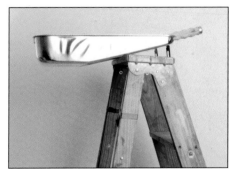

Look for ladders with built-in features that will increase their convenience.

PRIMING TIPS

Priming is an essential step for a good-looking, long-lasting paint job. At first glance, many primers may look like thinned paint, but primers are formulated to meet specific demands:

■ To adhere well to a variety of surfaces.

■ To seal stains and discolorations and prevent them from bleeding through the finish coat. This is especially important with latex finish coats, which otherwise are vulnerable to stain bleed-through.

■ To provide a uniform surface to which paint will adhere, giving the paint a better grip than it would on the bare surface.

■ To give the finished paint job a more uniform color and sheen, thereby making it more attractive. This is especially true on a porous surface or one with uneven porosity.

Primers go on easily and actually make the finish coat flow on smoothly too. They are less expensive than paint and in some cases can save you money by eliminating the necessity of applying a second top coat.

Primers are manufactured for specific applications. Choose the primer that fits the needs of your particular paint job (see "Picking the right primer," below right).

PRESTART CHECKLIST

☐ **TIME**
From 4 to 8 hours for a 10×12-foot room, depending on your painting experience and skill level

☐ **TOOLS**
Brushes, rollers, extension handle, ladder, paint buckets

☐ **SKILLS**
Using brushes and rollers

☐ **PREP**
Repair surfaces as necessary and mask unpainted surfaces to protect them

☐ **MATERIALS**
Primer

Spot-priming repairs

1 Repairs on a textured surface usually remove the texture, making the spot obvious when painted. To texture the repair, load an old paint brush with thinned drywall compound and spatter the wall. Dabbing the end of the bristles onto the surface will also help match the texture.

2 Spot-prime any areas of the walls, ceiling, or trim you have repaired. Brush the primer on liberally and smooth it out, but do not overbrush and thin the coating.

Picking the right primer

Type of primer	What it does
Stain-blocking primer	Protects the top coat against bleed-through of grease, dirt, rust, smoke residue, and water stains.
Drywall primer	Seals new drywall and joint compound to give the top coat of paint a uniform appearance. May also be suitable for new plaster.
Vapor-barrier primer	Minimizes passage of moisture through walls and helps elevate winter humidity levels and keep them consistent. High-adhesion interior primer for bathrooms, kitchens, and other damp rooms.
Enamel undercoater	Ensures maximum gloss and uniformity in the top coat when used under semigloss or gloss paint. For best results, lightly sand and clean dried primer before top coating.
Bonding primer	Adheres to slick or glossy surfaces such as glass, tile, and laminate or vinyl-coated paneling (but not countertops).
Concrete primer/ sealer	Provides a less-porous surface for painting. Reduces dust on interior concrete floors.

Priming and sanding walls

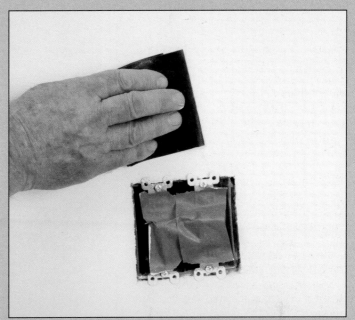

When preparing new drywall, use the same techniques as you would when painting a wall or ceiling, cutting in the edges with a brush and filling in the remaining areas with a roller (see pages 126–129). Work in sections so the primer cut into the corners does not dry before you roll the rest. Prime the entire surface with a PVA latex drywall primer or latex stain-blocking primer at a low spread rate, generally not more than a gallon per 450 square feet.

Most primers are formulated for the immediate application of paint when they're dry. With enamel undercoater, however, which is made for use under semigloss or gloss paint, you'll get better results with the top coat if you lightly scuff-sand the primer when it's dry. Use a sanding block, a light touch, and 150-grit sandpaper.

STANLEY PRO TIP

Tinting the primer

Tinting the primer the same color as the top coat primer can improve the coverage of your finish coat. The amount of tinting you can add is limited because primers don't work well when they carry too much pigment. Ask your paint supplier for the proper amount of tint to add.

Letting the primer dry

Drying times for primers vary with the type of primer, the surface, the spread rate, and the interior temperature and humidity.

Most primers feel dry to the touch in a short time period, a matter of minutes in some cases. "Dry to the touch," however, is misleading. Reading the manufacturer's recommendations for recoat or drying time will provide you with more specific information, but in most cases it's best to let the primer dry overnight.

Keeping the primer mixed

Paint products stay mixed for a longer time now than they used to, but insufficiently mixed primer is often hard to spot. Don't take chances—stir the primer each time you fill your paint bucket.

REFRESHER COURSE
Masking the trim

Apply painter's masking tape to the trim before priming. Press it into the corner where the trim meets the wall, sealing the edge with a plastic spatula and folding the extended edge of the tape over a plastic sheet to completely cover the window or door.

PAINTING CEILINGS

Painting a ceiling presents a slightly different challenge than painting a wall. That's because you're constantly working overhead—actually, upside down. Aside from some resulting perceptual differences that might take a little getting used to, ceilings will put different physical stresses on your body too. Painting ceilings can quickly tire neck, back, and arm muscles. Stay as relaxed as you can and stop for a moment as soon as something starts aching. Pushing through this period will only quicken your fatigue, and if you take short stops, you'll get used to the work faster.

Use a 4- to 6-foot extension pole on your roller and keep the roller head working out in front of you, not directly overhead. You'll find that position more comfortable and you won't get spattered as much. When the handle starts to approach vertical, step back so the work is in front of you.

When you're done write the paint color, the room, and the date you painted it on the back of a switchplate with an indelible marker. That will save the information if you need to touch up the surface in the future.

PRESTART CHECKLIST

☐ **TIME**
From 2 to 3 hours to paint a properly prepared 10×12-foot ceiling

☐ **TOOLS**
Paintbrushes, roller, extension handle, ladder, paint buckets, safety gear

☐ **SKILLS**
Painting with brushes and rollers

☐ **PREP**
Clean surface, repair holes and cracks, sand glossy paint, remove dust

☐ **MATERIALS**
High-quality interior latex paint

Painting a ceiling

1 If the walls and ceiling will be painted different colors, use 2-inch painter's tape to mask off the wall at the top where it meets the ceiling. This will keep the ceiling paint from getting on the wall when you cut in the edge of the ceiling. To protect the entire wall from spatters, slide a plastic sheet under the bottom edge of the tape, press the tape to the sheet, and let the sheet drape down across the wall (see page 120). If the walls and ceiling will be painted the same color, you can omit this step.

Making the sheen consistent

A consistent sheen across a drywalled surface will greatly improve the appearance of your work. Accomplishing this will depend on both proper preparation and application.

Feather out drywall joints so they are level with the surrounding surface. Compound that forms a raised joint will, when painted, reflect light differently than the rest of the wall, causing it to appear prominent. Sand the joints smooth with fine-grit sandpaper and look for flaws by viewing the surface at a low angle with good illumination.

Apply a PVA latex drywall primer or a latex stain-blocking primer at a sufficiently low spread rate, as recommended by the manufacturer. When you apply the top coat, do so at or below the manufacturer's recommended spread rate—an adequately thick film is required for a uniform sheen.

If you're rolling the paint, use a quality synthetic roller cover. It will put paint on more heavily and evenly than an economy roller. Keep your roller strokes as vertical as possible, avoid applying pressure, and keep the roller reasonably full of paint—if the roller makes a tearing sound, it means it's dry and you need more paint on it.

When painting with a sprayer, spray the first coat and roll the second coat. As an alternative, spray two coats and immediately back-roll the second coat. Rolling will provide a more uniform appearance, hide flaws more effectively, and allow you to touch up areas without making them noticeable.

Whatever method you use to apply the paint, let the first coat dry adequately (typically 4 hours or more) before applying a second coat. That will eliminate blistering and keep the roller from picking up flecks of the first coat from the surface ("roller picking").

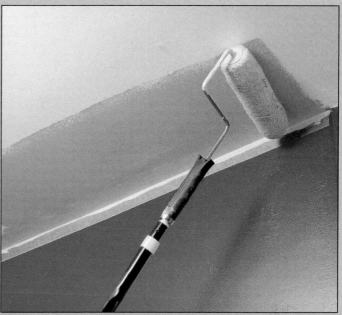

2 Using a 3-inch brush appropriate to the kind of paint you're applying (natural bristles for oil-base paints and synthetic bristles for latex paints), cut in the corners of the ceiling. Apply the paint liberally and brush it smooth, using the techniques shown on pages 54–55. Paint a band about 2 inches wide and 3 to 4 feet long on both legs of a corner. Proceed to step 3 while this band is still wet.

3 Using a roller equipped with an extension handle, roll the paint on the open corner section of the ceiling, blending it with the edges you just cut in. Proceed across the surface in sections approximately 3×3 feet, alternately cutting in and rolling to a wet edge until you've covered the entire ceiling.

STANLEY PRO TIP

Prime the roller

Before you roll your latex top coat on any surface, prime the roller by immersing it in water. Squeeze or roll out the excess water in a roller pan until the cover is just damp to the touch. Empty the water from the roller pan and pour in the paint.

WHAT IF...
I'm spray painting the room?

Spray painting a room is the quickest method for covering the surface, but you can end up with paint just about everywhere. Protect yourself from the overspray by wearing disposable paper overalls and taping the cuffs. Wear a paper painter's hat and keep paint out of your eyes with protective goggles.

Hiding the previous colors

Nothing looks better than a top coat that completely hides the previous colors on the wall. Using a high-quality paint is the best way to ensure complete hiding. Sometimes a high-quality paint can even do such an adequate job of hiding that you won't need a second coat. There are other factors that affect the hiding ability of paint.

■ Look on the label for the paint's "spread rate"—the area 1 gallon will cover. This is the manufacturer's recommendation; usually the paint will cover a little less. Don't push the paint to achieve the manufacturer's spread rate, and never exceed it.

■ Use colors, such as earth tones, browns, tans, and red tints, that have a natural tendency to hide better. Applying a light-color paint on a dark-color surface will decrease hiding. You'll get the best results with a color that is not completely different from the one already on the surface.

PAINTING WALLS

Painting a wall shouldn't tire you as quickly as painting a ceiling because you're working more at shoulder level (if you stand on a platform) or just slightly above, with a roller and extension handle.

The procedure for painting walls follows the same general principles as painting a ceiling—cutting in the edges with a brush, then filling in the balance with a roller.

Because the surface texture of brushed paint looks different than rolled paint, try to get the roller as close to the edge as possible to minimize what will be a noticeable difference.

Painting a wall (or ceiling for that matter) is a task made to order for two people, one with a brush, cutting in the corners in sections, and the other following with a roller and filling in. That way, tandem painters will eliminate any lap marks caused by applying rolled paint to an edge that's already dried.

A brush is the common tool for cutting in, but you may find using a paint pad easier. Paint pads leave a thicker coat of paint, so be careful the paint is not overly thick as it comes off the edge of the pad.

PRESTART CHECKLIST

☐ **TIME**
From 4 to 8 hours for a 10×12-foot room, depending on your experience and skill

☐ **TOOLS**
Brushes, rollers, extension handle, ladder, paint buckets

☐ **SKILLS**
Using brushes and rollers

☐ **PREP**
Prep and prime surface as necessary

☐ **MATERIALS**
Paint

Painting a wall

1 If you're painting the wall the same color as the ceiling, you don't need to mask off the ceiling. Different colors on the two surfaces, however, require you to mask the edge of the ceiling with 2-inch painter's tape. Make sure the ceiling paint is completely cured before masking it. Otherwise you risk pulling the ceiling paint off if it's too fresh. Starting in a corner (usually, but not always along the bottom of the wall) and using a 3-inch brush, cut in a band of paint about 2 inches wide, extending it 3 to 4 feet horizontally and vertically.

WHAT IF...
Humidity is too low?

When you're painting inside your house, you don't have to worry about rain pouring down your newly painted surface. You should, however, be mindful of the inside temperature and humidity. Interior paint goes on more easily and dries more uniformly in moderate temperatures and average humidities. Ask your supplier for the interior temperature and humidity ranges most suitable for your paint. You may need to adjust the thermostat, open windows, or add an exhaust fan to control the temperature. If the air is heavy with moisture (often the case when it's raining outside), you may be able to reduce the humidity by turning on the air-conditioning to a low level or bringing a dehumidifier into the room. To raise the humidity in a dry room, run a humidifier.

Cutting it close

The closer you can get the end of the roller to the corner of an adjacent surface, the less you'll notice any difference between cut-in paint and rolled paint. You can get really close by pulling the roller cover slightly off the end of the roller cage and painting carefully as shown.

2 Using the same technique, cut in any window or door on the wall that is close to your first cut-in area, masking the trim and cutting in the paint around it.

3 Starting at the cut-in window or door or the cut-in edge of the wall, roll the paint into the area between them, always painting to a wet edge.

4 Once you've filled in the area, finish it with light vertical strokes to smooth the paint and remove roller marks (see page 56). Alternate between cutting in and rolling until you've completed a wall. Don't take breaks or start a new can in the middle of a wall—you'll create a noticeable lap mark.

STANLEY PRO TIP

Textured paint

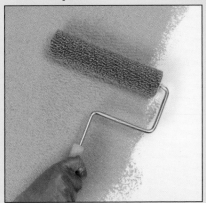

You can create various textures either by using textured paints or standard paints with textured rollers—or both. The depth of the texture and its pattern are controlled by a number of factors. Experiment on a test board before painting the wall (see page 10).

Let the paint dry

How much time you need to allow for latex paint to dry and properly cure depends on what you intend to do with it after it's applied. While paint may be truly dry to touch in minutes, you'll have to wait different lengths of time before recoating, cleaning, or masking.

Recoat time:

Generally you'll need to wait at least 2 hours before applying the next coat of paint. You may need to wait even longer if:

■ Conditions, such as high humidity or low temperatures, slow down the drying process.
■ You've applied the paint in a thick coat.
■ You've applied a heavily tinted paint (one with more than 8 ounces of colorant per gallon).

Any of the following conditions will tell you the paint needs to dry longer before recoating:

■ Blistering, wrinkling, or lifting
■ Uneven sheen

Time before cleaning

Normally you should wait 2 weeks or longer before cleaning the surface. Some manufacturers recommend 30 days, and the wait time is influenced by a number of factors:

■ Gloss paints have more co-solvent to evaporate and rely on getting maximum hardness from the binder, so they require longer drying than flat paints.
■ Cleaning with a wet sponge is less demanding than with a brush and detergent.

If your paint abrades, blisters, or changes its sheen or color when you try to clean it, you'll need to wait longer.

Masking

Allow 30 days before applying masking tape to new paint to prevent the tape from pulling up the paint. This extended dry time allows residual co-solvents time to evaporate so they won't bond to the tape adhesive.

PAINTING INTERIOR WINDOWS

Windows suffer an amazing amount of stress. Every time you open them, you are working against inertia and stressing the joints. What's even more damaging, however, is that windows are exposed to more changes in temperature and humidity than most other parts of the house. Those fluctuations can take their toll on both the structure of the window and its paint, so windows may need to be painted more often than interior doors or other trim.

To get started on the right track, gather all your tools at the window. Remove locks, curtain hooks, and other hardware so you'll have an uninterrupted surface.

If you're painting the windows in place, use care to keep paint from getting between the sash and the stops—where it can glue the surfaces together. Keep paint off the sash cords also.

Painting windows can take more time than you might think. It's always best to start the job in the morning so you can close the windows at night.

PRESTART CHECKLIST

☐ **TIME**
From 1 to 2 hours to paint a 23-inch, 12-light double-hung window, depending on your skills and experience—more if you are removing the sashes

☐ **TOOLS**
Sash knife, putty knife, 2-inch sash brush, utility knife, bucket

☐ **SKILLS**
Painting and masking double-hung window sashes

☐ **PREP**
Clean and repair surfaces

☐ **MATERIALS**
Masking tape and paint

Painting old double-hung windows

1 Gently work a stiff putty knife between the interior stops and the jamb. As you pry the stops free, take care not to dent them because you'll reinstall them later. Pull the nails through the back of the stops and save these pieces, or get replacement stops from your home center.

2 Cut the cords from the front (lower) sash; the weights will drop into the pocket in the wall. Then lift out the front sash. If your window has chains, use metal snips or bolt cutters.

WHAT IF...
My windows are new?

Press in on the jamb liner, and pull the corner of the lower sash out, just to the first grooves. Grasp the sash firmly at the top and bottom and push it in the opposite direction to compress the liner on the other side. With enough pressure, the sash edge will clear the liner. Pull that side toward you and remove the sash.

Remove
access door
for weight

3 Cut the cords and remove the upper sash. Remove the screw to open the door in the jamb that provides access to the weight pocket. Retrieve the weights so you can insulate the cavity. Replace the access door. If your jambs lack an access panel, leave the weights in place.

4 Remove the side and top parting stops, using a utility knife to cut the paint between the stop and jamb. You'll discard these stops, so don't worry about damaging them. Grab a stop with pliers and wiggle it out of its channel. Repeat with each stop.

PAINTING DOUBLE-HUNG WINDOWS IN PLACE

Raise the lower sash and lower the upper one so their respective top and bottom rails are completely out of their tracks. Using a trim brush, paint the inside edge

of the muntins around each pane on the top sash, then paint the frame of the top sash as far as you can go. Paint all the inside edges of the muntins on the bottom

sash, then paint the edges of the sash. Reverse the order of the sashes and paint the remaining parts of the top sash.

Painting old double-hung windows *continued*

5 Pull out the sash and place a piece of tape onto the jamb to mark the knothole position when the window is closed.

6 Make an easel from a ladder for easy sash painting. Open a wooden stepladder and lock the hinges. Drive #10×3-inch all-purpose screws into predrilled holes in the center of each leg of the ladder, using a level to keep the screws on the same plane. Set the sash on the screws. This will put the sash at an angle that makes it very comfortable to paint.

Get right to the finish

If you're installing new window sashes and the sashes are bare or primed wood, apply a finish coat before installing the new window. Otherwise the wood could start absorbing moisture or suffer damage from dirty hands. Besides, painting a window removed from its housing is much easier.

The minimum finishing schedule for paint should include at least one coat of high-quality primer followed by two top coats.

If you select a clear finish for the interior wood, water resistance is important. Water resistance helps protect the wood from damage due to contact with rain and condensation.

Don't paint or varnish the edges of the sash—the thickness of the film could make your windows difficult to operate. If you want to apply a finish to the edges of the sash, choose an oil finish that won't build a film thickness.

7 Using a trim brush or a sash brush and starting at a top pane, paint the inside edge of the muntins around the pane.

8 Continue painting the remaining muntins around each pane, taking care to remove excess paint that gathers in the bottom corners of each joint (see page 88).

9 When you have finished the muntins, paint the top and bottom rails, overlapping the joints on either end slightly. Then paint the vertical stiles. Painting in this order will eliminate crossed brush marks.

Check for concealed damage

After you've removed the sashes, carefully inspect the window jambs and sills before painting or installing new windows. If you see any evidence of insect infestation, such as mud tunnels or burrows in the wood, call a pest-control specialist for a thorough inspection and evaluation of the problem.

Probing the tracks and frame with the tip of a knife will quickly reveal punky wood, evidence of past water damage. Although sometimes called dry rot, the deteriorating wood fibers are the result of moisture from water infiltration.

Correct any problems before installing new sashes or reinstalling the old ones.

Don't paint the window shut

When you're painting any kind of window in place always be sure to keep paint from accumulating or seeping between sashes and stops. Newly painted double-hung windows are especially prone to this malady. If you do get paint between the surfaces, bend a piece of thin card stock and insert it in the gap. Run the card stock up and down a few times to remove as much paint as you can and keep the sashes moving (see Stanley Pro Tip, right).

STANLEY PRO TIP

Keep the sashes moving

If you're painting the windows in the frame, keep the sashes moving till the paint dries so the windows won't stick to each other. Use a putty knife to move the sashes and keep your fingers out of the paint.

Painting the casing and trim

1 Painting the inside of the frames is best done with the sashes removed. Paint or seal the inside track of the windows with a clear sealer. Then paint the top of the casing.

2 Use a trim guard to paint the outside edges of the window trim, or mask off the edge with blue painter's tape. Let the paint set up for about 20 minutes, then remove the tape when the paint is still wet.

3 Paint the inside edges of the front frame, then the face of the panels themselves. Finish the window trim by painting the top face and the sill and apron.

Removing paint from window glass

1 If you haven't masked the windows, you'll have to remove the paint from the glass. Wait until the paint has completely dried (usually the next day) and hold a stiff metal straightedge next to the frames and muntins. Score the paint next to the edge of the glass.

2 Use a single-edged razor blade or razor cartridge to remove the paint up to the scored line. Leaving a narrow edge of paint on the glass provides an additional seal against the outside elements.

Replacing the sash cord

Tie a figure-eight knot at the end of the cord and stuff it into the hole in the side of the sash. For added security, you can drive a small nail through the knot into the sash. Replace the moldings and touch up the finish if necessary.

Painting casement windows

1 Open the window and first paint the inside edges next to the glass. Then paint the top, sides, and bottom edges of the frame.

2 With the window still open, paint the jambs and window tracks, taking care to pull the brush up with a light downstroke to lift excess paint out of the bottom corners. Complete the job by painting the sill and apron. Let the paint dry thoroughly and close the windows. Open the windows the next day to complete the drying.

PUTTING THE PAINT ON IN ORDER

Painting casement windows

Painting awning windows

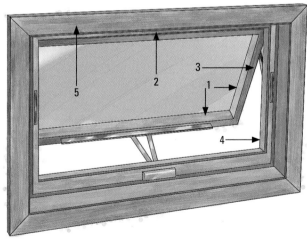

STAINING AND VARNISHING TRIM

Staining and varnishing require different techniques than painting. To start with, you can apply most stains with either a brush or a cloth. First lay a coat of stain on the wood in the direction of the grain. If the stain is not working its way into the grain, brush it across the grain and finish with brushstrokes parallel to the grain. It may look muddy at first—but that will clear up when you wipe off the excess. If it's too light, repeat the steps. For a light tone, first seal the wood with a prepared wood conditioner.

When you apply any clear finish to wood, start at one edge of the piece and work in the direction of the grain. Smooth out any ridges and pools in the finish while it's still wet. Finishes such as shellac and water-base varnish dry quickly, so you have to work quickly.

For greater visual appeal and durability, apply several coats of clear finish, rubbing with #0000 steel wool or very fine finishing sandpaper between each coat.

Applying stain

 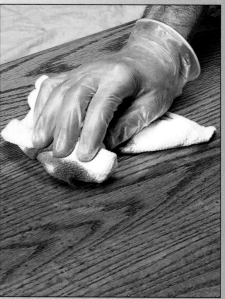

1 Mix stain thoroughly before using. With either a brush or lint-free cloth, apply it in the direction of the grain. Overlap your strokes slightly so you don't miss any spots.

2 Let the stain set up according to the manufacturer's directions, but before it begins to dry, wipe the entire surface to remove excess. This also forces the stain's pigment into the grain, enhancing contrast.

Remove the trim

For most paint jobs, it's actually easier to remove the baseboards and finish them on a work surface that's about waist high. If you paint or varnish either new or existing baseboards when they're on the wall, you're going to spend a lot of uncomfortable hours on your hands and knees.

Similarly, staining and finishing new window or door trim requires exacting application to keep the finish material off the walls.

Whenever you're finishing any new trim, stain it before putting it up.

Use a conditioner on softwoods

Softwoods, like pine and fir, have a pore structure that prohibits them from taking stain evenly. The result can often look blotchy. To make your stain coat even, first apply a wood conditioner made especially for this purpose.

Applying a clear polyurethane finish

1 Stir, don't shake, the polyurethane (or any varnish). For the smoothest application, use a disposable foam brush and work across the grain to fill the pores.

2 For the second coat, brush with the grain so any ridges won't be as visible. To avoid runs, don't load the brush when working near edges.

3 When the finish has thoroughly dried, go over it with #0000 steel wool or fine (320-grit) sandpaper. Repeat between coats.

4 Small flaws such as nicks and nail holes can be filled with a tinted filler stick of matching color after the finish has completely dried.

Applying penetrating oil

 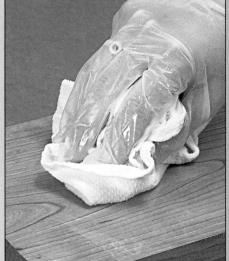 

1 When using any type of penetrating oil finish, pour a liberal amount onto the wood, then spread it with a lint-free cloth.

2 Let the oil soak in for about 10 minutes (read label directions). Wipe to remove excess oil. Allow the finish to dry before applying a second coat. Reapply until the wood will not absorb any more oil.

3 For a satin-smooth oil finish, rub the dry surface between coats with extra-fine (#0000) steel wool. Wipe off the entire surface after rubbing. When the oil has cured, apply paste wax for protection.

PAINTING INTERIOR DOORS

Painting doors is usually the last task of an interior painting project. When you get to this step, you can either paint the doors in the frame or take them down and paint them. Removing them takes a little more time but is easier in the long run, and the result will prove more satisfactory because you're working on an uninterrupted surface. And if you support the doors on sawhorses or some other horizontal structure, the finish will level itself out more smoothly.

No matter how you plan to paint the door, remove the knobs, lockset, striker plate, and any other hardware. That way you won't have to paint around them, which can leave swirls in the finish.

To remove the door, pull the hinge pins as shown. Then mask the hinge plates with two coats of rubber cement (see page 88) and set the door on a horizontal surface. If you support the door with screws driven into the top and bottom as shown below, you can flip the door (with a helper) and paint the other side before the first one dries. Using the screws as supports keeps the sawhorses from marring the wet paint.

PRESTART CHECKLIST

☐ **TIME**
From 1 to 3 hours, depending on your skills and experience

☐ **TOOLS**
Screwdriver, sawhorses, scraper, sanding block, sash brush, 2-inch brush

☐ **SKILLS**
Removing , sanding, priming, and painting a door

☐ **PREP**
Clean door and repair damaged areas

☐ **MATERIALS**
Drywall screws, primer (if necessary), putty, sandpaper, latex enamel

Door prep

1 To remove the door, start with the bottom hinge. Set the tip of a flat screwdriver just under the edge of the hinge pin and tap the pin until it comes away from the hinge plate. Repeat the process on the middle and top hinge. Friction will hold the door till you remove it.

2 Pull the door off the hinges and set it on its edge. Previous paintings invariably leave paint ridges on the edges of the door. These ridges can look distracting and cause the door to stick in the jamb. Use a chisel to remove excess paint. Sand the edges.

Interior door tips

1 Clean the surface, removing handprints, accumulated airborne cooking oil, etc. On glossy surfaces, use a TSP solution, and finish with a sanded scuff coat to promote adhesion of the new paint.

2 Remove the doors and place them on sawhorses for painting. This way you don't have to be concerned that the paint will sag or run.

3 Using a quality brush, apply the paint in heavy coats. Heavy coats help the paint flow out, but watch for runs and sagging, which are signs you're using too much paint. When using an HVLP sprayer, build up the paint to the proper thickness by applying several light coats.

"Handles" make flipping easy

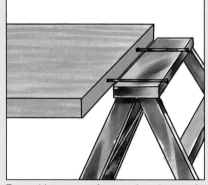

To provide supports for your door that won't mar any wet paint, predrill the ends of the door about 5 inches from each corner. Drive 10 d nails or #10×4-inch screws into the holes and support the door on them. When you've painted one side, grab the "handles" and flip the door.

Brushing a slab door

Using a roller

1 Brushing a slab door is much the same as painting a wall with a brush, although technically, you don't have to cut in the edges of the door. Apply the paint in sections, starting in an upper corner and smoothing the coat vertically with the final stroke. Make sure the final stroke goes beyond the edge.

2 On the next section, paint toward the wet edge, feathering it and finishing with a vertical stroke. Continue down the door, covering the entire surface. Finish with light upward strokes from bottom to top to blend the coat in. Carefully remove excess paint from the sides, top, and bottom of the door.

To paint a door with a roller, start in the center of the door and work outward. Paint the top half first, taking care to not start a stroke at the edges (which will push excess paint onto the sides of the door). Then paint the bottom half and finish with light strokes from bottom to top.

PAINTING SEQUENCE FOR A PANELED DOOR

1. Paint the inside edges of a paneled section.

2. Paint the raised panels.

3. Paint the face of each interior vertical panel, then each interior horizontal panel.

4. Paint the top and bottom rails, extending the paint slightly beyond the joints.

5. Paint the faces of the vertical stiles on both sides of the door.

6. Paint the edges of the door and the jamb.

Painting sliding doors

1 Carefully mask off the glass with blue painter's tape. If possible, mask both sides of the door and paint them as one project.

2 Following the sequence illustrated below and beginning with the stationary panel, paint one vertical edge, then paint the top of the frame. Next paint the opposite edge and bottom of the same panel. Move the sliding section about an inch from the edge of the jamb and paint it in the same order. Leave the sliding section open until the paint dries.

STANLEY PRO TIP

Keep the doors moving

When painting sliding doors, keep the sliding section open until the paint dries and move it slightly about every half hour to keep the paint from forming a seal along the top and bottom tracks.

Because doors are such a prominent design element, any flaws will be immediately noticeable. Paint them in one session and smooth the paint with continuous strokes to eliminate lap marks.

WHAT IF...
You have sliding closet doors?

Like any door, you can paint sliding closet doors (or pocket doors) in place, but you'll get easier application and a better-looking surface if you remove the doors. To remove sliding doors, grasp both sides of the door and lift up and push its rollers off the track.

PAINTING SEQUENCE FOR A SLIDING DOOR

Painting fixed louvers

1 Using a 1½-inch trim brush, work the paint into the inside edges on both sides, brushing out the excess.

2 Starting at each end of a louver, pull the paint back across the louver, toward the center. Fill in the center, and finish with a continuous stroke from one end to the other.

Spray painting louvered doors

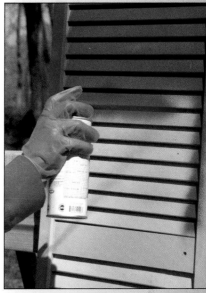

If you're painting with a spray can or power spray equipment, keep the spray head moving and spray a misting coat. Let it dry, then spray another thin coat.

Painting adjustable louvers

1 Using the same techniques for fixed louvers (see above), open the louvers fully and apply paint to both inside edges of the frame.

2 Wedge the louvers open to keep them stationary. Paint one side of the louvers, flipping the frame to paint the opposite edge. Then paint one side of the frame.

3 Turn the frame over and paint the opposite side of the louvers and the bar. Then paint the unpainted side and edges of the frame.

PAINTING A BASEMENT WALL

Whatever your reasons for painting a basement wall—to help waterproof it or simply to make it more attractive—it's important that you first fix problems that are allowing water to migrate through the wall.

Condensation, the mildest form of water problem, doesn't originate on the outside. It forms when the cooler temperatures of water pipes and walls condenses the moisture from warm-weather air and leaves it on the surface. Increasing the ventilation, insulating the pipes, or installing a dehumidifier will relieve condensation.

To control seepage from groundwater, install new gutters or fix the existing ones and slope at least 4 feet of the soil away from the foundation so water runs away and doesn't seep through the walls. Sealing the interior surface of the walls with hydraulic cement and patching the holes can also cure some seepage problems. If neither of these methods work, consult a drainage specialist.

PRESTART CHECKLIST

☐ **TIME**
About an hour to prepare and paint a 6×8-foot wall, not counting drying time required for repairs and caulk

☐ **TOOLS**
Wire brush, small sledge and cold chisel, trowel

☐ **SKILLS**
Brushing walls, keying cracks, and applying liquid waterproofing agents

☐ **PREP**
Check for moisture and eliminate outside seepage

☐ **MATERIALS**
Hydraulic cement, muriatic acid, waterproofing agent

Painting a masonry wall

1 Using a wire brush, remove as much loose mortar and paint as you can. Remove efflorescence (salts that leach to the surface of the wall and appear as a white deposit) with muriatic acid, following the manufacturer's instructions. Rinse the wall and let it dry.

2 Using a small sledge and cold chisel, key the cracks in the wall—hold the chisel at an angle and undercut the edges of the crack so the bottom of the crack is wider than the opening. Keyed cracks help keep the patching cement in place. Vacuum the crack to remove the dust.

WHAT IF...
Your wall has large cracks?

Backer rod

Press a foam backer rod into the crack before applying hydraulic cement or a high-quality urethane caulk. The backer rod puts a "bottom" in the crack and gives the caulking a surface to adhere to.

Removing efflorescense

Efflorescence is a powdery coating of salts in masonry materials brought to the surface by water migrating from the interior of the material. You'll have to remove it before you paint a basement wall. Mix a solution of muriatic acid and water, strictly following the instructions on the label. Wearing old clothes, gloves, and eye protection, scrub the surface with a stiff-bristled brush.

Caulking wide cracks

3 If the area is not already wet, mist it with a spray bottle. Then force a small amount of hydraulic cement into the crack with a trowel and smooth it down. Apply hydraulic cement where the wall meets the floor also.

4 When the hydraulic cement cures, brush on two coats of a high-quality masonry or waterproofing paint.

Plug wide cracks with hydraulic cement or urethane caulk. Press foam backer rod into a wide crack before caulking.

Applying the final coat

For best results, apply the first coat with a nylon or polyester bristle brush, the second coat with a brush or masonry roller. Work the paint thoroughly into the pores of the masonry, then back-roll the area.

Roll a second coat over the wall. If you see seepage after several days, tiny pores or pinholes are still open. Apply an additional coat to these areas.

Open windows and use an exhaust fan to provide adequate ventilation. Where good cross-ventilation is not possible, a latex product might be less noxious.

EXTERIOR DRAINAGE SYSTEM

KEEPING THE BASEMENT DRY

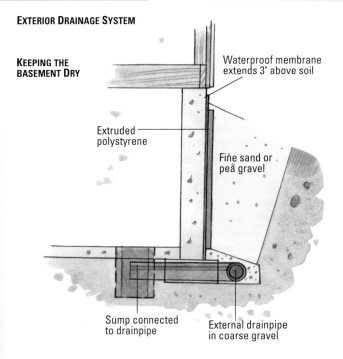

Waterproof membrane extends 3" above soil

Extruded polystyrene

Fine sand or pea gravel

Sump connected to drainpipe

External drainpipe in coarse gravel

PAINTING A BASEMENT OR GARAGE FLOOR

Painting a basement floor can take many forms. You can paint it simply to cover the dull gray color of concrete, or you can add some fun to your basement by painting any number of decorative elements—bowling lanes, shuffleboard or other floor games, or the logo of your favorite team. No matter how you paint your floor, you need to make sure that it's clean, smooth, and defect free.

Scrape off hard surface debris, then sweep the floor with a stiff-bristled garage broom. Next mix up a solution of water and concrete cleaner to label directions. Once spots are cleaned, power-scrub the entire floor, using a stiff-bristled hand brush along the walls. Then rinse thoroughly.

Manufacturers make a variety of paints suitable for floors. Epoxy paints are some of the most durable and come in one-part or two-part formulations. Let two-part epoxies stand for the prescribed time and use them within the recommended time.

PRESTART CHECKLIST

☐ **TIME**
From 30 to 45 minutes per square yard to prepare the surface, plus another 15 minutes to paint each section

☐ **TOOLS**
4-foot level, hammer, cold chisel, margin and mason's trowels, grinder, sanding block, vacuum, stiff-bristled brush, broom, rented floor-cleaning machine, paintbrushes

☐ **SKILLS**
Using a level, troweling, grinding with power grinder, cleaning and painting concrete

☐ **MATERIALS**
Hydraulic cement, muriatic acid, rubber gloves, epoxy or other paint suitable for floors

Preparing the floor

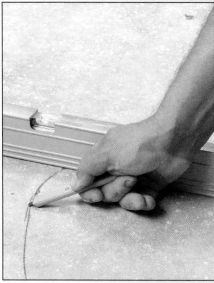

1 Divide the slab into imaginary 6-foot sections and check each section with a 4-foot level. Mark cracks, high spots, and other defects with a carpenter's pencil. Cracks may be a sign of a structural defect. Some may be repairable. Others may require professional help.

2 Use a small sledge and a cold chisel to open small cracks so you can fill them. If possible, angle the chisel into each side of the crack to create a recess wider at the bottom of the crack than on top. This will help hold the patching cement more securely.

Painting the floor

1 Prepare the floor as necessary, then sweep or vacuum it thoroughly to remove dust.

2 Prepare a cleaning solution according to manufacturer's instructions and scrub the floor thoroughly. Rinse and let it dry for 4 hours. Prepare a 10-to-1 water/muriatic etching solution and power-scrub the floor. Rinse twice and let the floor dry overnight.

3 To fill depressions in the slab, pour a small amount of self-leveling compound into the depression and trowel it level. Add compound until the surface is level. Feather the edges level with the floor.

4 Grind down any high spots you have marked using a grinder equipped with a masonry-grit abrasive wheel. A right-angle grinder makes this job go quickly. Hold a vacuum hose near the grinder to remove the dust as you work. Vacuum and damp-mop the surface thoroughly.

5 Protect the lower portions of the walls by draping plastic sheets about 2 feet up the wall, holding them in place with painter's tape.

3 If your floor paint calls for a primer, apply it according to the manufacturer's instructions and let it dry completely. Then prepare your paint, mixing two-part epoxy and letting it set as directed by the manufacturer.

4 Starting in a corner opposite a door and using a 4-inch brush, apply the first coat, using the same technique you would use for any other surface. Lay the paint in sections and finish each section with parallel strokes.

5 Let the first coat dry as prescribed on the label, then roll on the second coat. Let the paint dry at least 4 hours before using it for light foot traffic, and 7 days for full use and to park vehicles in a garage.

PAINTING A WOOD FLOOR

Although wood floors are commonly finished with stains and clear varnishes, painted floors can add a special touch to any room. Today's floor paints are durable and attractive, and you can use them as a single-color element in the room or as a base for other decoration, such as stencilling.

Painted floors need preparation, and the steps are pretty much the same for wood that is varnished, already painted, or bare.

- Remove mildew with a 3-to-1 water-bleach solution.
- Scuff-sand glossy areas (mill glaze on new wood, gloss paints on painted floors, and varnished wood).
- Remove deteriorated paint and make repairs to the flooring.
- Clean the floor thoroughly to remove dirt and grease.
- Prime and paint the floor.

Apply a primer recommended for floors—apply latex primer for latex floor paint or an alkyd primer for latex, alkyd, or polyurethane floor paint.

PRESTART CHECKLIST

☐ **TIME**
From 30 to 45 minutes per square yard to prepare the surface, plus another 15 minutes to paint each section

☐ **TOOLS**
4-foot level, hammer, sander, vacuum, screwdriver or cordless drill and screwdriver bits, paintbrushes, roller with extension handle

☐ **SKILLS**
Using a level, cleaning, repairing, and painting wood

☐ **MATERIALS**
Bleach, sandpaper, primer and floor paint, patching compound

Painting a wood floor

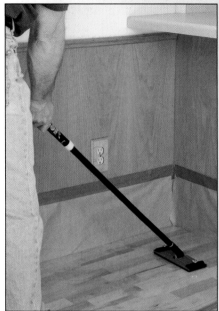

1 Remove mildew and let the floor dry. Then scuff-sand glazed or glossy surfaces with 120-grit sandpaper and a pad sander. Make other repairs as necessary, then vacuum and clean the surface.

2 Using the primer recommended for both the kind of existing floor surface and the finish top coat, cut in the primer along the edges of the floor with a 3-inch brush. Start in a corner and on each leg of the corner, paint a band about 4 feet long.

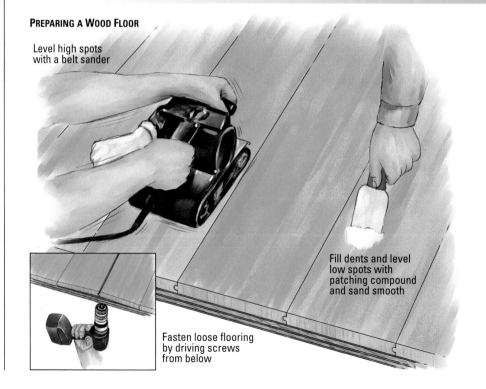

PREPARING A WOOD FLOOR

Level high spots with a belt sander

Fill dents and level low spots with patching compound and sand smooth

Fasten loose flooring by driving screws from below

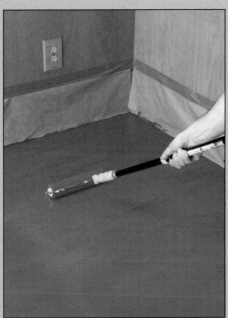

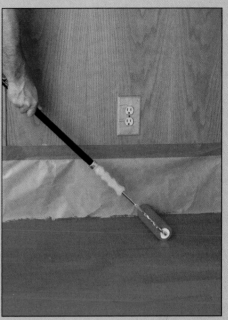

3 Using a medium-nap roller, apply the primer in the section you've just cut in, rolling the paint as close to the edge of the wall as possible and working with the grain.

4 Working in the same 4×4-foot section, roll the primer against the grain. This will spread primer into any floor irregularities.

5 Finish the section by rolling lightly with the grain, and lifting the roller at the end of each stroke (see page 56). Move to the next section, cutting in and rolling in the same fashion, always working toward a wet edge. When the primer is dry, use the same techniques to apply paint to the floor.

Decorative techniques

STENCILING

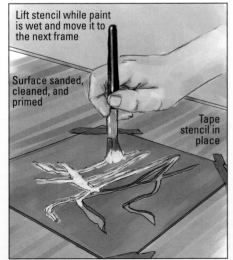

Lift stencil while paint is wet and move it to the next frame

Surface sanded, cleaned, and primed

Tape stencil in place

A painted floor provides a literal canvas of opportunities for the application of decorative techniques. The three shown here are among the

COMB PAINTING

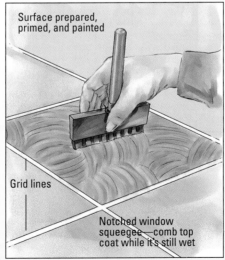

Surface prepared, primed, and painted

Grid lines

Notched window squeegee—comb top coat while it's still wet

easiest of perhaps a hundred different effects you can create on a painted floor. With some techniques, such as stenciling, it will help to

SPATTER PAINTING

Spatter succeeding colors after each color has dried

Surface prepared, primed, and painted

sketch out your pattern first. With others, like spatter painting, you can exercise your creativity.

STAINING OR VARNISHING A WOOD FLOOR

Finishing a wood floor requires a number of preparation steps, but nothing beats the final appearance of a wood floor with all its warmth and richness.

If you're planning to refinish an existing floor, before you do anything, pull up a floor register to make sure you have enough wood for another sanding. Standard hardwood strip flooring can be sanded several times, but if your floor is only slightly more than ½ inch thick, consult a professional. The same goes for engineered flooring. It can be refinished, but its top layer is quite thin.

Take inventory of the existing floor and mark and repair popped nails and damaged areas. Because depressions in an old floor are inevitable, they'll show up as you're sanding them. Mark them so you can resand them if necessary.

Even if your floor is brand new and unfinished, it will still require some sanding and preparation. In almost all cases, it's easier to use a pad sander rather than a drum sander.

PRESTART CHECKLIST

☐ **TIME**
2 to 4 days, depending on conditions and size of the floor and your skills and experience

☐ **TOOLS**
Pry bar, putty knife, hammer, pad sander, random orbit sander, vacuum, finish applicator, paintbrush

☐ **SKILLS**
Preparing, sanding, and finishing wood

☐ **MATERIALS**
Finishing nails, wood putty, stain, sandpaper, varnish

Finishing a wood floor

1 Remove shoe molding and baseboard (if desired). Rough-sand the floor with a heavy-grit paper, keeping the sander moving and working with the grain. Change sandpaper often to keep the cutting surface fresh. A sander equipped with a dust-removal system will speed the work.

2 When the floor is sanded to a rough-cut smoothness, fill the entire surface with a wood filler recommended by your floor products retailer. Let the filler dry.

SHOE MOLDING
Save the moldings

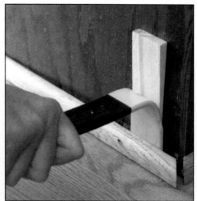

Shoe molding (and baseboards too) will invariably suffer some damage from the sanding machine. To avoid replacing the moldings and baseboards with new material (which will also require finishing), remove them with a flat prybar.

STANLEY PRO TIP

Down to the nitty gritty

When you're refinishing a wood floor, begin sanding with a heavy grit and work with successively finer grits until the floor is smooth enough to take a finish. (An improperly sanded floor will show scratches immediately upon application of the finish.)

On existing floors with dents and other signs of wear, you may need to use the following grits in succession—36-grit, 50-grit, and then 80-grit. On new floors, start with a medium paper such as 100-grit and move up to finer grits such as 150-grit and higher. Run your hand over the floor surface as you work to reveal any slight imperfections. Although you will want to increase the grit as you sand, using abrasive finer than 220-grit can create a burnished surface that won't accept stain evenly.

3 Rough-cutting the floor will leave the edges slightly higher than the main body of the floor. To even out this difference in floor levels, scrape down the edges so they're level with the sanded surface. Change blades often and pull the scraper toward you with firm pressure on the wood.

4 Buff the floor with a 100-grit screen to remove any remaining imperfections, and to bring the floor to a consistent level from edges to center, leaving the surface at its finished smoothness. Vacuum thoroughly and remove dust with a tack cloth.

5 Stain the floor (optional) with a rag or the applicator recommended, removing the excess if required. Let the stain dry. Using a lamb's wool or other suitable applicator, apply the finish coats, letting each coat dry. Scuff-sand and vacuum each dried coat before applying the next one.

USING A DRUM SANDER

1. Start here and sand a section two-thirds the width of the floor.

2. Then sand the remaining one-third on the other side of the room.

Drum sanders require a specific technique to produce a smooth surface. Start about two-thirds of the way along the length of one wall and sand with the grain. Push the sander forward and overlap its next path slightly, pulling it toward you. After sanding the section, turn the sander around and repeat the process.

Choosing the right finish

Interior stains are generally wiping stains applied to bare wood with a protective clear top coating.

Wiping stains:
■ Applied to bare wood with a rag or brush in maximum 2-foot sections. Let stand 5 minutes; wipe excess with rags; dry overnight.
■ Darkness will depend on stain, color, porosity of wood, time left on before wiping, how hard it is wiped, and number of applications.
Oil Finishes are based on drying oils such as tung or linseed oil.
■ Applied to bare wood, often over wiping stain, with brush or rag. Let stand for 5 minutes; wipe excess with rag; dry overnight. Repeat with additional coats.

■ Provide a rich, satin finish and moderate water resistance.
Varnishes—solvent base
■ Applied to bare or stained wood with natural bristle, nylon, or polyester brush.
■ Stir matte finishes without making foam; do not shake.
■ Let first coat dry 24 hours. Sand first coat to ensure adhesion.
Varnishes—water base
■ May be milky white in the container but dry clear.
■ May appear more like plastic than solvent-based varnish.
■ To remove whiskers that come up when applying the coating, predampen bare wood, let dry 20 minutes, and fine-sand, going with the grain.

PAINTING VINYL FLOORING AND CERAMIC TILE

If your old vinyl flooring or ceramic tile is looking a little tired and you'd like to spice up its appearance while you're redecorating the room, consider painting the surface. You can easily paint both vinyl flooring (sheet flooring and tile) and ceramic tile with the proper preparation, and paint is much cheaper than the expense of tiling over the existing floor.

This treatment, however, is not recommended for ceramic tile shower and tub walls but is perfectly acceptable for other walls in the bathroom—those that don't get directly wet. The key to success is very careful preparation and the use of the right primer and paint.

The preparation techniques and products shown here apply to both materials—first removing mildew, cleaning, and scuff-sanding the surface. You will not need to use a deglossing agent on ceramic tile, however.

Use high-quality primers and paints made specifically for vinyl or ceramic. Get recommendations from your paint supplier.

PRESTART CHECKLIST

☐ **TIME**
About 3 hours for a 10×10-foot floor, not including drying time for primer and paint

☐ **TOOLS**
Sanding block and/or pad sander, paint rollers and brushes, stencil pattern (optional)

☐ **SKILLS**
Preparing and painting vinyl or ceramic tile flooring

☐ **MATERIALS**
Sandpaper, deglossing agent, cleaning solution, bleach, primer, paint

Painting vinyl flooring

1 Remove any mildewed areas by scrubbing them with a 3-to-1 water-bleach solution, letting it soak in for 20 minutes, then rinsing it. Then scrub the floor thoroughly to remove grease and dirt.

2 To provide a slightly roughened surface that will help the paint adhere, scuff-sand the flooring with 150-grit sandpaper and a pad sander. Wipe the floor with a damp rag. Then remove any remaining gloss with a deglossing agent (see below).

STANLEY PRO TIP: **Deglossing (for vinyl only)**

Almost all vinyl flooring, both tile and sheet flooring, comes with some kind of pattern embossed in it. Because a major portion of this pattern lies slightly below the rest of the flooring, scuff-sanding might not be successful in getting at and removing the gloss in the depressions. Since paint won't adhere to these small glossy indentations, you'll end up with a pattern of "holes" in your paint job. You'll need a deglosser to remove this final bit of gloss in the original flooring.

Because different products call for different application methods, be sure to read the instructions carefully and wear gloves and protective glasses for caustic solutions.

Apply the solution full strength. Don't dilute it. Saturate a coarse cloth (an old terry-cloth towel makes a good applicator) and working in sections, rub the surface in a circular motion. Fold and resaturate the cloth frequently to prevent redepositing grease or

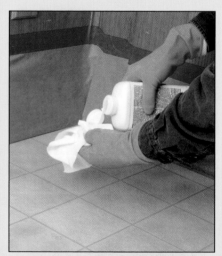

wax. When the deglossed surface is dry to the touch (about 10 minutes), it's ready for priming. You'll get the best adhesion if you prime within an hour of deglossing.

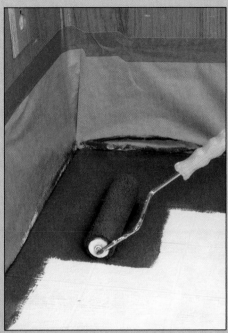

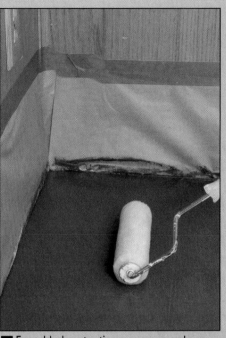

3 Apply a thick coat of latex stain-blocking primer, first cutting in the edges with a brush, then filling in the rest of the surface with a roller. Sand the primer when it's dry, then apply a second coat if you need to further level the surface.

4 Paint the floor, cutting in and brushing. For walls, use a quality latex kitchen and bath paint in a satin, semigloss, or gloss finish. For floors, use a latex satin-finish floor paint or a semigloss oil-base or polyurethane floor paint.

5 For added protection, you can apply an acrylic floor sealer. Check with your paint distributor to find a product compatible with the floor paint you have applied.

Coloring the grout (for ceramic tile only)

If you don't want to go to all the trouble of painting an entire surface finished with ceramic tile, try coloring the grout instead. Colorants made specifically for grout can dramatically alter the color scheme of the floor. First chip out any loose grout with a hammer and cold chisel, and vacuum out the loose dust. Patch the repaired spots with the same grout as the original, finish it with a striking tool, and let it cure. Then mix up the colorant and apply it to the grout with a narrow brush. Repeat the application to darken the color.

Stencil a pattern over the final coat

Painted floors provide perfect backgrounds for stenciled patterns. Tape the stencil to the floor and paint the pattern with a stencil brush. Stencilling will also help hide areas that might show remnants of the vinyl or ceramic texture.

PAINTING STEPS

Some structural elements in the interior of a home just naturally become focal points. Fireplaces are one such example. Staircases are another. Because they play so dominant a role in the design of a room, staircases deserve special attention.

In many older homes with painted stairs, you'll find quality hardwoods under the paint. You may want to first decide whether to strip the paint and refinish with a stained and varnished surface, or simply repaint it. This is a decision you should make when you're planning the room, so the finish and color of the staircase will fit harmoniously into the overall appearance of the space.

To find out what kind of wood is hidden by the paint, scrape the paint from an inconspicuous spot. If you don't recognize the wood, call in a carpenter.

Even with an expensive hardwood, you still might not want to go to the trouble of removing the paint. Experiment with a section, applying stripper and removing the paint. If the paint was applied over undamaged varnish, stripping it will only be messy, not difficult. If the varnish had deteriorated, however, the paint may lie in the grain of the wood, and removing it may require extensive and careful work with stiff brushes and stripper.

PRESTART CHECKLIST

☐ **TIME**
Will vary with the size of the staircase and the complexity of its design

☐ **TOOLS**
Putty knife, preparation tools as required

☐ **SKILLS**
Repairing and preparing wood, and refinishing or painting

☐ **PREP**
Repair and clean damaged surfaces

☐ **MATERIALS**
Sandpaper, painter's tape, paintbrushes, roller, primer, paint

Painting a staircase

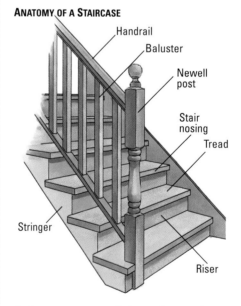

1 Carefully mask off the steps with heavy butcher paper and painter's tape. Starting at the top of the stairs and using a 2-inch trim brush, paint the handrail first, working the brush carefully to get paint on all the surfaces. Finish each section by brushing with the grain.

2 If the balusters will be painted a different color than the rest of the staircase, make sure to mask them off carefully where they meet the steps. If everything will be the same color, keep a dampened cloth handy to wipe up drips and spatters. Even though they might be the same color, they'll dry as lumps.

ANATOMY OF A STAIRCASE

Handrail
Baluster
Newell post
Stair nosing
Tread
Stringer
Riser

Stairways can pose painting problems different from other projects—chiefly those associated with height. Use ladders to reach outside surfaces. Don't hang over the railing to paint one side. It's dangerous and you're bound to miss spots.

3 After you have finished painting the handrail and balusters, start at the top of the steps and paint the underside of the first nosing. Then paint the first riser.

4 Paint the tread next and continue down the steps in the same order, applying paint to every other step. Leaving alternate steps unpainted will allow you to use the stairs while the paint dries. When the paint is dry, lightly tape 4-inch squares of cardboard to the painted stairs and paint the remainder. The cardboard will remind family members which treads they can step on.

When you're painting a stairwell, you might find the upper walls out of reach, even with an extension handle. And without some kind of platform, cutting in the edges at the ceiling will be impossible. Make yourself a scaffold platform with two ladders as shown, clamping the plank to a step on the top ladder. Adjust the other ladder until the plank is level.

Painting the lower walls may require only one stepladder and a scaffold plank. Make sure the plank is level and clamped to the ladder. Move the plank down the ladder and steps as you work.

PAINTING CABINETRY

Painting built-in cabinetry and bookcases is a time-consuming job because of the many surfaces. Paint built-ins after you've painted the wall.

Remove adjustable shelves and paint them first so they'll be dry when you're ready to reinstall them. If possible, paint them in another room to get them out of your way, and support their edges with nails driven into predrilled holes in the ends. That way, you don't have to wait for one surface to dry before painting the other one. Be sure to remove the shelf supports before you paint the inside of the cabinet.

You can paint the cabinet doors either on or off the cabinet, but removing them makes painting easier. Remove the hardware from both the cabinet and the doors.

If you prefer to leave the doors on, as shown here, you probably won't need to paint the interior of the cabinets. If you do, paint them from the inside out as shown in the illustration at right.

Remove drawer hardware and stand the drawers on their backs. Paint the fronts and leading edges, but don't paint any other part of the drawer or the tracks inside the cabinet. For cabinets with fixed shelving, paint them in the order shown at right.

PRESTART CHECKLIST

☐ **TIME**
From 1 to 2 days, depending on size of cabinet installation and your skill level and experience

☐ **TOOLS**
Screwdriver, pliers, paintbrushes, rollers

☐ **SKILLS**
Preparing and painting wood cabinetry

☐ **PREP**
Clean, repair, and sand surfaces

☐ **MATERIALS**
Sandpaper, primer, paint

Painting cabinets

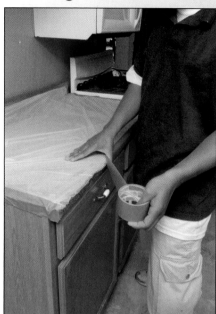

1 Prepare the cabinets as you would any other surface, cleaning mildewed spots and washing the entire surface to remove dirt and grease. Repair or replace damaged wood and cover any surface you want protected.

2 Since paint won't stick to glossy surfaces, scuff-sand them with 150-grit sandpaper or use a commercial deglossing agent. Apply the deglosser in sections small enough that you can paint them within an hour. Applying paint within an hour after the deglosser will give you better adhesion.

PAINTING A CABINET

Numbers show painting sequence

Remove drawers; paint fronts only.

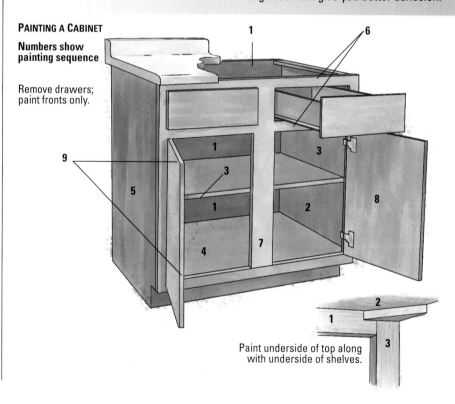

Paint underside of top along with underside of shelves.

3 Open the cabinet doors and paint the reverse side with a brush, holding the door open with your free hand. Paint the interior of all the cabinet doors, and leave them open. Use the techniques shown on pages 88 or 89, depending on whether you have slab doors or raised-panel units.

4 While the inside faces of the doors are drying, paint the front edge of the shelving and the cabinet frame.

STANLEY PRO TIP

Contour sanding

To get your sandpaper into all the contours of paneled doors, use a contoured sander, a small sponge wrapped with sandpaper, or a commercial sanding sponge.

Painted cabinets can bring a vintage look to any kitchen. Gloss white is a traditional finish for cabinetry, but you can paint the doors and face frames different colors for a stylish effect. The interiors of wall cabinets with glass doors can be painted to match or contrast too.

Painting cabinets *continued*

5 When the front faces of the doors are dry, close them and paint the stiles and rails of the frame, always painting the longest piece of the structure last to avoid crossed brush strokes.

6 Paint the sides and other open areas of the cabinets. You can speed this application with a roller, but if you do, back-brush the rolled paint to level it and make its surface consistent with the rest of the unit.

Painting with the doors removed

1 Using a cordless drill or manual screwdriver, remove the hinges from the frame and door. Set the doors aside in the areas where you plan to paint them.

2 If you're painting the inside of the cabinets, follow the order illustrated on page 154. If you're not painting the interiors, paint the face frame with a trim brush.

3 Support the doors in a fashion that will make painting them as easy as possible. Paint the contours first, then roll the paint on the faces of the doors and back-brush.

7 If you're painting the back wall under the wall cabinets, cut in the edges first, just as you would any other wall.

8 While the cut-in edges are still wet, fill in the remainder of the wall. You can use a roller here without going to the trouble of back-brushing, but you may find it more convenient to apply the paint with a 7-inch or smaller roller.

Tighten up

Cabinet doors get a lot of abuse, which can take their toll on the door hinges and work the hinge screws loose. When a screw works loose, it means that some of the wood on the frame or door has been gouged away by the screw threads.

Before you remove the doors, push them gently up and down and watch for movement of the hinges on the wood. Mark those locations with a small piece of tape and remove the doors. Then go back to your marked spots and insert one or two stick matches in the loose holes, applying a thin coat of carpenter's glue to the matches before you insert them. Let the glue dry for about 20 minutes before you paint the frames. When you reinstall the doors, you should be able to tighten the screws in the filled holes without predrilling. Use a manual screwdriver or a cordless drill with the clutch set on the lowest setting.

STANLEY PRO TIP

Time to update hardware

Repainting cabinets provides a perfect opportunity for replacing the hardware and making the style of your kitchen design take on a whole new look. Consider replacing pulls with knobs and knobs with pulls or using hardware with a slightly different style on the doors and drawers.

You can shop for your hardware at any number of retail outlets, and you'll be amazed at the variety offered on Internet sites. Purchase the hardware before you start your paint job, and fill and sand any holes that will no longer match before you paint.

After the paint has dried and with the doors and drawers in place, predrill the mounting holes for the new hardware, if required, using a level when installing pulls.

HOW TO PAINT A BOOKCASE

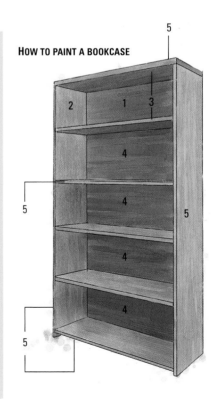

HOW TO PAINT JUST ABOUT ANYTHING

There once was a time when using paint to change the color of some objects was simply out of the question. Technology kept inventing materials faster than paint could be made that would stick to them. And paint may have also suffered from the prevalent but false notion that it simply wasn't appropriate for certain surfaces. The color of concrete or ceramic yard ornaments, for example, was frequently perceived as simply immutable—it was made in the color it was supposed to be.

Whatever real or imagined limitations may have applied to paint in the past are today fairly well put to rest. Whether you want to paint an old cast-iron toy, a plastic lawn chair, a solid concrete yard ornament, a wicker rocking chair, an ornate iron fence, old vinyl shutters on your house, or even your child's half-worn sneakers, there's a modern paint that will do the job.

The conditions for paint to stick to a surface are pretty much the same no matter what the material. It must be free of mildew, dirt, and grease; it must provide some "traction" or a "tooth," (something a little rougher than bright and shiny) for the paint to stick; and it must be primed with a solution that minimizes the chance of interfering elements (like rust) occurring or reoccurring. That means that no matter what you're painting, preparation steps will be about the same. Paints and application techniques, however, will vary.

For example, metals are best painted with paints formulated for metals, plastics with "plastic" paints, fabrics with "fabric" paints, and so on. Different surfaces will also require different painting techniques. Painting stucco, for example, will mean spraying paint from several directions so all parts of the surface and all the small recesses get covered. The same is true for other rough textures, such as wicker furniture and anything woven, as well as complicated pieces like chairs and toys.

Painting an object in multiple colors can produce attractive results, but multicolor paint schemes take patience in order to look professional. Mask off sections around the area you want to paint using masking tape and paper. Then paint the section. To paint another color, remove the tape and repeat the process, masking off the first color only when it is fully dry.

Modern paints and a variety of techniques allow you to paint just about any surface.

CHAPTER PREVIEW

Painting iron and steel furniture and ornaments
page 160

Painting plastics
page 166

Painting wood furniture
page 168

Special applications
page 170

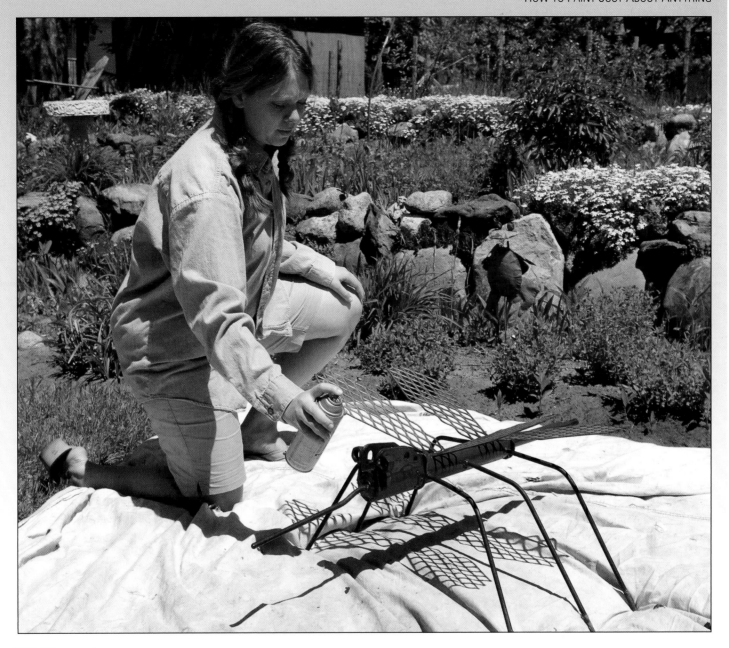

Whitewash, distemper, and milk paints
page 172

Painting a swimming pool
page 174

PAINTING IRON AND STEEL FURNITURE AND ORNAMENTS

No matter what kind of structure defines your first painting project, if you are involved with painting long enough, sooner or later you're likely to run into some kind of metal object whose surface needs refreshing. Many of these will be made from ferrous metals—iron or steel. With the exception of stainless steel, the primary element that begins their deterioration is rust, the oxidation of the surface brought on by exposure to air and moisture.

Rust can not only eat away at the metal and spoil its appearance, it can undermine any primers, paints, or other coatings applied to protect it.

Rust can start on bare metal more quickly than you might imagine—immediately when an unprotected surface is exposed to moisture in any form. Your objective, then, is to stop any rusting that has begun and to keep moisture and air from getting to the metal after painting. To prepare ferrous metals, you'll need to remove both the rust and any peeling paint.

On smaller jobs, use a scraper and a wire brush—the scraper to take off heavy rust and loose paint, the brush to remove the rust residue. On larger jobs, use power brushing and disk sanding with aluminum oxide paper.

These steps will leave the surface covered with small particles of rust and dust, which should be removed before you apply any coating. Brush them off with a soft-bristled brush, scrub the entire surface with a detergent-and-water solution, then rinse it thoroughly with clean water. Cleaning will also remove any mill oil (a residue from the manufacturing process), which can interfere with the paint bond. Prime the surface with a top-quality latex rust-inhibitive metal primer as soon as it dries. Brush or spray the primer at the recommended spread rate and apply a second coat to get the maximum resistance to corrosion.

Top-coat the metal with a high-quality acrylic latex paint. It can last as much as two to four times longer than conventional alkyd paints without serious cracking or fading.

An ornate iron fence and railing is the highlight of the entrance to this traditional home. Keeping such decorative items in tip-top condition is not difficult with the proper preparation and the use of high-quality primers and paints.

Painting ornamental iron

1 Examine the surface thoroughly and remove loose rust as you come across it. Use new wire brushes of different sizes to get into as many of the small corners as possible. Where the brush won't fit, slide aluminum oxide sandpaper or strips of emery cloth to strip off the rust.

Painting iron and steel

Prep	Remove all loose rust and paint using wire brushes, emery cloth, scrapers, cold chisels, and aluminum-oxide sandpaper as appropriate to reach all the contours of the material. Brush the resultant dust and rust particles off the surface with a soft brush and scrub the entire surface with a detergent-and-water solution. Rinse the surface thoroughly with clear water and let it dry. Then apply a coat of rust inhibitor, if compatible with your primer.
Prime	Brush, roll, or spray a high-quality latex corrosion-inhibitive primer on the surfaces you have repaired. Let the first coat dry and apply a second coat. If you spray or roll on the primer, back-brush it immediately, which will work the paint into the surface and create a better bond. Back-brushing the primer before it sets up will also remove any drips.
Paint	When the second coat has fully cured (see label instructions), apply two top coats of high-quality acrylic latex paint, allowing sufficient drying time between coats

2 When removing loose paint from flat surfaces, use a chisel scraper or stiff putty knife. Chipped paint can be surprisingly stubborn. If necessary, remove it with a sharpened cold chisel and hammer, taking care not to dent or bend the material.

3 Using a top-quality latex rust-inhibiting primer, brush all surfaces from which you removed paint or rust. Work the brush into all the contours of the metal.

4 When the primer is dry, finish-coat the surface with two coats of a top-quality acrylic latex paint.

ALTERNATE PREPARATION TECHNIQUES

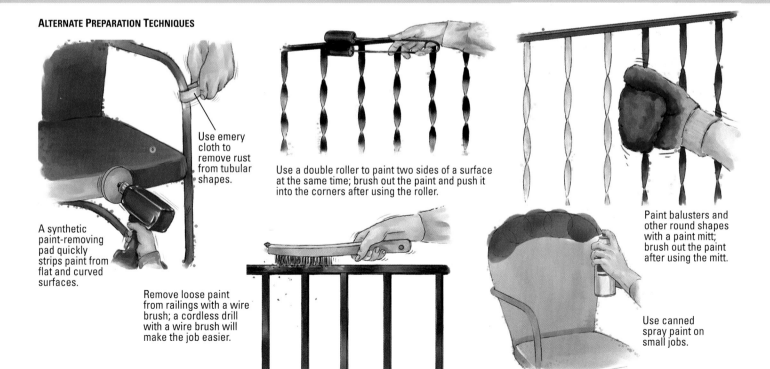

Use emery cloth to remove rust from tubular shapes.

A synthetic paint-removing pad quickly strips paint from flat and curved surfaces.

Use a double roller to paint two sides of a surface at the same time; brush out the paint and push it into the corners after using the roller.

Remove loose paint from railings with a wire brush; a cordless drill with a wire brush will make the job easier.

Paint balusters and other round shapes with a paint mitt; brush out the paint after using the mitt.

Use canned spray paint on small jobs.

Painting a metal file cabinet

Set up your home office—or any office for that matter—in style with colorful file cabinets. Although you can find colorful cabinets at commercial outlets, you can also transform your existing "institutional" models into a bright arrangement sporting your own color scheme.

1 You can paint the cabinet with the drawers removed or leave the drawers in. Remove or mask off the handles and hardware. Then mask the interior sides of the drawer and spray paint the cabinet and edges of the drawer face. Apply a mist coat first, then several light coats.

2 Using the spray technique shown on page 57, paint the front face of the drawer. If masked, remove the tape from the hardware while the paint is still slightly wet. If you've removed the hardware, wait until the paint has dried completely, then reinstall the hardware.

Ornate iron outdoor furniture is full of spaces that make rust removal and rejuvenation very difficult with standard tools. Taking such objects to a local sandblaster is a much more effective way to prepare them for painting. Be sure to prime the surface immediately and use a top-quality acrylic latex paint for the top coat.

There's no rule that says outdoor yard ornaments have to be adorned in standard colors. Spice up your landscape with interesting objects painted in an array of different, contrasting colors. In the outdoors, you can literally throw any rules to the wind.

Painting a barbeque grill

1 Using a new wire brush, remove rust and loose and charred paint. For especially stubborn areas, scrape the paint off with a wide putty knife or scraper. Sand the rough spots smooth and scuff-sand the surface.

2 Wipe the entire surface clean with a rag dampened with mineral spirits. If areas of grease still remain, clean them with an oven cleaner, rinse thoroughly, and let the surface dry. Wear rubber gloves, old clothing, and eye protection when using oven cleaner.

3 Using a high-quality high-temperature spray paint made for renewing barbecue grills, spray the exterior surface with several light coats until you achieve a consistent sheen over the entire surface.

PAINTING RADIATORS

Even though radiators don't get as hot as barbecue grills, the heat they generate can deteriorate standard interior paints. You can apply a high-temperature paint with a brush made specifically for radiators, but spraying them is more effective. Cover the floor with plastic sheeting and tape the edges down. Then protect the wall by slipping a large piece of cardboard behind the radiator and taping it in place. Spray several light coats.

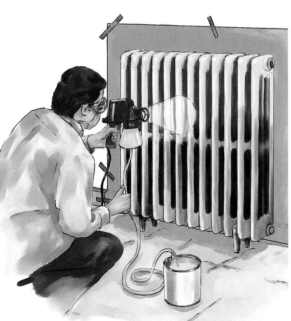

A coating of high-temperature paint can make your old wood stove look brand new. These paints come in a wide range of temperature applications, so be sure to ask your supplier for the paint rated for the amount of heat generated by a stove.

Painting Iron and Steel Furniture and Ornaments *continued*

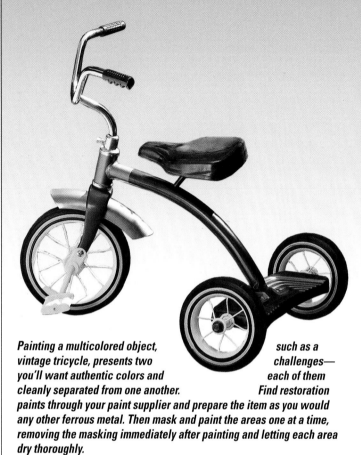

Painting a multicolored object, such as a vintage tricycle, presents two challenges— you'll want authentic colors and each of them cleanly separated from one another. Find restoration paints through your paint supplier and prepare the item as you would any other ferrous metal. Then mask and paint the areas one at a time, removing the masking immediately after painting and letting each area dry thoroughly.

Customizing mailboxes will both individualize them and create a colorful display. First set the mailbox on a drop cloth outdoors or in a large enough area to keep any overspray off other surfaces. Wire-brush all loose paint and rust and sand smooth. Clean the mailbox with soap and water, then rinse and let it dry. Using a spray metal primer, spot-prime any bare metal and areas that were rusted. Remove or mask off the flag with plastic and masking tape. Then spray the entire surface with an enamel rust-inhibiting paint. Start with a mist coat, let it dry, then follow with several light coats to avoid drips and sags. Remove the masking and/or reattach flag and refasten the mailbox to its post.

Painting aluminum furniture

Prep	Older aluminum furniture with factory finishes may show excessive chalking with age. In severe cases a deteriorated finish can leave bare metal exposed. Unprotected aluminum surfaces will quickly oxidize, exhibiting a heavy powdered residue. Use a nonmetallic scouring pad to remove any oxidation. Then, using 320-grit sandpaper, smooth the edges of painted or finished areas to ease the transition between them and bare metal. Scrub the surface with a detergent-and-water solution, or power-wash it to remove dust, loose paint, dirt, and chalk. Then rinse the surface clean and let it dry thoroughly.
Prime	Apply a corrosion-resistant acrylic latex primer to areas of bare metal.
Paint	Finish with two coats of top-quality acrylic latex paint.

Spraying is an ideal way to paint an ornate object like this chair, but you can brush-paint it too. Use a brush that will fit into the spaces on complex areas so you can paint the edges. You can use a wider brush on larger areas, such as the rim around the seat, to minimize brush marks.

Even galvanized utilitarian objects, such as watering cans, can make your gardening chores more pleasant if you dress them up with a coat of paint. Clean the surfaces thoroughly before painting and use primers and paints made specifically for use on galvanized metals.

Galvanized metal poses a special problem because the galvanization makes it difficult for paint to adhere to the surfaces. Wipe the surface with a degreasing cleaner and use conditioners made specifically for new metal such as gutters, downspouts, and flashing. Weathered galvanized metal will hold primers, but it's best to use specialized primers made specifically for galvanized metal.

Painting galvanized surfaces

Prep	For finished galvanized surfaces, remove all loose paint and rust with a wire brush, using care to minimize scratching the surface. Using 320-grit sandpaper, smooth the edges of painted or finished areas to ease the transition between them and bare metal. 　　Scrub the surface with a detergent-and-water solution, or power-wash it to remove dust, loose paint, dirt, and chalk. Then rinse the surface clean and let it dry thoroughly. 　　For unfinished galvanized metal, wipe the surface with a degreasing cleaner, rinse, and let dry.
Prime	Apply an acrylic latex rust-inhibitive primer.
Paint	Finish the job by applying a top-quality acrylic latex paint. Do not apply an alkyd (oil-base) paint directly to galvanized metal.

Metal storage bins are great tools for helping you stay organized. Transform them into decorative accents to brighten up your desk or shelving. Finish them with primer and two coats of paint to keep them from chipping in use.

PAINTING PLASTICS

Plastics are perhaps the most difficult surfaces to paint. Their chemical composition and smooth surface do not promote good paint adhesion, and the fact that plastics can expand and contract at a greater rate than many paints leaves them vulnerable to flaking paint, even when you think you have the coating securely adhered.

With proper preparation and specialty products, however, you can paint plastics and not have to worry about the durability of the finish.

For interior walls (tiled with plastic tile, for example, or finished with other plastic products), apply a high-adhesion latex stain-blocking primer. For bathroom and kitchen walls not subject to constant exposure to water, use a top-of-the line interior latex paint. Shower walls and similar surfaces do not make suitable candidates for paint.

For extra insurance against peeling and cracking, ask your paint dealer about primers and paints made specifically for plastic surfaces. They will give you a great deal of versatility in transforming drab outdoor objects into attractive ornaments.

Painting plastic lawn furniture

1 Wash the object thoroughly with a mild detergent solution and let it dry. Then lightly scuff with 220-grit sandpaper.

2 Using a spray primer and top coat formulated for plastics, prime the surface, let it dry, then paint it. Spray multiple light coats, letting them dry completely before applying each succeeding coat.

Painting plastics

Prep	First get rid of any mildew by scrubbing the areas with a 3-to-1 water/bleach solution. Keep the area wet for about 20 minutes, then rinse it off. Clean the object thoroughly with detergent and warm water. Rinse and let dry. Scuff-sand the surface with 200-grit sandpaper to give it tooth, which will help the paint stick better. Wipe off the sanding dust with a damp cloth and let it dry.
Prime	Apply a high-adhesion latex stain-blocking primer to interior walls. For outdoor furniture, spray-prime with specialized plastic primers formulated specifically for adhesion to plastics.
Paint	Paint interior walls with a top-quality acrylic paint and outdoor furniture with spray paints made for plastics.

Painting PVC trim

To paint PVC trim, wash, rinse, and let dry. Scuff-sand (220-grit) and wipe clean. Prime with acrylic latex primer recommended for exterior PVC surfaces and top-coat with 100-percent acrylic latex paint using a high-quality sash or trim brush. Do not paint trim darker than its original color—that way you'll avoid potential warping.

Spray painting tips

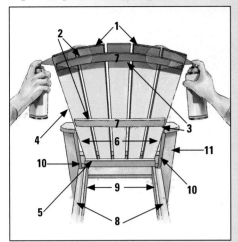

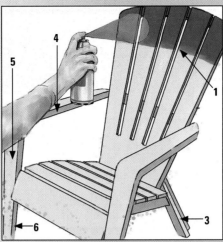

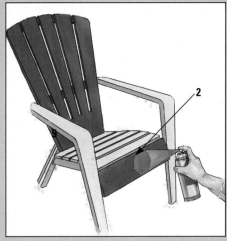

When spraying furniture, paint the bottom as shown below. Then turn the chair upright and paint in the order shown. The best way is to paint as much of the object as you can see from one side, then reverse

your position and paint as much of the surface as you can see from the other side. Applying paint in this order will ensure that you get full coverage and will eliminate drips. Apply the paint in light coats and

repeat the process, completing one side and then the other. Let this complete coat dry before applying the next one.

Turn the object upside down and support it on a flat surface, preferably at about shoulder height, so you can keep a good view of the surface and avoid bending down to paint it. Paint the underside from different angles to assure complete coverage. Let the paint dry, then turn the object right side up and continue painting.

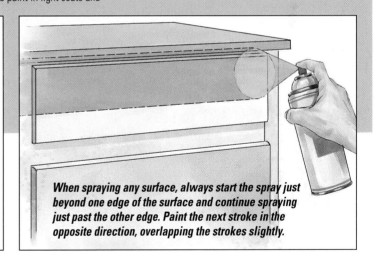

When spraying any surface, always start the spray just beyond one edge of the surface and continue spraying just past the other edge. Paint the next stroke in the opposite direction, overlapping the strokes slightly.

When spraying a surface with a roughened texture, spray one coat from one angle and other coats from other angles for full coverage.

Spray paint protocol

- Test the spray on a piece of paper taped to a wall.
- Hold the can as perpendicular to the surface as possible.
- Tack coat the first pass for about 50-percent coverage. This gives the next coats something to adhere to.
- Apply the paint in numerous light coats, not one heavy coat.
- Shake the can periodically during the paint job.

- "Orange peel" means you've applied the paint too thick or on too warm a surface. Smooth mild orange peel with fine rubbing compound. Wet-sand severe orange peel, smooth with rubbing compound, and recoat.
- Runs and sags mean the paint is too thick or the surface is too cold. Remove dried runs with #400 or #600 sandpaper and paint again.

PAINTING WOOD FURNITURE

If you're in the market for new furniture or looking for a way to spice up one or two pieces you already have, paint may just be the answer you're looking for. Buying furniture off the showroom floor is expensive, and so is hunting for finished antiques. Painting the furniture can save you money and time.

The preparation techniques for painting wood furniture vary somewhat, depending on whether the surface is already painted or not. Existing paint must be smooth and have enough tooth for the new paint to adhere. You'll also have to carefully scrape off flaked or damaged paint and sand the edges of the remaining paint so the new coating won't highlight the edges of the old paint.

Unpainted wood also requires sanding to a smooth surface. You can tell when the surface is smooth enough by using cotton gloves. Once you've sanded and dusted the surface to a level you believe is satisfactory (using successively finer sandpaper grits), gently draw a gloved hand across it. If the surface needs more sanding, the cotton glove will catch on the wood fibers.

Painted furniture makes the perfect addition to a child's room and provides an inexpensive way to brighten up the space. Recoat existing painted items or purchase new unfinished furniture.

Painting wood furniture

Prep	For painted wood, wash the surface with a mild detergent to remove dirt and grease. Do not overwet the wood. Let the surface dry and gently scrape away loose paint with a narrow putty knife, taking care not to dent or scratch the wood. Sand the edges of the remaining paint around bare wood so they're as level as possible. Scuff-sand any glossy surfaces. For new, unfinished wood, start with coarser sandpaper (80 to 100 grit, depending on the surface) and brush off the dust and loose abrasive particles. Using progressively finer grits (up to about 220 or 250), sand with the grain of the wood, not against it. Wipe the dust off the wood using a cloth dampened with mineral spirits
Prime	When working with painted wood, prime any bare spots and let them dry. For new wood, prime the entire surface with a spray primer recommended by your paint dealer.
Paint	Spray-paint the furniture in the color of your choice, using a high-quality latex acrylic or epoxy paint.

White paint helps this large entertainment center blend in with the walls so it seems less overwhelming in the room.

Old furniture from the attic or thrift store becomes a decorator accent item with a bright coat of paint. Careful preparation is essential for a smooth finish on old wooden furniture.

Instead of painting furniture a single solid color, you can add style with a two-tone (or more) color scheme. Here dark blue and light blue highlight the stained and varnished wood parts to create a unique table.

For outdoor wood furnishings, prepare the item as instructed (left), prime it if necessary, and top-coat it with a semigloss or gloss exterior latex or acrylic enamel.

WHAT IF...
I want to spray my own color?

Although paint manufacturers supply spray paint in a wide variety of colors, you may not be able to find one that's just exactly what you want. For example, you may want to paint a wood chair an off-shade of a color already in the room, and although you can have the paint store mix just the right color, you'll get it in a quart or gallon, not a spray can. Here's where you need an aerosol-driven spray device.

Aerosol canisters have been around for a long time in the auto-body-repair business so you can find them at an auto-body supply shop or general automotive supply stores. All you need to do is thin the paint according to the

manufacturer's instructions (do not overthin it), pour the thinned paint into the jar, screw on the aerosol unit, and spray away.

The jars are reusable, and generally you need to purchase only one in a kit complete with a canister. Replacement canisters are usually sold as separate items.

SPECIAL APPLICATIONS

Some painting projects don't fit neatly into any one category, but you'll find specialty paints for many different kinds of objects and surfaces. There are paints formulated specifically for farm implements, for automobile engines, and for appliances; paints that glow in the dark, or with colors that make your hunting gear blend into the landscape; paints that keep you from slipping on stairs, as well as paints that you can stick magnets to, others that will turn any flat surface into a blackboard, and metallic paints that finish an object in gold, aluminum, or silver.

   With the proper preparation and the right products for the job, modern technological improvements have made sure there's almost no surface that won't take and hold a coat of paint.

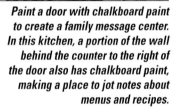

Paint a door with chalkboard paint to create a family message center. In this kitchen, a portion of the wall behind the counter to the right of the door also has chalkboard paint, making a place to jot notes about menus and recipes.

To get your boat ready for the hunting season, first get the right colors for its intended use. Camouflage kits are available from large sporting goods retailers and come in several color combinations. Most kits also include stencils for creating the correct painted shapes. Prepare the surface of your boat as you would any other metal, plastic, fiberglass, or wood surface, using the techniques shown on the previous pages. Prime as necessary and paint the entire surface with a base coat. Then apply stencils and paint the boat in your desired color scheme.

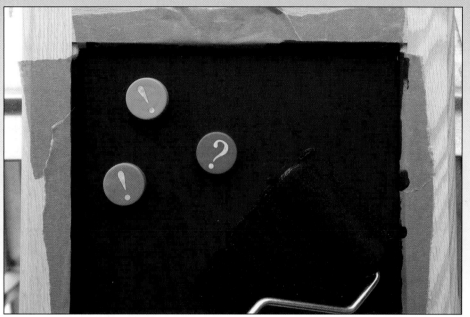

Here's another option for creating a message board, a visual memory center, or an entire wall that makes a giant magnetic game space for the kids. Smooth surfaces are the best for magnetic objects—prepare the surface using the appropriate techniques shown on earlier pages. Paints formulated specifically for this purpose contain iron particles and will probably give you better results than powders added to standard paints. Roll the paint on the wall as you would a primer, let it dry, and top-coat it with a latex paint in the color of your choice.

Prime and paint your container garden to help bring the plant colors to life. Seal the pots with a primer made for masonry surfaces and spray the top coat with colorful epoxy paints.

Make your backyard ornaments—fountains, birdbaths, decorative statues, and other items with sculpted contours—stand out in the outdoors with a coat of paint. Prepare the surfaces using the techniques illustrated on earlier pages, and paint the items with the paint recommended by your paint dealer.

An amazing number of surfaces can be made safer with antislip paints—step treads, ladders, stairwells, boat loading docks, decks, pool decks, and ramps—just to name a few. Mask the areas you don't want painted and spray-paint two coats for longer wear.

WHITEWASH, DISTEMPER, AND MILK PAINTS

Milk paint, a traditional finish, is historically correct for many antiques, including this Windsor chair.

Whitewash, distemper, and milk paints are old-time formulations that are still in use today in professional and DIY historic restoration work and when a subtle, antique effect is desired for new or old furniture.

■ **Whitewash,** usually an exterior paint, is a mixture of water and lime, which forms a plasterlike coating. All kinds of binders—salt, sugar, flour (rice, wheat, rye, or buckwheat), starch, varnish, glue, skim milk, whiting, brown sugar, vegetable oil plasticizer, casein, formaldehyde, borax, or sulfate of zinc—have been added over the years to improve its durability and reduce chalking. Alum would harden the coating and keep it from rubbing off, and tintings—earth pigments, brick or stone dust, indigo, and bluing—counteracted the tendency of some binders to yellow.

■ **Distemper paints** were mixed in two categories, depending on the binder used. Glue-bound distemper was usually produced from powdered chalk and a gelatinous sizing, such as rabbit-skin glue, although there were many substitutes for both the chalk and the glue. Modern formulations can include white glues and other synthetics. Distempers were often used as decorative paints over new lime plaster or previously painted interior walls. The addition of oil and emulsifier created a more durable coating—the predecessor of today's oil-base paints.

■ **Milk paint,** a mix of lime, casein (the protein component of milk), clays, and any of a variety of earth pigments, makes a rich, lustrous, and complex finish that improves with time. It was used as a coating for furniture, producing interesting textures and degrees of tinting across the surface.

Each of these old-time paints produce subtle shadings that have an allure all their own. Because of this built-in patina, they are frequently used in modern applications.

All these paints were home-mixed from materials readily at hand. You can brew your own following the traditional recipes shown below and opposite. Commercially prepared powdered mixes that generally require only the addition of water are also available.

Recipes for whitewash

Whitewash for woodwork

■ Make lime paste by soaking 50 pounds of hydrated lime in 6 gallons of clean water or by slaking 25 pounds of quicklime in 10 gallons of boiling water. Either will make about 8 gallons of paste.

■ Dissolve 15 pounds of salt or 5 pounds of dry calcium chloride in 5 gallons of water. Combine with the lime paste and mix thoroughly. Thin with fresh water as necessary. **CAUTION—adding water to quicklime releases tremendous amounts of heat and can cause the water to boil violently**. Take proper precautions.

Whitewash mix for plaster

■ Make lime paste by soaking 50 pounds of hydrated lime in 6 gallons of clean water or by slaking 25 pounds of quicklime in 10 gallons of boiling water. Either combination will make about 8 gallons of paste.

■ Soak 5 pounds of casein in 2 gallons of water for about 2 hours or until thoroughly softened.

■ Dissolve 3 pounds of trisodium phosphate in 1 gallon of water. Add to the lime paste and allow the mixture to dissolve.

■ Allow both the lime paste and the casein to thoroughly cool.

■ Stir the casein solution into the lime paste.

■ Just before using, dissolve 3 pints of formaldehyde in 3 gallons of water; *SLOWLY* add this solution to the whitewash; stir frequently; thin the mixture as desired.

Milk paint is sold as a dry powder. Mix it into water to make the paint.

You can apply whitewash like a stain—wipe it on and wipe it off. This method results in a faded, well-worn look that suits furniture and accessories.

To enhance the impression of age on furniture finished with whitewash or milk paint, rub away some of the finish on raised features to simulate wear. Use fine sandpaper after the paint has dried.

Recipe for milk paint

■ Mix 2 teaspoons of low-fat sour cream in 1 liter of nonfat or 2 percent milk, whip it well, and keep it warm until it thickens (a day or two).

■ Warm up the mixture or add lemon juice or vinegar to curdle it. Separate the curds by pouring the mix through a cheesecloth.

■ Dissolve 1 tablespoon of ammonium carbonate in ¾ cup of warm water and add it to the mix. This is the binder for the milk paint, but it will lose its strength quickly if not kept refrigerated.

■ Add pigment and extenders to the binder up to a 75 percent proportion. Make a paste of the extender, pigment, and water, then add the binder. For a glazed surface, thin the paint with water.

Whitewash gives the ceiling in this room a distinctive, old-time look. The finish is a perfect fit for a country decorating style.

PAINTING A SWIMMING POOL

Like any other large structure, swimming pools require periodic maintenance. The best time to perform these chores is in the early part of the year, when the weather is still relatively cool and you can refill the pool immediately after the new paint cures.

Inspect the pool for cracks, chips, and other needed repairs. Repair hairline cracks in a concrete pool with a coat of the proper chlorinated rubber or epoxy swimming pool paint. For slightly larger cracks, use an epoxy patching compound made specifically for concrete pools.

In fiberglass pools, hairline cracks that don't open to the substrate may not need repair—they're a sign of inevitable weathering. Repair larger cracks with a fiberglass patch kit. Fix cracks in fiberglass pools immediately; water can quickly damage the substrate and rot it. Buy fiberglass patch kits at swimming pool dealers, auto body supply houses, and watercraft retailers. Follow the instructions that come with the kit.

Hire a pool-care pro to repair cracks wider than ⅛ inch or longer than 1 foot.

PRESTART CHECKLIST

☐ **TIME**
From 1 to 3 days, depending on pool size and your skills and experience

☐ **TOOLS**
Utility knife, paint roller with extension handle, roller pan, sandblaster (optional) respirator, paintbrushes, safety goggles, garden sprayer

☐ **SKILLS**
Preparing a masonry surface, repairing existing cracks and applying paint

☐ **PREP**
Drain pool, patch cracks, remove flaking paint, fill holes

☐ **MATERIALS**
Muriatic acid, pool paints

Preparing a swimming pool

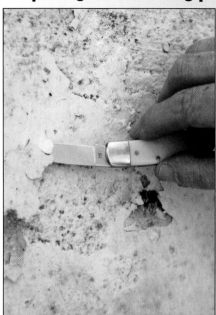

1 Determine what kind of existing paint you have on the pool walls. Loosen the edge of a peeling piece, pull it off, and take it to your dealer and have it tested. It is always best to continue recoating the pool with the same kind of paint.

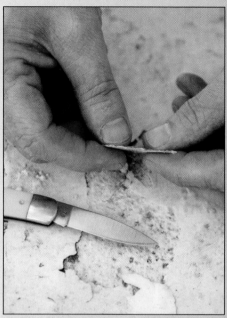

2 Determine how many coats are already on the walls of your pool. Painting over a coat or two of both rubber and epoxy paints is fine, but you'll likely run into adhesion problems with more coats than that. It's best to sandblast the pool to bare concrete.

SAFETY FIRST
Relieving hydrostatic pressure

As an in-ground pool is being drained and therefore the water pressure against the interior of the walls reduced, hydrostatic pressure from ground water can build up on the exterior of the walls.

This pressure from the outside can cause serious damage if it's not properly released while you're emptying the pool. Hydrostatic forces can be strong enough to float the pool out of the ground or can seriously crack the walls and physically move them.

To avoid this damage, many in-ground pools are equipped with pressure-relief valves, which allow ground water to be slowly released into the pool and drained away with the pool water.

If you can't locate the pressure-relief valves or aren't sure your pool has them, consult a pool builder, the previous pool owner, or a pool professional to determine whether you have them and where they're located.

This is of special concern to anyone owning a pool located next to a body of water in any low-lying land.

If your pool is located in an area with an extremely high water table, you may need to attach a hose to the pressure-relief valve so you can continuously remove the incoming groundwater while the pool is empty and until you've finished with your repairs and painting and can refill the pool.

3 Drain the pool and remove all debris. Scrape off loose paint (a high-pressure power washer will help). Cut out cracks in the pool shell to a ¼-inch depth with a diamond saw or grinder. Chip out loose cement. Caulk the cracks, and patch any large chips with hydraulic cement.

4 Wearing old clothes, boots, eye protection, gloves, and a respirator, and working in sections, apply a coat of 50-50 water-muriatic acid solution mixed according to the manufacturer's instructions. Let the acid soak in for the required time, then scrub the surface with a stiff brush.

5 Rinse the acid off the walls with a steady flow of clean water from a garden hose, and wash the pool down with TSP solution to neutralize any remaining acid. Apply the paint you have chosen using rollers and brushes and making sure that you have plenty of ventilation.

STANLEY Pro Tip

Draining the pool

■ Stop adding chemicals to the water three or four days before draining. Check the pH.
■ Attach a long hose to the drain line so it will drain into your lawn or trees (not the neighbor's). Run the pump until the lawn appears nearly sodden. Turn off the pump and wait several hours. Repeat until the pool is empty.
■ Check with local officials before you allow large amounts of water to run into the storm sewers. It may be illegal.

Paints for pools

Paint is perhaps the most common of swimming pool finishes. It is attractive, comes in many colors, makes maintenance and cleaning relatively easy, and is inexpensive compared to other coatings.

When you're shopping for pool paint, you'll find three kinds:
■ Epoxy paint is best for new pools and for those previously painted with epoxy paint. It is long lasting, durable, and will stand up to UV rays, automatic pool cleaners, and chemical treatments. With proper surface preparation, an application epoxy paint will last about 7 to 10 years.
■ Chlorinated rubber-based paint is not as durable as epoxy paint, but is a dependable, easy-to-use, inexpensive coating. It is easy to apply, comes in many colors, and properly applied has an expected life span of about 3 to 5 years.

■ Water-based acrylic pool paint can be used on any type of surface, is easy to apply, and cleans up with water. It's the ideal choice for pools that get a lot of use and that require regular repainting. It should last about 2–3 years.

Within each of these categories, swimming pool paints come in a broad range of prices. You get what you pay for both in quality and durability. Whatever paint you use, follow the manufacturer's instructions and heed the recommended safety guidelines. You might need a respirator when using some paints in poorly ventilated areas.

Apply paint with a 3/8-inch nap roller. Start in the deep end of the swimming pool and work your way to the shallow end. Wait 2 to 4 hours before painting the second coat.

Wait 5 to 7 days before filling the swimming pool. If it rains, remove any standing water. If the rain lasts more than an hour or two, add a day to the cure time.

APPLYING STAIN & VARNISH

A careless finishing job can ruin the appearance of the most careful work. On the other hand, a skillful finisher can often make less-than-perfect woodworking look better. It always pays to put your best efforts into finishing.

Why finish?
Wood grain has powerful allure. Clear finishes let you see the wood and give its grain a rich look. Stains, too, play a part, changing the color and highlighting the grain. Stain can make inexpensive wood look like an exotic species.

Clear finishes, however, do more than make wood look beautiful. Finishes protect wood and wood products from absorbing or expelling moisture too fast, which can lead to warping, cracking, and loose joints. Finishes also protect wood from dirt, oxidation, spills, and stains. You can wipe off dirt from a finished surface that would otherwise penetrate and stain bare wood.

Don't skimp on prep work
The final look of a beautiful wood finish is the result of careful preparation that goes down several layers.

After careful sanding, remove all dust before you stain, dye, or apply the first varnish coat. Lightly sand between coats, remove the dust, and keep your work area as clean as possible.

Where to finish
If you have a shop, you can do most of the finish preparation at your workbench, including dust-producing activities such as sanding. But it's a good idea to clean a special area just for applying the finish and drying it, so dust and dirt won't mar your results. Or designate a room or part of the basement or garage. (Stay away from the furnace or water heater, as dust and finish fumes can be flammable or explosive.) Be sure you have good ventilation and bright lighting.

A poor finish results from second-rate preparation. Take the time to do it right.

CHAPTER PREVIEW

Preparing wood
page 178

Stain, dye, and varnish
page 180

Stripping paint and varnish
page 184

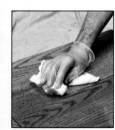

Applying stain, dye, and clear finish
page 186

PREPARING WOOD

Make the wood as smooth and perfect as possible to ensure a great finish. Find and fill defects, conceal unsightly edges in plywood, and sand thoroughly.

Detecting defects

Natural defects in wood include tiny, solid knots; thin splits or cracks; and minuscule pest holes. Inspect your wood carefully for these and note them. If you find them on hardwood that will be stained and clear finished, it's best to wait until after you've completed the finishing to take care of them. Then apply a colored putty that matches the final finish. If you repair blemishes before staining and finishing, the repair will probably take stain and finish differently than the wood and will be more obvious.

As an alternative, you can fill small gaps and other minor imperfections before applying the clear finish. One way to do this is to mix some of the wood's own sawdust with a bit of the finish and fill with that. Fine dust from sanding is best; the dust-collecting bag or cup of a finishing sander is a great source. You can also purchase a commercially prepared stainable filler in a matching color.

Use a commercial filler or exterior patching compound to smooth the rough edges of softwood plywood you plan to paint. Then sand the repair. For hardwood plywood, use iron-on veneer tape of the same wood species. In some cases moldings can both conceal the edge and add style.

Sand smooth

Do all final sanding with orange-colored, open-coat garnet sandpaper. Dust won't clog it as easily as closed-coat papers, and the garnet particles fracture as you use them, producing an increasingly finer grit. For hand-sanding, "A" weight paper works best. Wrap it around a sanding block so the surface you're working on remains flat as you smooth it.

The higher the grit number, the finer the grit. For most work, start with 100-grit, then use 150-grit, and end with 220-grit. Clean the surface of the wood between sandings with a vacuum, a tack cloth, or a paper towel lightly dampened with a solvent such as mineral spirits.

Filling

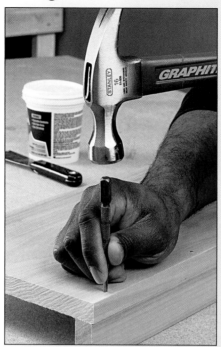

1 Use a nail set and a hammer to drive the head of finishing nails below the surface. Press wood filler into the hole, let it dry, then sand flush.

2 Softwood and softwood plywood often have blemishes that will show through a finish. To prevent this, apply wood filler with a putty knife, then sand when dry.

Edges

Wood filler: Softwood plywood edges usually look rough. Before painting plywood edges, spread wood filler in the voids and sand smooth when dry. Exterior patching compound also works well.

Veneer tape: Easily applied, heat-activated veneer tape neatly covers hardwood plywood edges. Simply trim it with a utility knife, and use an iron set on medium-low heat to adhere the tape.

Sanding

A belt sander quickly smooths large surfaces, such as plywood sheets. It is aggressive, however, so keep it moving. If held too long in one place, it can dig into the wood and cause a low spot.

Orbital finishing sanders do a fine job on hardwoods. They are lightweight and maneuverable and are handy for small areas and narrow parts. With a random-orbit sander, you can sand in all directions across the grain and not leave swirl marks.

A sanding block produces the best results when hand-sanding. Purchase one or make one from a piece of scrap wood. Change paper frequently.

The right abrasive

Select the correct grit for the woodworking job at hand.

Grit	Uses
36–80	Surfacing rough wood
60–100	Rough-sanding saw marks
80–320	Sanding contours
120–320	Smooth sanding
240–600	Sanding between coats

Open-coat papers in garnet or aluminum oxide last longer and cut faster.

STANLEY PRO TIP: **Dampen hardwood for final sanding**

Get a super-smooth surface on hardwoods by dampening them with water before the final sanding. Moisten a lint-free cloth and wipe down the wood. This raises the "hairs" in the grain so you can remove them with fine sandpaper for a silky-smooth surface.

STAIN, DYE, AND VARNISH

The chart on page 183 tells you what to expect from several types of finishes. The photos on the opposite page illustrate what some popular finishes look like when they're applied to commonly used materials.

What to have on hand

You won't need all the items shown below for each type of finish. Applicators, for instance, differ with the type of finish you select. The personnel in the finishing department at a home center or hardware store can help you find what you need.

Brushes are either foam, synthetic bristle, or natural bristle. Natural bristle works best when applying oil-base products. You can use a **roller** with water-base coatings, but it will add texture. Lint-free **cheesecloth** is an optional applicator for stains and clear finishing oils.

Steel wool in the fine (#000) and finest (#0000) grades smooths a finish between coats. Don't use it with water-base finishes—small metal particles left on the wood will rust. Woven **abrasive pads** perform like steel wool, and you can use them on all finishes.

Fill sticks repair minor surface imperfections, while **wood filler** handles larger ones. **Putty knives** are useful for filling large surface defects.

Working with stains and dyes

Choosing the right tone for your wood is a major decision—changing your mind exacts a heavy price in both materials and labor. Make sample strips of your leading color candidates before making your final choice.

Making samples means more than dipping skinny sticks into a can of stain. Take actual pieces of your wood (cutoff ends work nicely), sanded to the same degree that your finished wood will be, and apply the stain to the sample pieces, just as you would to the finished product.

Wipe on the stain, then apply the same number of clear coats that you'll brush on later. Use a permanent marker to identify each board with the color and brand of the stain you're testing.

If you're working with trim, make certain that you're judging the samples under the lighting conditions of the room. If you've already selected a wall color, go ahead and paint the room or at least paint a good-size swatch to help you visualize how the paint and stain colors work with each other. Don't make a snap decision. Instead view the samples at different times over several days.

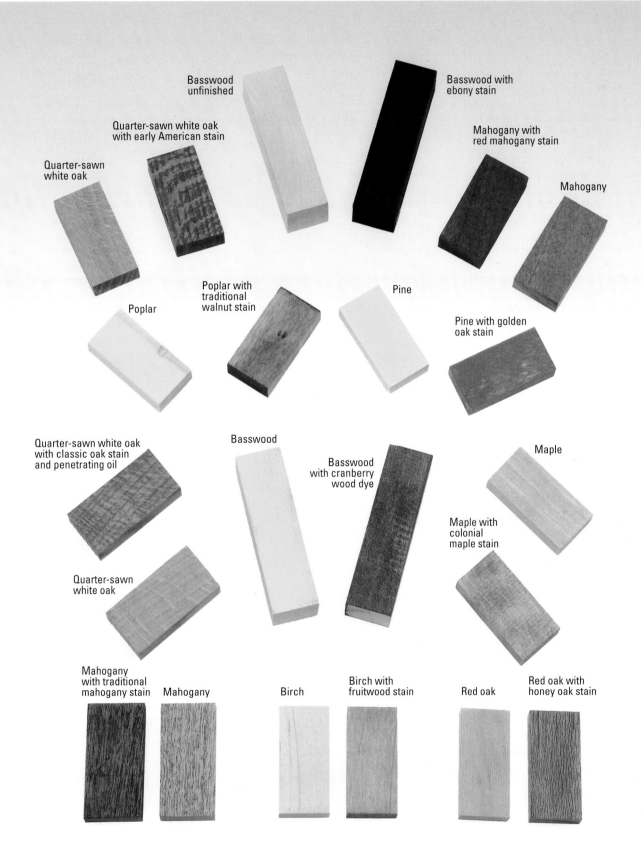

Basswood
unfinished

Basswood with
ebony stain

Quarter-sawn white oak
with early American stain

Mahogany with
red mahogany stain

Quarter-sawn
white oak

Mahogany

Poplar with
traditional
walnut stain

Pine

Poplar

Pine with golden
oak stain

Quarter-sawn white oak
with classic oak stain
and penetrating oil

Basswood

Maple

Basswood
with cranberry
wood dye

Maple with
colonial
maple stain

Quarter-sawn
white oak

Mahogany
with traditional
mahogany stain

Mahogany

Birch

Birch with
fruitwood stain

Red oak

Red oak with
honey oak stain

STAIN, DYE, AND VARNISH *continued*

Oil stains are easy to use, but on softwoods, such as pine and fir, you may need a wood conditioner to prevent blotching. If you can't achieve the exact look you want with off-the-shelf colors, you can custom-mix a stain. Several cautions: Stir well to ensure consistent results, mix stains only of the same type and from the same manufacturer, and keep careful notes of precise measurements so you can duplicate the tone later.

Dyes are less likely than stains to produce blotching. If you use a dye that mixes with water, prepare the wood by wiping it with a barely damp cloth. Let it dry. Then, using 220-grit sandpaper, remove the whiskers of wood raised by the wetting before you proceed with the dye coat.

You also can choose dyes that dissolve in denatured alcohol. Alcohol dries quickly—especially in hot weather—so make certain you allow enough working time to achieve smooth coverage. Whenever you work with solvents, provide plenty of ventilation and exercise extreme caution to prevent fires.

Clear finishes

Many people believe that successful wood finishing has more to do with alchemy than chemistry. And taking a quick glance at the wide range of clear wood finishes, you may think it will take a miracle to help you choose the right one.

The ideal finish would combine fast and easy application; quick drying; simple touch-up and repair; complete resistance to moisture, solvents, and abrasion; and low cost. Unfortunately there is no one finish that exhibits all these qualities. So choosing a finish involves trade-offs—you select the qualities that are most important to you and decide whether you can do without the others. Familiarity with the major categories of finishes will narrow your search.

Varnish

Generally speaking, a varnish is your best choice as a clear finish for both interior woodwork and many furniture projects. But selecting varnish involves further choices. Varnish is not a single finish; it's an entire family of products. And like any family, each member exhibits distinctive traits and characteristics.

Prepare samples with the same care that you'll use on finished wood so that you can accurately preview the tones.

Using a prestain conditioner can help prevent oil-base stains from blotching your lumber, like the pine sample above. Follow label directions and ensure identical timing of the conditioner step for consistent results.

Stir gently to minimize bubbles

Vigorous stirring whips air bubbles into the finish, which can cause a problem on your woodwork. If the tiny bubbles don't have time to pop and level out before the finish dries, they can impart "fish-eyes" and a gritty feel to the surface.

The flattening agents in a semigloss finish may sink to the bottom of the can during long storage, so gently lift the paddle as you stir to put these tiny particles into suspension.

A gloss finish doesn't have these fine grains, so stirring is barely needed.

STANLEY PRO TIP

Freshness counts

Ready-mix finish has a shelf life—even if the can has never been opened. Old shellac thickens, and polyurethane that's past its prime may refuse to dry. Chemists formulate water-base finishes so that the products can survive a few (but not an unlimited number of) freeze-thaw cycles during wintertime shipment. Summertime transport can subject finishes to extreme temperatures inside sealed trucks.

Check the container for an expiration date—a common sight on shellac containers. If the varnish cans at your local store are covered with dust, go to a paint store that turns inventory more often.

Water-base varnish is environmentally friendly because it does not contain a high proportion of volatile solvents. Some water-base products are completely free of volatile solvents. Water-base varnishes are easy to apply with a foam brush, but you have to be careful to minimize bubbles in the finish. (See "Stir gently to minimize bubbles," opposite.) And a water-base varnish doesn't yellow as many solvent-base varnishes do.

A brush is the usual applicator for solvent-base varnish (although foam brushes work well with some formulations). Choose a quality brush for best results. Buy the best brush you can afford—high-quality natural bristles and sturdy construction. Although a high-quality brush can give you a severe case of sticker shock, the resulting finish will quickly show you made the right choice. Cleaned promptly after each use, it will last for years.

Wipe-on varnishes range from thick gels to free-flowing liquids; the one you choose is largely a matter of personal preference. But whichever type you select, be sure to apply it with a lint-free cloth. Worn-out white cotton T-shirts are ideal. Beware of colored fabrics because they may impart a slight tint to your finish. Synthetic fabrics don't flow on the finish as evenly, leaving streaks and lines in the finish.

Oil and oil/varnish blends

The so-called pure oil finishes—linseed oil, mineral oil, and tung oil—don't contain dryers, so they may remain sticky and emit odors for an extended time.

But you'll also find oil-and-varnish finishes that contain dryers. These blends each have different characteristics in both their application methods and drying times. Some oil/varnish finishes are sometimes called penetrating oils (but don't confuse this term with the product that loosens rusty bolts). Some common categorical names include Nordic Oil and Danish Oil.

Applying either pure or blended oils is easy. Simply flood the surface with a liberal amount of product (a brush works fine), let it soak in according to the manufacturer's instructions, then wipe off the excess with soft cloths.

Oil finishes offer protection to the wood without building a surface film and they're also easy to repair. They are not, however, as durable and resistant to wear as a film-forming varnish. Oil finishes can require a long finishing schedule—over several days—which may be a reason for you to choose another finish for trimwork. They are excellent finishes, however, for furniture.

To maintain an oil finish, recoat annually.

Lacquer

Many professional finishers choose lacquer because it dries rapidly, which produces two important advantages: airborne dust has little time to settle on a wet surface, and the finisher can apply multiple coats in a day.

For large-scale work, lacquer requires a high-quality spray system that can be a substantial investment for occasional use. For small-scale work, you can use aerosol cans. Wear a respirator to protect yourself from fumes during spray application. Effective ventilation is an absolute necessity because the vapors can be explosive. Unfortunately, lacquer finishes can fail when exposed to moisture or even excessive heat and humidity.

Shellac

Shellac shares lacquer's fast-drying advantage but isn't as durable, and water and other liquids can stain or damage it easily. But shellac is still valuable as a sealer coat for wood and is compatible with most varnishes. (Check with the finish manufacturer or conduct your own test in an inconspicuous area.) Seal wood end-grain with shellac to minimize absorption of stain or finishes.

FINISH FEATURES

Not all finishes perform or apply equally. Note the comments following each type to aid in your selection. Finishes described are normally available at home centers and hardware stores.

Type of finish	Description	Application	Comments
CLEAR SURFACE FINISHES			
Lacquer	Moderately durable, lustrous	Best sprayed	Many coats, flammable, bad odor, fast drying
Varnish	Durable, clear	Natural-bristle brush	Flammable, bad odor, slow drying, yellows
Polyurethane varnish	High durability/protection	Natural/synthetic/foam brush	Flammable, bad odor, slow drying
Water-base varnish	Durable, no color, easy cleanup	Synthetic/foam brush, spray	Nonflammable, fast drying
Shellac	Easy to apply, difficult cleanup	Natural-bristle brush	Low protection, needs wax, many coats, flammable
PENETRATING FINISHES			
Danish oil	Easy to apply, enhances grain	Natural-bristle brush or cloth	Low protection, many coats, slow drying
Tung oil	Easy to apply, low luster	Natural-bristle brush or cloth	Low protection, many coats, slow drying

STRIPPING PAINT AND VARNISH

Some finishing projects will require only minimal preparation. Painted trim or furniture whose surface is in good condition may need only a good cleaning or some scraping and sanding. Items in rough condition, with multiple layers of paint poorly applied or some of which are coming off, will need stripping, no matter what kind of finish you're reapplying. This is especially true of wood trim and a necessity if you're changing from a latex to an oil-base finish, or vice versa, or restoring a painted antique to its original unpainted state.

Stripping solutions come in a variety of forms, from "cold" (with minimal health, fire, and environmental concerns) to "hot" (fast acting but posing potential health and environmental risks, therefore requiring careful precautions).

No matter what kind of stripper you are planning to use, wear heavy rubber gloves, eye goggles, old clothing, long-sleeved shirts, and a respirator. Do not use solvent-base strippers in a room with an open flame (a stove, water heater, or furnace pilot light, for example), and provide your workspace with ample cross-ventilation.

Set up a receptacle for disposing of the finish you remove—an old paint can is a good choice, but several thick layers of newspaper will allow you to spread out the removed finish in a relatively thin layer so the stripper can quickly and completely evaporate from the old finish. Once evaporated, you can safely dispose of the dried finish in plastic bags. Check with your trash removal agency to see whether the dried residue can be included in your regular trash pickup or if it must be taken to a special drop-off location.

If you use rags in any part of the stripping process, soak them in water and hang them outside to dry before disposing of them. Solvent-base strippers, especially, are prone to spontaneous combustion if wadded up in a closed container (like a trash bag) before the solvent has completely evaporated.

Stripping varnish

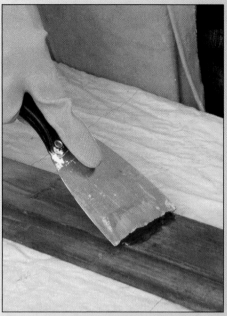

1 Using an old natural-bristle brush (some strippers will melt synthetic bristles), apply the stripper in a heavy coat, brushing in one direction only. Rebrushing stripper will only remove it before it can do its work. Apply stripper to an area only as large as you can remove before it dries.

2 Leave the stripper undisturbed on the surface until bubbles begin to appear. Then wait longer. Most modern formulations will remove multiple coats of paint if you let them work long enough. Then scrape the paint up with a putty knife, depositing it in a metal disposable can or on newspapers.

Using refinisher

Certain solvent formulations are sold as furniture "refinisher." Most of these products contain the same solvent mixes as strippers but without the thickening agents.

Refinishing solutions are not made for paint removal, but they do remove varnishes and other clear finishes quickly.

To use a refinisher, pour a small amount of the solution into a pie tin or other small container. Soak a pad of #0000 steel wool in the refinisher and apply it to the surface, removing the finish with light circular scrubbing motions. Squeeze the dissolved varnish back into the refinisher and reapply until the finish is removed.

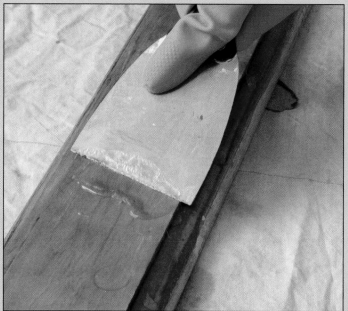

3 Reapply a thinner coat of stripper and let it stand until it completely softens any remaining paint and varnish left on the wood. Then scrape up the varnish and paint flecks with a wide putty knife, taking care not to gouge the wood (wet wood fibers gouge and tear very easily).

4 While the surface is still damp from the stripper residue, wash it several times with denatured alcohol. Use a pad of #0000 steel wool or a fine abrasive pad to clean the residual stripper from the surface. Be sure you get it all. Residues will interfere with your finish coatings.

Types of stripping agents

Chemical paint removers come in many formulations, each with different strengths, benefits, and hazards. Some, like refinishers, have the thin consistency of solvents and are made for quick removal of varnishes and clear finishes but not paint. Others are enhanced with waxes and varying proportions of thickeners that slow their evaporation and help them cling to vertical surfaces.

■ **Methylene-chloride** strippers have one advantage that other solvent strippers do not—they are nonflammable. In fact, when added to other solvent strippers, methylene-chloride makes them nonflammable also. This chemical, however, is harmful when inhaled and must be used with ample ventilation.

Methylene-chloride strippers work from the bottom up—they seep through the paint and remove it from the wood. The result is that the paint comes up in sheets, meaning you'll tend to use less of this product than others.

■ **Solvent strippers** work from the top down—they dissolve the finish layer by layer until they reach the wood. The paint you remove comes off as a "goo," not in layers. Although these strippers work more slowly, they don't evaporate as quickly as other strippers and don't raise the grain as much as water-base strippers. Pure solvent strippers are flammable, but many solvent products will contain a small amount of methylene-chloride to make them nonflammable.

■ **Caustic strippers** contain strong alkaline solutions, such as lye, and literally "eat" the finish off the wood. If you've run into a milk-painted antique, this is the only kind of stripper that will remove the milk paint. Caustic strippers form a rubbery coating on the surface. When you're ready to remove the paint, most of it will come up in a single sheet. These strippers are less messy and can remove many layers of paint.

Caustic strippers are water-base, so they won't catch fire, but they are very harmful to skin and mucous membranes. These serious chemicals require appropriate protection, including good ventilation. In addition, caustic strippers will eat into the wood fibers and darken the wood if left on too long, so they require careful monitoring.

The least aggressive and easiest stripping solution to work with is a water-and-citrus-base product that is nontoxic, releases little odor, and is environmentally friendly. It works well but it takes a lot more time—often as much as 24 hours—to be effective. It can also raise the grain of the wood, which might require additional sanding.

Even though new products make stripping faster, easier, and safer, be sure to wear safety goggles, latex gloves, long sleeves, and a dust mask or respirator. Check for lead paint before beginning work (see page 116).

APPLYING STAIN, DYE, AND CLEAR FINISH

Nothing brings out the natural beauty of wood grain better than one of several coloring agents followed by multiple coats of a clear finish.

To an extent, penetrating oils will color the wood—some more than others. Tung oil, for example, will have only a mild effect on the color and contrast of the wood. Natural (untinted) Danish oils will darken the wood somewhat, but you will achieve the largest color change with boiled linseed oil. Applied in a 50/50 solution of oil and mineral spirits or turpentine, this oil will initially impart some of its amber color to the wood. Then, over time, linseed oil darkens to a rich golden color with exposure to air and light.

The effect of stains and dyes on wood grain is more pronounced. Stains are a mixture of pigment in some kind of liquid carrier, and pigments, because they are large particles, stay suspended in the carrier but are not dissolved by it. Dyes, on the other hand are dissolved by their carrier, generally water or alcohol. The dye particles, therefore, are microscopic and almost indistinguishable from the carrier. Because of this difference, stains and dyes behave differently on wood, and their effect on grain pattern is likewise different.

Because pigments are thick, they are absorbed less by the denser portions of the wood and more by the areas containing open grain. If you apply stain to oak, for example, and then wipe off the excess, the areas of open grain will appear much darker than the surrounding wood. If you dye the same piece of oak, the entire surface will take on an evenness of tone, because the smaller dye particles penetrate all areas of the wood just about equally.

For all these pronounced differences in their final appearance, stains and dyes go on pretty much the same. Flood the surface, give the colorant the proper penetration time, then wipe off the excess.

Applying stain

1 Mix stain thoroughly before using. With either a brush or lint-free cloth, apply it in the direction of the grain. Overlap your strokes slightly so you don't miss any spots.

2 Before the stain begins to dry, wipe the entire wood surface to remove excess. This also forces the stain's pigment into the grain, enhancing its contrast.

Applying varnish

1 To properly load a brush, dip the bristles into the finish up to about one-third of their length. Touch the tip of the brush against the sides of your container and put a little pressure on the bristles to let the excess flow out.

2 Starting at one edge of the work, hold your brush at about a 45-degree angle and apply just enough pressure to deflect the bristles and release the varnish. Pull the brush slowly and in a straight line along the grain.

Applying wood dye

1 Apply the dye liberally to the surface using a brush, foam brush, rag, or sprayer.

2 Let the dye remain on the surface for the time period recommended by the manufacturer, then wipe off the excess with a rag before the dye dries.

Applying penetrating oil

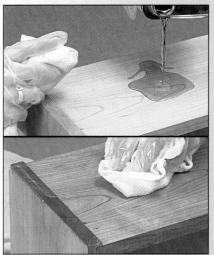

When using any type of penetrating oil, pour a liberal amount onto the wood, then spread it around with a lint-free cloth. Let the oil soak in for about 10 minutes, then wipe off the excess. Allow the finish to dry 24 hours before applying a second coat. Reapply until the wood will not absorb any more oil.

3 As you approach the end of the workpiece, put slightly more pressure on the bristles, but don't change the angle of the handle or bristles.

4 Keep the brush moving in the same line until you reach the end of the workpiece and lift the brush in one smooth motion as you clear the edge.

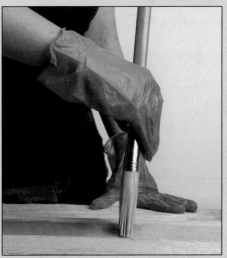

5 Scrape the brush against the inside lip of the container, which will unload the remaining varnish. Then, with the brush held at almost 90 degrees to the surface, run just the tip of the bristles lightly through the varnish from one end to the other.

GLOSSARY

Acrylic: A synthetic resin used as the binder in high-quality latex paint.

Additive: Any ingredient added to a paint to improve a specific performance.

Adhesion: The ability of a paint to stick to a surface.

Alkyd: A synthetic resin used as solvent in oil-base paints.

Binder: The agent in a paint that adheres the pigment to the surface.

Blocking: The tendency of low-quality painted surfaces to stick together when dry. **Breathable:** A paint that allows water vapor to pass through.

Burnishing: An increase in gloss caused by rubbing the painted surface.

Casein paint: Paint containing milk protein as a main ingredient.

Ceiling paint: A thick, flat, high-hiding paint made especially for ceilings.

Chalking: Formation of a fine powder on a painted surface.

Complementary colors: Colors opposite each other on the color wheel, e.g., blue and orange.

Custom color: A specialty color mixed by a paint retailer.

Cutting in: Applying a narrow band of paint in corners of walls and ceilings.

Deglossing: Roughing the surface of paint to promote better adhesion.

Distemper paint: Paint made from powdered chalk and animal or synthetic glue.

Drywall primer: A primer formulated for use on drywall.

Efflorescence: White salt deposits brought to the surface by water inside masonry material.

Eggshell: A soft paint sheen.

Elastomeric wall coatings: Extremely flexible paint made for covering small cracks in masonry.

Enamel: A paint with high binder content that dries to a hard, smooth finish.

Factory finish: A paint made without tinting.

Fiber cement siding: A high-density material made from cement and fiber and formed into siding and soffits.

Flagging: Split ends on paintbrush bristles.

Flat: A nonreflective paint sheen.

Glazing compound: A puttylike material that holds glass in windows.

Gloss: A shiny paint sheen.

Green paints: Paint with most or all harmful chemicals removed.

Hiding: A paint's ability to cover a previous coat.

Hue: Pure color—red, blue, and yellow.

HVLP: High-volume, low pressure; a kind of paint sprayer.

Kitchen and bath paint: Paint with low spattering and extra mildewcide.

Ladder jacks: Brackets attached to ladders to support a scaffold plank.

Lap mark: A visible overlap in paint.

Latex paint: Water-base paint.

Lead paint: Paint made prior to 1978 containing lead as a primary ingredient.

Leveling: The ability of a paint to flow out smoothly.

Light: A pane of window glass.

Masking: Protecting a surface that isn't to be painted.

Matte: Flat sheen.

Mineral spirits: Petroleum-base thinner for oil-base paints.

Monochromatic: A color scheme employing one color in various intensities.

Muriatic acid: Dilute hydrochloric acid used for cleaning masonry.

Natural-bristle brush: A paintbrush made from the hair of an animal, e.g., boar's hair.

Painter's tape: A masking tape that can be removed without leaving residue.

Pigment: The finely ground materials that give paint or stain its color.

Primary color: See "hue."

Primer: A base coat applied to help paint adhere.

Resin: A soluble substance that cures to a hard surface.

Respirator: A device made with fine filters to remove harmful chemicals and dust from breathing.

Satin: A low-luster sheen.

Scrubbable: Paint that can be cleaned with water, detergent, and a brush.

Sealer: An undercoat applied over porous surfaces.

Secondary colors: Colors created from equal amounts of two primary colors—orange, purple, and green.

Semigloss: A slightly reflective paint sheen.

Shade: A darker version of a color.

Sheen: The degree of reflectivity of a paint.

Solvent: The liquid component of paint.

Stain-blocking primer: A primer that prevents stains from bleeding through the finish paint.

Standard mix: One of a multitude of colors premixed at the factory.

Synthetic-bristle brush: A brush with bristles made from nylon or polyester.

Tertiary colors: Colors formed from equal amounts of a primary color with one of its secondary colors.

Tint: A lighter version of any color.

Triadic colors: Colors at equidistant points on the color wheel., e.g., greens, oranges, and purples.

Tone: A subtle version of a color made by adding gray.

Tooth: A surface coarseness that improves adhesion.

TSP: Trisodium phosphate, a cleaning and deglossing agent.

Turpentine: A thinner for oil-base paints derived from natural pine resins.

Uniformity: Even appearance of color and sheen.

Vapor-barrier primer: A primer that retards the transfer of moisture to the paint.

Vinyl: A synthetic resin used as a binder in latex paints.

Washable: Paint that can be cleaned with a mild detergent, water, and a sponge or rag.

Wet edge: The undried edge of paint.

Whitewash: A heavy exterior paint made from water and quicklime.

Wood conditioner: A liquid product that makes the application of stain on softwoods more even.

INDEX

A–B

Accent color, 10, 18
Additive, 31, 52, 84
Airless spraying, 50, 85
Alligatoring, 42
Aluminum, 37, 44, 71, 91
Analogous colors, 6, 7
Antislip paints, 171
Barbecue grill, painting, 163
Baseboards, masking, 120
Basement
  floor, 144–145
  wall, 142–143
Bead lines, removing, 56
Binder, 30, 33
Bleach, 60, 68, 71, 150
Blistering, 40
Blocking, 41
Board and batten siding, 70, 90
Boxing the paint, 52
Brick, repairing mortar joints, 72
Brush
  cleaning, 58–59
  foam, 47, 137
  holding, 54
  inspecting, 46
  loading, 53
  natural-bristle, 46
  painting with, 54–55
  preconditioning, 58
  quality, 47
  sizes, 47
  for stains, dyes, and varnishes,
    180, 183
  synthetic-bristle, 46
  wire, 73, 142, 160–161, 163
  wrapping in plastic bags, 59
Burnishing, 40

C

Cabinetry, 24, 154–157
Camouflage kits, 170
Casing, painting, 134
Caulking joints, 72–73
Cedar shingles, 92–93
Ceilings, 34, 39, 111, 126–127
Ceramic tile, grout coloring, 151
Chain link, painting, 95
Chalkboard paint, 170
Chalking, 42, 60
Chlorinated rubber paint, 175
Cleaners, 60–61

Cleaning
  basement floor, 144
  brushes, 58–59
  deck surface, 98–99, 100
  new paint, 129
  rollers, 59
  techniques, 110
  walls, 110
Clear finish
  applying, 186–187
  choosing, 182–183
  for deck, 100–101
Color
  accent, 10, 18
  analogous, 6, 7
  complementary, 6, 7
  connecting rooms with, 10
  for exteriors, 64
  favorite, as starting point, 9
  focal points vs. backdrops, 9
  grout, 151
  hiding previous, 127
  mixing options, 18
  monochromatic, 7, 10
  neutrals, 7, 10
  pigment, 30
  primary, secondary, tertiary, 6
  quick solutions, 10
  room size, perception, 11
  scheme, 8–11, 64, 104
  shades, tints, and tones, 6
  style and, 12–13, 16
  testing, 10, 97
  tips, 11
  triadic, 7
  value, 6, 22
  warm and cool, 6, 8
  wheel, 6–7
  white, 10
Colored putty, 178
Comb painting, 147
Complementary colors, 6, 7
Concrete block, 73, 90
Concrete primer/sealer, 37
Contractors, 26–27
Corner roller, 56
Corner sprayer, 57
Coverage, 65, 105
Cracking and flaking, 41, 43
Cracks, keying, 142
Crayon marks, 61
Cutting in, 128–129

D

Danish oil, 183, 186
Deck

clear finish, applying, 100–101
finish selection, 96–97
lightening wood, 97
painting, 98–99
prefinishing, 101
preparation, 98–99, 100
weathered look, 96
Design, 4–27
  color, 6–11
  furniture, trim, and
    accessories, 24–25
  styles, 12–13
Distemper paints, 172
Door
  cabinet, 154–157
  handles for, 138
  interior, 138–141
  louvered, 141
  masking trim, 121
  paneled, 88, 89, 139
  preparation, 138
  slab, 88, 139
  sliding, 140
Drop cloth, 67
Drywall
  installing new, 111
  repairing, 112–113
Drywall compound, 115
Dust, 106–107
Dust mask, 121
Dyes, 180–182, 186, 187

E

Easel, painting, 132–133
Eaves, painting, 82
Edges
  finishing, 178
  unsticking painted, 61
Efflorescence, removing, 60, 72,
  142
Elastomeric wall coatings, 39, 90
Epoxy paint, 39, 144–145, 175
Estimating paint, 64–65, 104–105
Extender pigments, 30
Exteriors, painting, 62–101
  brushing top coats, 85
  color choice, 20–23
  decks and porches, 96–101
  doors, 88–89
  fences and gates, 94–95
  ladders and scaffolding, 74–81
  lead-based paint, 62
  masonry, painting, 90–91
  masonry, preparation, 72–73
  planning and estimating, 64–65
  primers and sealers, 36–37

problems and cures, 42–43
shingles, 92–93
shutters, 89
siding, painting, 84–85, 90, 91
siding, preparation, 68–71
site preparation, 66–67
soffits and fascia, 82–83
time required, 65
weather, influence of, 65
windows, 86–87
Eye protection, 121

F

Fabric softeners, 58
Fascia
  painting, 82
  replacing damaged, 70
Fences, 94–95
Fiber cement siding, 91
File cabinet, painting metal, 162
Filler stick, 137
Filling defects in wood, 178
Filling nail holes, 116–117
Finishes and finishing, 176–187
  applying stain, dye, and
    varnish, 186–187
  benefits of, 176
  clear finish, 100–101
  decks and porches, 96–101
  filling defects, 178
  interior windows, 132
  location for, 176
  prefinishing, 101
  sanding, 178–179
  sealer, 100–101
  selecting stain, dye, and
    varnish, 149, 180–183
  stain, 100–101, 136–137
  stripping paint and varnish,
    184–185
  testing color, 97
  trim, 136–137
  UV blockers, 96
  varnish, 136–137
  wood floor, 148–149
Fixtures, masking, 106–107
Flat paints, 34, 35
Flattening agents, 182
Floetrol, 52, 84
Floor
  basement or garage, 144–145
  decorative techniques, 147
  vinyl flooring, 150–151
  wood, painting, 146–147
  wood, staining or varnishing,
    148

Furniture, 24–25
  aluminum, 164
  iron and steel, 160–165
  plastic, 166–167
  whitewash and milk paints for, 172–173
  wood, 168–169

G–H
Galvanized surfaces, painting, 165
Garden ornaments/structures, 24, 162, 165, 171
Gates, 94–95
Glass, removing paint from, 134
Gloss, removing, 61, 117
Gloss paints, 34, 35, 117
Grout, coloring, 151
Hardware
  holes, matchsticks in, 107
  keeping track of, 66
  masking, 88
  updating, 157
Heat gun, 119
High-temperature paint, 39, 163
High volume low pressure (HLVP) spraying, 51, 99
Humidity, 104, 128
Hydraulic cement, 142
Hydrogen peroxide, 61
Hydrostatic pressure, 174

I
Interiors, painting, 102–157
  basement walls, 142
  cabinetry, 154–157
  ceilings, 126–127
  choosing, 34–35
  cleaning and sanding, 110
  color choice, 14–19
  design gallery, 14–19
  doors, 138–141
  floor, basement or garage, 144–145
  floor, staining and varnishing, 148–149
  floor, wood, 146–149
  humidity and temperature effects, 104
  ladders and work platforms, 122–123
  planning and estimating, 104–105
  primers and sealers, 36–37
  priming, 124–125
  problems and cures, 40–41

protecting surfaces, 120–121
room preparation, 106–107
smoothing textured surfaces, 111
steps, 152–153
trim, preparation, 116–119
trim, staining and varnishing, 136–137
vinyl flooring, 150–151
wallpaper removal, 108–109
walls, painting, 128–129
walls, preparation, 112–115
windows, 130, 135
Iron
  painting furniture and ornaments, 160–165
  preparation of, 44
  primer for, 37

K–L
Kitchen and bath paints, 39
Lacquer, 183
Ladder
  choosing, 75
  extensions, 77
  indoor use, 122–123, 152–153
  protecting surfaces from, 76
  raising, 76–77
  safety, 74, 76, 122
  sloping ground, use on, 77
  3-to-1 rule, 76
  types, 74–75
Ladder boots, 76
Ladder jacks, 78
Lapping, 43
Lead, 62, 116
Lid, cleaning paint can, 53
Louvers, 141

M
Magnetic surfaces, 171
Maintenance, 60–61
Masking
  ceilings, 126
  exterior, 84–88
  floor edges, 120
  hinges and hardware, 88
  indoor, 106–107
  new paint, 129
  outdoor structures, 66, 67
  tapeless, 87
  trim, 121, 125
  windows and doors, 121
Masonry
  painting, 90–91
  preparing surfaces, 44, 72–73

primers and sealers for, 37
  wall, 142–143
Message board, 170–171
Metal
  painting furniture and ornaments, 160–165
  preparation of, 44
  primer for, 37
  rust encapsulators, 39
Mildew, 31, 60, 68, 110
Milk paint, 172–173
Mixing, 18
Moldings, removing, 148
Monochromatic colors, 7, 10
Mood, color effect on, 8
Mortar
  concrete patching, 73
  joints, repairing, 72
  skimcoat, 72
Muriatic acid, 72, 175

N–O
Nail holes, filling, 116
Neutral colors, 7, 10
Oil finishes, 149, 183, 187
Orange peel, 167

P
Paint
  boxing, 52
  chemistry of, 30–31
  choosing, 34–35
  drying, 31, 129
  environmentally friendly, 105
  interior vs. exterior, 33
  latex vs. oil, 31
  mixing, 52
  old, 53
  for pools, 175
  pouring, 53
  quality, 32–33
  specialty, 38–39, 170
  storing, 59
  textured, 38–39, 129
Paint incompatibility, 42
Paint mitt, 95, 161
Paint pad, 47, 55
Patching cement, 144
Patching compound, exterior, 69
Peeling, 43
Penetrating oil, 137, 183, 187
Penetrol, 52, 84
Pigment, 30
Planning, exterior painting, 64–65
Plants, protecting, 67

Plaster
  repairing, 114–115
  whitewash mix for, 172
Plastics, painting, 166–167
Plastic sheeting, 67, 106, 145
Polyurethane, 182. *See also* Varnish
Pool paints, 175
Porch, 96–99. *See also* Deck
Pots, painting, 171
Power wash, 68, 71, 99
Preconditioning brushes, 58
Preparation, 44–45
  aluminum furniture, 164
  deck and porch, 98–99, 100
  door, 138
  exterior site, 66–67
  floor, 144–145
  galvanized surface, 165
  iron and steel, 160–161
  plastic surfaces, 166
  primers and sealers, 36–37
  room, 106–107
  siding, 68–71
  swimming pool, 174–175
  trim, 116–119
  wood floor, 146
  wood furniture, 168
Prestain conditioner, 182
Primers and priming, 36–37
  for aluminum furniture, 164
  choosing correct, 124
  drying time, 125
  exterior, 69, 84
  for galvanized surfaces, 165
  for iron and steel, 160–161
  mixing, 125
  for plastic, 166
  spot repairs, 124
  tinting, 125
  wall, 124, 125
  for wood furniture, 168
Professional painter, 26–27
Protecting surfaces, 120–121
Protective gear, 121
Putty, applying with spatula, 117
PVC trim, painting, 166

R
Radiators, painting, 163
Recoating, 129
Refinisher, 184
Repairs
  aluminum siding, 71
  basement floor, 144–145
  basement wall, 142–143

board and batten siding, 70
concrete block, 73
drywall, 112–113
efflorescence, 60, 72, 142
fascia, 70
filling nail holes, 116–117
mortar joints, 72
plaster, 114–115
stucco, 73
touch-ups, 61
trim, 116–117
wood siding, 69
Respirator, 121
Roller
  bead lines, removing, 56
  for concrete block, 90
  corner, 56
  double, 161
  extension handle, 127
  loading, 56
  marks, 41
  nap or pile, 48, 49
  painting with, 56
  power, 49
  priming, 127
  quality, 49
  for sealer, 101
  for sheen consistency, 126
  size, 48
  soffit painting with, 83
  stipple, 38, 41
  for wood floor, 147
Room preparation, 106–107
Rust, 160
Rust encapsulators, 39
Rust-inhibiting primer, 161, 165

S
Safety
  electrical, 106
  hydrostatic pressure, 174
  ladder, 74, 76, 122
  lead paint, 62, 116
  protective gear, 121
  scaffolding, 81
Sagging, 40
Sanding
  cabinetry, 154, 155
  contours, 119, 155
  dampening wood prior to, 179
  grit number, 148, 178, 179
  sanders, 69, 149, 179
  vinyl flooring, 150
  walls, 110
  wood floor, 148, 149
Sash cord, 134

Satin finishes, 34, 35
Scaffolding
  exterior, 74
  indoor, 123
  ladder jacks, 78
  safety, 81
  setting up, 79–81
  toggle pins, 79
Sealer
  choosing, 36–37
  deck, 96–97, 100
  floor, 151
Semigloss paints, 34, 35
Shade, color, 6
Sheen, 126
Shellac, 182, 183
Shingles, painting, 92–93
Shutters, painting, 89
Siding
  aluminum, 71
  board and batten, 70, 90
  fiber cement, 91
  painting, 84–85
  preparation, 68–71
  staining cedar, 93
Site preparation, 66–67
Soffits, 82–83
Solvent, paint, 30, 105
Spatter painting, 147
Specialty paint, 39, 170
Spraying
  airless, 50, 85
  application tips, 51
  conventional, 50
  corners, 57
  cup, 50
  deck, 99, 101
  fence, 94
  high volume low pressure,
    51, 99
  iron and steel, 161–165
  louvered doors, 141
  plastic surfaces, 166–167
  protective clothing for, 127
  for sheen consistency, 126
  shingles, 93
  siding, 85
  stucco, 91
  technique, 57
  wood furniture, 168–169
Stain-blocking primer, 37, 69, 93,
  110, 151
Stains and staining
  applying, 186
  cedar siding, 93
  choosing, 34, 149, 180–182

deck, 96–97, 100
interior trim, 136–137
scrubbing paint stains, 61
varnishing, 148–149
wood floor, 148–149
Steel wool, 180
Stenciling, 147, 151
Steps, painting, 152–153
Storing paint, 59
Strippers and stripping, 119,
  184–185
Stucco
  painting, 91
  preparation of, 44
  repairing, 73
Studs, finding wall, 115
Style, 12–13, 16
Swimming pool, 174–175

T
Talcum powder, 61
Tannin-blocking primer, 84
Test board, 10
Texture, 38, 111
Tint, color, 6
Tinting primers, 125
Toggle pins, 79
Toilet, removing, 113
Tone, color, 6
Touch-up paint, 61
Triadic colors, 7
Trim
  design, 24
  masking, 84, 120–121, 125
  painting, 34, 54
  patching, 118
  preparation, 116–119
  PVC, 166
  staining and varnishing
    interior, 136–137
  window, painting, 134
Trim guard, cleaning, 58
Trisodium phosphate (TSP), 110,
  118

U–V
Ultraviolet (UV) blockers, 96
Undercoater, latex enamel, 37
Unsticking painted edges, 61
Value, color, 6, 22
Vapor barrier primers, 37
Varnish
  applying, 186–187
  choosing, 34, 149, 182–183
  freshness, 182
  interior trim, 136–137

stripping, 184–185
Veneer tape, 178
Vinyl
  deglossing, 150
  flooring, 150–151
  siding, 71, 91
  wallpaper, 108
  windows, 71
Volatile organic compounds
  (VOCs), 31, 105

W
Wallpaper, removing, 108–109
Walls
  basement, 142–143
  cleaning, 110
  focal-point and backdrop, 9
  paint choice for, 34–35
  painting, 128–129
  priming, 125
  protecting, 120
  repairing, 112–115
  sanding, 110, 125
  smoothing textured, 111
  studs, locating, 115
Weather, 65
White, 10
Whitewash, 172
Window
  aluminum and vinyl, 71
  casement, 135
  casing and trim, 134
  damage, checking for, 133
  double-hung, 130–133
  finishing, 132
  glazing, 86
  masking trim, 121
  masking without tape, 87
  painting exterior, 86–87
  painting interior, 130–135
  painting shut, 133
  removing paint from glass, 134
  sash cord, 134
Wire brush, 73, 142, 160–161, 163
Wood
  decks and porches, 96–101
  floor, finishing, 148–149
  floor, painting, 146–147
  furniture, 168–169
  preparation of, 44
  primers and sealers for, 36–37
  siding, preparing, 68–69
  whitewash for, 172–173
Wood conditioner, 136
Wood filler, 148, 178
Wood patch, 118

KNOWLEDGE IS
THE BEST TOO

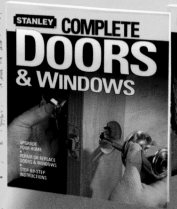

CONSTRUCT

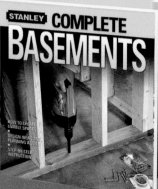

REJUVENATE

PLAN & REPAIR

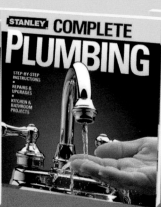

ENHANCE

MAINTAIN

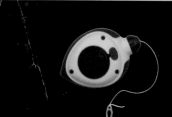